Laughter as Politics

Series Editors: Alex Thomson, Benjamin Arditi, Andrew Schaap
International Advisory Editors: Michael Dillon, Michael J. Shapiro, Jeremy Valentine

Offering New Perspectives on Contemporary Political Theory, books in this series 'take on' the political in accordance with the ambivalent colloquial sense of the phrase – as both an acceptance and a challenge. They interrogate received accounts of the relationship between political thought and political practice, criticise and engage with the contemporary political imagination, and reflect on the ongoing transformations of politics. Concise and polemical, the texts are oriented towards critique, developments in Continental thought, and the crossing of disciplinary borders.

Titles in the *Taking on the Political* series include:

Polemicization: The Contingency of the Commonplace
Benjamin Arditi and Jeremy Valentine

Cinematic Political Thought
Michael Shapiro

Untimely Politics
Samuel A. Chambers

Speaking Against Number: Heidegger, Language and the Politics of Calculation
Stuart Elden

Post-Marxism versus Cultural Studies
Paul Bowman

Post-Foundational Political Thought: Political Difference in Nancy, Lefort, Badiou and Laclau
Oliver Marchart

Democratic Piety: Complexity, Conflict and Violence
Adrian Little

Gillian Rose: A Good Enough Justice
Kate Schick

Ethics and Politics after Poststructuralism: Levinas, Derrida and Nancy
Madeleine Fagan

Space, Politics and Aesthetics
Mustafa Dikeç

History and Event: From Marxism to Contemporary French Theory
Nathan Coombs

Immanence and Micropolitics: Sartre, Merleau-Ponty, Foucault and Deleuze
Christian Gilliam

Shame: A Genealogy of Queer Practices in the 19th Century
Bogdan Popa

Visions of Council Democracy: Castoriadis, Arendt, Lefort
Benjamin Ask Popp-Madsen

Laughter as Politics: Critical Theory in an Age of Hilarity
Patrick T. Giamario

https://edinburghuniversitypress.com/series-taking-on-the-political.html

Laughter as Politics

Critical Theory in an Age of Hilarity

Patrick T. Giamario

Edinburgh University Press is one of the leading university presses in the UK. We publish academic books and journals in our selected subject areas across the humanities and social sciences, combining cutting-edge scholarship with high editorial and production values to produce academic works of lasting importance. For more information visit our website: edinburghuniversitypress.com

© Patrick T. Giamario, 2022

Edinburgh University Press Ltd
The Tun – Holyrood Road
12(2f) Jackson's Entry
Edinburgh EH8 8PJ

Typeset in 11/13 Sabon by
IDSUK (DataConnection) Ltd

A CIP record for this book is available from the British Library

ISBN 978 1 4744 9154 9 (hardback)
ISBN 978 1 4744 9156 3 (webready PDF)
ISBN 978 1 4744 9157 0 (epub)

The right of Patrick T. Giamario to be identified as the author of this work has been asserted in accordance with the Copyright, Designs and Patents Act 1988, and the Copyright and Related Rights Regulations 2003 (SI No. 2498).

Contents

Acknowledgements — vi

Introducing Gelopolitics — 1

1. The Laughing Body Politic: The Counter/sovereign Politics of Hobbes's Theory of Laughter — 39

2. Beyond A/gelasty: Adorno's Critical Theory of Laughter — 65

3. Over a Barrel: Ellison and the Democratic Politics of Black Laughter — 95

4. The Best Medicine? Repoliticising Laughter for Contemporary Feminist and Queer Politics — 123

The End of Laughter? Gelopolitics and the New Agelasty — 160

References — 173
Index — 198

Acknowledgements

If this book has an 'origin' – a discrete event that made its theoretical intervention possible – it was reading a passage from Jean-François Lyotard's *The Differend* in the autumn of 2012. Lyotard writes that 'Politics is tragedy for the authorities, comedy for the people. The respecting of the event which comic laughter is should be granted its ontological dignity' (Lyotard 1988: 144). There is much in this quotation with which the present book takes issue (e.g., Lyotard's conflation of laughter and comedy and his focus on laughter's 'ontology'), but at the time it struck me as saying something obviously true and important: political theorists and philosophers have not given laughter its due as a site of politics in the social order. This basic insight has guided me from the very earliest stages of writing *Laughter as Politics*.

I am fairly certain I never would have read Lyotard if it were not for Sam Chambers's graduate seminar 'Language, Order, Action' at Johns Hopkins University. Assigning *The Differend* – an extremely dense text that most political theorists would have considered dated by then – was probably the single most consequential thing Sam ever did for me. I am heavily indebted to him for this and the many other intellectual doors he opened, and the pages that follow are the product of his scholarly influence and unwavering professional support. The book is similarly indebted to the larger Political Theory community at Hopkins. The fruits of seminar discussions and conversations with Bill Connolly, Jennifer Culbert, Jane Bennett, P. J. Brendese and Emily Zackin appear throughout the book in ways large and small. I am especially grateful to Zach Reyna and Tripp Rebrovick for close readings and challenging questions on early chapter drafts. Sincere and bountiful thanks also go to Mike Albert, Angus Burgin, Stephanie Erev, Chris Forster-Smith, Nina Hagel, John Hoffmann,

Lawrence Jackson, Roger Maioli and Jon Masin-Peters who all offered careful and illuminating feedback on large sections of the book.

While this book originated in my PhD study at Johns Hopkins, it came to fruition at the Political Science Department at the University of North Carolina at Greensboro. Every junior scholar should be as lucky as I am to teach in such a supportive department. My colleagues' encouragement and guidance has been essential to the book's completion. Special thanks to Department Head Greg McAvoy for always going the extra mile to secure research time, assistance and funding; Fabrice Lehoucq for sage publishing advice; and Susan Shelmerdine in the Classical Studies Department for several crucial Greek translations. Stellar research assistance was offered by three undergraduate Political Science students: Shannon Behn, Walter Combs and Andrea Santolim Geller.

Fellowships from the Alexander Grass Humanities Institute and Project in American Pluralism, as well as a Dean's Teaching Fellowship from the Krieger School of Arts and Sciences, were essential resources for this project at Hopkins. I also benefited greatly from two Scholars' Travel Grants from the UNC Greensboro College of Arts and Sciences, as well as funding from the Office of Research and Engagement to index the book.

Many thanks to the 'Taking on the Political' series editors Andrew Schaap, Ben Arditi and Alex Thomson for 'taking on' this book and offering such helpful feedback. Great thanks also to the editorial team at Edinburgh University Press, especially Ersev Ersoy, Gillian Leslie, Caroline Richards and the manuscript's anonymous reviewers. Their comments made this a much better book.

Endless gratitude is due to my parents, Joan Buckley and Ron Giamario, for their unshakeable support in this and all my endeavours. Insofar as anything I say in this book is comprehensible, I owe it to my mom for teaching me how to write and my dad for keeping the peace.

Finally, deepest personal thanks are reserved for Ayla Amon. The origin of this book's argument may have been a 2012 graduate Political Theory seminar at Johns Hopkins, but my capacity to bring it to life originated in the 2007 undergraduate Italian class where I met Ayla. A fierce intellectual interlocutor, meticulous proofreader and steadfast partner, she is the book's *sine qua non*. I hope the finished product is worthy of her innumerable contributions to it.

Introducing Gelopolitics

agelast, n. A person who never laughs; one who has no sense of humour.

Etymology: < Middle French *agelaste* person who never laughs (1539; 1552 in Rabelais [. . .]) < ancient Greek ἀγέλαστος not laughing < ἀ- A-prefix + γελασ- , stem (also seen in γελαστός laughable, γελαστής laugher) of γελᾶν [*gelân*] to laugh [. . .] + -τος, suffix forming verbal adjectives.

Oxford English Dictionary (brackets added)

On 4 January 2019, the *New York Times* published an op-ed titled 'We Need to Keep Laughing' (Egan 2019). Its author, Timothy Egan, warns that the American people are in danger of losing their sense of humour in the Trump era. Amid the unrelenting onslaught of reactionary rhetoric, official corruption and deadly policy, it has become tempting to adopt the 'dour cast' of comedy-sceptical college campuses and the now laughter-free White House Correspondents' Dinner. This is a problem, Egan argues, because laughter is 'our best weapon' against leaders like Donald Trump. Laughter pierces the thick web of deception that would-be authoritarians arrogantly weave around themselves; it confirms that the emperor really has no clothes. About comedy, Egan writes: 'Mr. Trump hates this stuff. More than anything, he fears ridicule. It's the necklace of garlic against the vampire. [. . .] The mockery gets to him because deep down, he knows he's a fraud' (Egan 2019). From Egan's perspective, as soon as citizens take dangerous politicians as seriously as they take themselves, the battle has been lost. Egan consequently endorses the anti-Trump comedy of *Saturday Night Live* and Stephen Colbert, concluding that 'the antidote to a long day of White House lies is a long late night of comedy'.

On 5 July 2019, the *Guardian* published an opinion piece titled 'Donald Trump Wants to Be a Dictator. It's Not Enough Just to Laugh at Him' (Freedland 2019). The author, Jonathan Freedland, contends that rather than crippling Trump, laughter actually strengthens his political position. It does so by transforming scandalous events that ought to prompt forceful democratic responses – separating migrant families, hosting military parades, rejecting election results – into throwaway laugh lines. Instead of leading to a clearer vision of political reality, the liberal television and Internet satire machine makes it *less* likely that citizens recognise and respond to the slow erosion of democratic norms. 'We hesitate to see it for what it is,' Freedland writes, because 'the laughter gets in the way.' 'All those giggles served to obscure' the dire reality of the situation. Indeed, the pleasurable highs provided by the culture of satire perversely incentivise ever larger doses of political wrongdoing and extremism. For Freedland, fighting authoritarianism need not always be fun, and those looking to resist Trump and Trump-like figures would do well to laugh a bit less often.

To laugh or not to laugh? This has indeed been the question amid a global rise in far-right political activity in recent years, whether it be Trumpism in the United States, the Brexit campaign in the United Kingdom, or Jair Bolsonaro's presidency in Brazil (Mudde 2019; Stanley 2020; Traverso 2019). Egan and Freedland represent the two sides of an ongoing debate about laughter's place in political communities featuring high levels of what William Connolly calls 'aspirational fascism' (Connolly 2017).[1] Laughter is believed to be either the aspirational fascist's kryptonite – the reaction they fear the most and that will precipitate their demise – or their very condition of possibility – the grist for the right-wing grievance mill powering their political coalitions and thus a weapon too dangerous for liberals and leftists to wield. Is fascism uniquely vulnerable or uniquely impervious to laughter? Does a politics predicated on the violent elimination of difference collapse or draw energy from a confrontation with its own absurdity? The challenge posed by contemporary neofascism is, in a crucial sense, the challenge of knowing whether or not to laugh.

The dispute exemplified by Egan and Freedland is by no means new. The question of laughter's place in the *polis* has occupied political thinkers and actors since the earliest days of the Western political tradition. In Plato's *Republic*, Socrates worries that laughter will distract citizens from the requirements of justice. He demands that the guardian class 'shouldn't be lovers of laughter [. . .]. For when a man lets himself go and laughs mightily, he also seeks a mighty change to accompany his condition' (Plato 1991: 388e). Because comic poetry features untrustworthy imitations of earthly and divine life, the laughter it stimulates leads citizens astray from their natural functions (394c–395d). Laughter 'produces a bad regime in the soul of each private man' (605b), and for that reason, a just *polis* must strictly regulate comedy (Plato 2016: 816b–816c, 935d–936a). While Plato reveres Socratic irony and allows for laughter directed against whatever is foolishly or unjustly ordered (Plato 1991: 337a, 452d), these exceptions merely prove the rule, as the origin of such laughter in philosophical natures indicates its unavailability to the public at large. Plato advocates a political life largely devoid of laughter – what Rabelais would call an *agelastic* politics, or a politics without *gelōs* (γέλως), without laughter (Bakhtin 1984: 267).

Some 2,300 years later, Jean-François Lyotard endorses this very same 'irrational', popular laughter as the condition of justice, arguing that

> [t]he 'people' is not the sovereign. It is the defender of the differend against the sovereign. It is full of laughter. Politics is tragedy for the authorities, comedy for the people. The respecting of the event which comic laughter is should be granted its ontological dignity. (Lyotard 1988: 144)

According to Lyotard, social and political life features a multiplicity of *differends*, or disputes that cannot be resolved due to the lack of a common language game (xi). For instance, a differend exists between the Platonic philosopher-king and the many because the latter necessarily mistake opinions for truth (Plato 1991: 493a–494a). Lyotard contends that justice involves 'bearing witness' to the differend by inventing idioms that allow for the expression of previously inexpressible wrongs (Lyotard 1988: 13, 141). A just political life begins with and proceeds through laughter because only laughter deflates the pretensions of a single language game (e.g., that of philosophy or of an authoritarian's speech) to exhaust the possibilities of language. Lyotard believes that popular laughter – the laughter of those silenced by the differend – protects the *polis* against unjustified claims to discursive closure and completeness. To Plato's staunchly *agelastic* republic, Lyotard counters with an unapologetically *gelastic* political vision.

For Plato, the harmony and stability of the *polis* requires keeping the distractions of laughter at arm's length, while for Lyotard, laughter exposes the illusory nature of all such 'harmony' and 'stability'. Their positions do not, however, indicate a progressive march of political theory from ancient agelasty to postmodern gelasty. On the contrary, Plato and Lyotard exemplify rival camps in an age-old dispute over laughter, one that has in different periods pitted the gelastic Dionysus against the agelastic Apollo; the gelastic Sarah against the agelastic Abraham; Aristophanes against Plato; Rabelais against Benedict; Nietzsche against Hobbes; Bataille against Hegel; Foucault against Habermas; Butler against Nussbaum; Jon Stewart against Tucker Carlson; and most recently, the *Times*'s Egan against the *Guardian*'s Freedland.

The enduring salience of this debate over laughter's place in the *polis* reflects how laughter, as Mikhail Bakhtin puts it, 'has a deep philosophical meaning [. . .]; it is a peculiar point of view relative to the world' (Bakhtin 1984: 66). One's position on laughter reveals something essential about what Sheldon Wolin calls their 'political metaphysic', or conception of the basic terms and challenges of political life (Wolin 2004: 16). Agelasts who fear the bodily and linguistic disruptions posed by laughter tend to turn to transcendent notions like justice, God and reason to secure the *polis*, while gelastic theorists typically embrace the material and conceptual messiness of laughter as reflecting the nature of political life itself. The history of political thought understands laughter to be either the antithesis of a properly political life or its very lifeblood; the political vice or virtue par excellence; the source of a community's troubles or its hope for salvation. 'To laugh or not to laugh?': this has been and continues to be the question.

Laughter as Politics poses a straightforward challenge: suppose this is the wrong question? What if the historical dispute between gelastic and agelastic political theories – manifest today in the debate over whether or not to laugh at aspirational fascists – obscures a more fundamental and consequential set of political questions surrounding laughter itself? What if instead of trying to determine the place of laughter *in* politics, we consider laughter *as* a site of politics in its own right? How does laughter operate politically? What does it actually *do* in the *polis*? How does laughter express and shape the terms of citizenship? How does it build and entrench structures of power and hierarchy, especially those associated with race, sex and gender? Why are certain types of laughter deemed 'polite', 'rational' and 'civilised', while others are labelled 'rude', 'irrational' and 'primitive'? How do the rules governing the timing, movements and targets of laughter emerge, and what are their political effects?

Once we begin asking these questions – as I do in the following chapters on Thomas Hobbes, Theodor Adorno, Ralph Ellison and a collection of thinkers on feminist politics and human sexuality like Judith Butler and Sigmund Freud – it becomes clear why the prevailing 'to laugh or not to laugh?' framing is inadequate. The *polis* that commentators like Freedland and Egan and philosophers like Plato and Lyotard envision as either constraining or encouraging laughter has itself been shaped by, through and in laughter. The question of laughter's place in the *polis* overlooks how the *polis* as we know it – a political community organised around a particular conception of citizenship, hierarchy and the good life – is constituted by practices of laughter. The political-theoretic task, then, is to determine how laughter does this, why it is so effective in doing so, and the political opportunities and dangers it presents. When we study laughter as itself a site of politics, questions about its place in the *polis* – like whether we should laugh at far-right political figures – appear in an entirely new light.

The Laughing Animal

> Man is by nature a political animal [*zōon politikon*].
>
> Aristotle, *Politics* (1996: 1253a3)

> Mankind [. . .] is the only one of the animals that laughs [*to monon gelān tōn zōōn anthropon*].
>
> Aristotle, *On the Parts of Animals* (2001: 673a7)

These two short quotations from Aristotle illustrate what is at stake in shifting away from the dispute between gelastic and agelastic political visions, or what I will call the 'a/gelasty dispute'. The first is familiar to political theorists (or indeed any student of politics), as it is perhaps *the* foundational argument in the Western political tradition (Bennington 2009; Chambers 2003, 2018). According to Aristotle, the human animal's unique status as *political* rests on its possession of *logos*, or the capacity for reasoned speech. Unlike the mere voice or noise (*phōnē*) that issues from non-human mouths, the human *logos* performs the specifically political work of establishing shared prudential ends and normative aspirations:

> Man is the only animal who has the gift of speech [*logos*]. And whereas mere voice [*phōnē*] is but an indication of pleasure and pain, and is

therefore found in other animals [. . .] the power of speech [*logos*] is intended to set forth the expedient and inexpedient, and therefore likewise the just and the unjust. And it is a characteristic of man that he alone has any sense of good and evil, of just and unjust. (Aristotle 1996: 1253a10–16)

The most important political thinkers since Aristotle – Aquinas, Hobbes, Marx, Heidegger, Arendt, Fanon, Derrida, Foucault and Habermas – all engage, contest and recast this basic argument. Doing political theory after Aristotle means grappling with the relationship between the human, *logos* and public life.

While the second quotation is not nearly as famous, it proves quite consequential when considered alongside the first. In addition to possessing *logos*, Aristotle argues that humans are the only animals that laugh; they are, we might say, the laughing animal (*zōon gelon*). Yet *logos* and laughter are not natural allies. In laughter, reasoned speech 'intended to set forth the expedient and inexpedient [. . .] the just and the unjust' devolves into what Descartes describes as 'an inarticulate and explosive cry' (Descartes 1989: 84). Numerous commentators describe how humans appear to be at their least 'human'- and most 'animal'-like when they descend into a fit of chuckling, chortling, cackling, guffawing or giggling (Beard 2014; Critchley 2002; Eagleton 2019; Parvulescu 2010; Scott 2015). But even if laughter does not qualify as *logos*, Aristotle's insistence that laughter is the exclusive property of the human animal and that the movements of the diaphragm in laughter 'produce perception' and 'act and move thought' (Aristotle 2001: 673a1–5) suggests we should not dismiss laughter as mere *phōnē*. Stephen Halliwell concludes that laughter for Aristotle involves a complex 'body–mind interaction [that] can operate in either causal direction' (Halliwell 2008: 315), and David Appelbaum describes laughter as a 'double movement': a shattering of *logos* that nonetheless reverberates with meaning (Appelbaum 1990: 21; see also Eagleton 2019: 4). Laughter, in short, troubles Aristotle's foundational distinction between the *logos* that marks a properly human, political life and the *phōnē* exterior to it. As an eruption of *phōnē* that paradoxically retains an essential connection to thought and speech, laughter disturbs the smooth functioning of the human *logos*, calling its very nature into question.

With these two claims, Aristotle opens the door to an alternative mode of theorising the relation between laughter and politics to that offered by the a/gelasty dispute. If humans are political animals due to their possession of *logos*, then laughter's destabilisation of the distinction between *logos* and *phōnē* plays a decisive role in establishing, contesting and modifying the bounds and contours of that political existence. Laughter is not simply an experience for the *polis* to manage; in shaping and reshaping *logos*, it is central to the very constitution and maintenance of the *polis* itself. By highlighting how the human subject's nature as a political animal hinges on its status as a laughing animal, Aristotle raises the possibility of an account of *gelopolitics*. Gelopolitics (literally 'laughter-politics') refers to the concrete practices of and regulations around laughter (γέλως; *gelōs*) that express, shape and alter the life of the *polis*. A funny-sounding word for an oftentimes funny subject, gelopolitics – pronounced like geopolitics, except with an 'l' – indicates that laughter not only affects and is affected by politics but is a site of politics in its own right. 'Gelopolitics' captures how laughter and politics are not exogenous to one another but rather unfold through one another. A study of gelopolitics explores laughter as a key experience through which a particular distribution of *logos* and *phōnē* – or notion of what counts as rational, truthful speech and who qualifies as a rational, truthful speaker – emerges, entrenches and transforms itself.

This book's study of gelopolitics is motivated by the simple fact that the question of laughter today is not one of *if*, but *how*. Decades of political-theoretic debate between proponents of an agelastic politics oriented towards the construction of a just political order through rational agreement[2] or deliberation aimed at mutual understanding[3] versus those promoting a gelastic politics featuring destabilising forces like comedy,[4] carnival,[5] irony,[6] humour[7] and parody[8] seem almost quaint in the contemporary context. At the start of the third decade of the twenty-first century, political life and discourse are relentlessly comedic, carnivalesque, ironic, humorous and parodic.[9] We live in an Age of Hilarity, and if we ever had the luxury of speculating on the utility or danger of laughter in politics, we no longer do. Politics today *is* gelopolitics. The following section considers several dispatches from the Age of Hilarity that showcase its political dangers and opportunities. The remainder of the Introduction reviews the dominant discourses of gelopolitics and their weaknesses, proposes an alternative theoretical framework for making sense of and intervening in the Age of Hilarity, and previews the chapters that follow.

The Age of Hilarity

> Everything is changing in America. People are taking their comedians seriously and the politicians as a joke.
>
> Will Rogers (1932)

Laughter as Learning

A few weeks before the 2014 World Cup football tournament, comedian John Oliver dedicated an episode of his HBO programme *Last Week Tonight* to a blistering attack against FIFA, the international association that governs the tournament. Using a series of absurd analogies and humorous quips, Oliver introduced the World Cup's corrupt practices to an American audience largely unfamiliar with FIFA but increasingly interested in international football. For example, after showing a clip where FIFA chairman Sepp Blatter defends the organisation's non-profit status by claiming that its $1 billion holdings are merely a 'reserve', Oliver responds, 'A reserve? A reserve of a billion dollars? When your rainy day fund is so big that you have to check it for swimming cartoon ducks, you might not be a non-profit anymore!' (Oliver 2014).

There is nothing especially memorable about Oliver's FIFA sketch, and this is precisely the point. In the early twenty-first century, it is exceedingly normal for citizens to learn about and engage with political issues by laughing at them. In the 2000s, young Americans reported Jon Stewart's *The Daily Show* and Stephen Colbert's *The Colbert Report* to be their primary news sources (Cosgrove-Mather 2004; Rasmussen Reports 2009). The success of Stewart and Colbert led to a proliferation of political satire programmes in the 2010s (e.g., the shows hosted by John Oliver, Samantha Bee, Larry Wilmore and Michelle Wolf) as well as the overt politicisation of previously staid network talk shows (e.g., CBS's *The Late Show* and NBC's *Late Night*). Similar developments are also under way beyond the United States. In the last decade, television networks in Canada, Germany, India, Iran, Israel, Japan, Pakistan, Portugal and the United Kingdom have all launched *Daily Show* spinoffs (Balapurwala 2015; Cardoso 2009; Hughes 2017; Iqbal 2011; Marx 2012).

Not simply a reaction one has to political events or controversies, laughter has become a key medium through which subjects learn about, engage with and respond to political issues and processes. Political scientists and media scholars have demonstrated the impact of laughter on public opinion about political figures and awareness of current events.[10] For example, Tina Fey's *Saturday Night Live* portrayals of Sarah Palin during the 2008 US presidential campaign were associated with steep declines in Palin's approval ratings (Baumgartner, Morris and Walth 2012), and exposure to *The Daily Show* and *Last Week Tonight* has been shown to increase viewers' knowledge of political and current affairs (Becker and Bode 2018; Young and Hoffmann 2012). Politicians have sought to capitalise on this educative efficacy of laughter by making comedy shows regular stops on the campaign trail (Garcia 2015). Perhaps most memorably, Barack Obama rescued the 2014 Affordable Care Act enrolment period with a viral appearance on Zach Galifianakis's absurdist web series *Between Two Ferns* (Epstein 2014). In 2016 Donald Trump boosted his campaign's mainstream appeal by appearing on Jimmy Fallon's *Tonight Show* (Itzkoff 2017), and in 2020 the Democratic presidential candidates all made pilgrimage to Stephen Colbert's *Late Show* (Stelter 2019). Contemporary life features a gelopolitics of education and engagement: citizens learn about and grapple with political issues through laughter.

Laughter as Violence

On 7 January 2015, two militants broke into the offices of the French satirical magazine *Charlie Hebdo* and killed twelve people, including the magazine's editors and five cartoonists. The attack originated in a dispute over laughter. For years, *Charlie Hebdo* had published irreverent caricatures of the Prophet Muhammad to mock what its editor called the 'totalitarian religious rhetoric' of 'Islamic fascism' (Biard 2015). The magazine viewed laughter as a non-violent means of defending the secular French public sphere from an allegedly intolerant religious orthodoxy. Following the attacks, virtually the entire French political and cultural establishment and its foreign allies united around the slogan #JeSuisCharlie, and laughing at Islam became something of a liberal political duty. *New York* magazine's Jonathan Chait announced that 'the right to blaspheme religion is one of the most elemental exercises of political liberalism' (Chait 2015) and the *Guardian*'s Martin Rowson demanded that 'we must not stop laughing at these murderous clowns' (Rowson 2015).

Many Muslims living in France and elsewhere interpreted the *Charlie Hebdo* cartoons differently. From their perspective, the sketches of Muhammad were the latest example of Western imperialism, colonialism and racism against Muslims. As French sociologist and anthropologist Didier Fassin noted:

> The caricatures were one more affront in a long list. Indeed, whereas satire has long been a way to mock and challenge the powerful, in the case of the French magazine, it only added insult to injury, targeting an already stigmatized and discriminated group, constantly exposed to Islamophobia as well as racism and xenophobia. (Fassin 2015: 7; see also Jackson 2015; Kay 2016; McGrogan 2017)

The laughter generated by the cartoons antagonised (and thus reproduced) the 'enemy' against which *Charlie Hebdo* claimed to be defending French liberalism. If, as the magazine's supporters insist, laughter is a key weapon in the 'war on terror', then it is one that helps create, sustain and intensify the divisions at the very root of that 'war'.

The *Charlie Hebdo* attack, along with the 2005 Danish cartoon controversy (Kuipers 2011), suggests the existence of a gelopolitics of struggle and contestation. Who or what counts as laughable, how it feels to laugh and be laughed at, and the histories of these meanings and practices constitute major axes around which contemporary political conflicts emerge and play out. Laughter is a multifaceted stake and weapon in political struggles: it incites, marginalises, attacks, defends, empowers and humiliates. By entering into, intensifying, and at times reconfiguring relations and structures of power, laughter today has become, as Lauren Berlant and Sianne Ngai claim about comedy, 'freshly dangerous' (Berlant and Ngai 2017: 235).

Laughter as Rupture

In October 2013, the BBC's Jeremy Paxman interviewed actor and comedian Russell Brand about his recent assignment as a guest editor for the British political magazine *New Statesman* (Brand and Paxman 2013). The interview began with Paxman questioning Brand's credentials for the assignment, and it quickly morphed into a debate over the form that political discourse should take amidst mounting global economic, social and environmental crises:

> *Jeremy Paxman*: Russell Brand, who are you to edit a political magazine?
> *Russell Brand*: Well, I suppose like a person who's been politely asked by an attractive woman. I don't know what the typical criteria is. I don't know many people that edit political magazines. Boris [Johnson], he used to do one, didn't he? So I'm a kind of a person with crazy hair,

quite a good sense of humour, don't know much about politics – I'm ideal.
Paxman: But is it true you don't even vote?
Brand: Yeah, no, I don't vote.
Paxman: Well, how do you have any authority to talk about politics then?
Brand: Well, I don't get my authority from this pre-existing paradigm which is quite narrow and only serves a few people. I look elsewhere for alternatives that might be of service to humanity. Alternate means, alternate political systems.
Paxman: They being?
Brand: Well, I've not invented it yet, Jeremy! I had to do a magazine last week. I've had a lot on my plate. But I say, but here's the thing you shouldn't do: shouldn't destroy the planet, shouldn't create massive economic disparity, shouldn't ignore the needs of the people.

Paxman continues quizzing Brand on his reasons for not voting and concludes that Brand's indifference towards voting means that he does not care about democracy. Brand rejects this accusation and insists on his commitment to a different vision of democratic politics:

Paxman: You're calling for revolution!
Brand: Yeah! Absolutely. Absolutely. I'm calling for change. I'm calling for genuine alternatives.
Paxman: There are many people who would agree with you.
Brand: Good!
Paxman: The current system is not engaging with all sorts of problems, yes. And they feel apathetic, really apathetic.
Brand: Yes.
Paxman: But if they were to take you seriously, and not to vote –
Brand: Yeah, they shouldn't vote, they should – that's one thing they should do, don't bother voting. [. . .] We know it's not going to make any difference. We know that already.
Paxman: It does make a difference.
Brand: So like I have more impact at West Ham United cheering them on, and they lost to City, unnecessarily, sadly.
Paxman: Well now you're being facetious.
Brand: Well, facetiousness has as much value as seriousness. I think you're making the mistake of mistaking seriousness for the –
Paxman: You're not going to solve world problems by facetiousness.
Brand: We're not going to solve them with the current system! At least facetiousness is funny.
Paxman: Sometimes.

In this rendition of the a/gelasty dispute, Paxman demands that political discourse be serious and rational, while Brand insists it needs a dose of fun and mischievousness. What conception of gelopolitics informs Brand's gelastic argument? According to Brand, *being funny* or *laughable* has a political efficacy that exceeds that of Paxman's 'serious', programmatic discourse. When Brand responds, 'At least facetiousness is funny', he suggests that the laughter he produces achieves something that other forms of discourse cannot, namely a loosening of the stranglehold that the prevailing political-economic system has on the collective imaginary. Laughter makes it possible (and pleasurable) to conceive of alternative modes of social, political and economic life. Brand considers the agelastic discourse to which Paxman dedicates himself as failing precisely on this count: it assumes that existing institutional forms exhaust the space of political possibility. The Paxman–Brand interview reveals a third form of gelopolitics: a gelopolitics of disruption and transformation. Laughter alters the very terrain of political discourse and action by interrupting the ordinary ways subjects see, understand and inhabit the world in common. While Brand does not foresee the darker potentialities of this mode of gelopolitics as they have since manifested themselves in figures like Donald Trump and Boris Johnson, he holds that a democratic politics worth its salt must be a gelopolitics in this way.

Laughter as Escape

In April 2019, comedian Volodymyr Zelensky was elected president of Ukraine in a landslide victory. Zelensky was well known to Ukrainians as the star of the satirical television programme *Servant of the People* (2015–19) in which he played Vasyl Holoborodko, a high school history teacher who is unexpectedly elected president after his rant about government corruption goes viral online. 'Who's there to vote for?' an exasperated Holoborodko asks. 'It's always the lesser of two assholes and it's been this way for 25 years. If I could have just one week in office, I would show them!' (Schwartz 2019). Zelensky brought Holoborodko's persona to life by running a modest, Instagram-based campaign attacking the incumbent government. Describing himself as 'a simple man who's come to destroy this system', Zelensky refused to commit to any ideology or policy proposals: 'No promises, no disappointment', he insisted (Fisher 2019). (However, as tends to be the case with early twenty-first-century politicians who brand themselves as non-ideological, Zelensky has a proclivity for neoliberal technocracy, quoting Reagan that 'government is not the solution to our problem; government is the problem'; Chappell 2019.) In his inauguration speech, Zelensky remained vague on what he hoped to accomplish in office, declaring only that 'All my life I tried to do all I could so that Ukrainians laughed. That was my mission. Now I will do all I can so that Ukrainians at least do not cry any more' (Chappell 2019).[11]

The idea of a hard-charging, truth-telling, incorruptible comedian serving in elected office has become a powerful political trope in recent years. In the mid-2000s, fans of Jon Stewart and Stephen Colbert regularly implored the comedians to run for president. (This idea formed the premise of the 2006 film *Man of the Year*, where Robin Williams plays a political satirist who seeks the presidency.) In 2008, Colbert actually took the plunge, launching a month-long presidential primary campaign in his home state of South Carolina. That same year, former *Saturday Night Live* cast member Al Franken was elected to the US Senate from Minnesota. Meanwhile, Icelandic comedian Jón Gnarr was elected mayor of Reykjavik in 2010; television comedian Jimmy Morales was elected president of Guatemala in 2015; and comic actor Marjan Šarec became Prime Minister of Slovenia in 2018. If we consider Donald Trump to be a certain kind of comedian – as I will in the next section – then the notion that the solution to intractable political problems is putting a comedian in charge reached its zenith in 2016. Today it is not too far-fetched to predict, as economist Tej Parikh has, that 'comedians will soon rule the world' (Parikh 2019).

The comedian-turned-politician defeats the establishment not by winning office, but by discrediting it. The presence of a professional jokester on the ballot or in government exposes the existing political order to be a joke; only in a broken system could the line between comedian and statesman become so blurred.[12] Those who vote for a comedian hope that someone who understands and indeed *embodies* the joke into which politics has devolved can yield something better. Yet Zelensky's programme – which, like that of most comedians who run for office, consists of virtually nothing besides his own comedic performance – raises severe doubts. Zelensky's gelopolitics is the mirror image of Brand's: rather than prompting the imagination of and striving for new forms of social, economic and political organisation, laughter anesthetises the public to the pain of existing life. As Zelensky pledges: 'I will do all I can so that Ukrainians at least do not cry any more.' While a disempowered establishment may mean that tears will no longer be possible, the minimalist goal of 'no disappointment' means that nothing else will be either. The case of Zelensky indicates the existence of a gelopolitics of escape, wherein laughter offers citizens a reprieve from the challenges and opportunities of political life.

Laughter as Affect

At the 2011 White House Correspondents' Dinner, President Barack Obama and comedian Seth Meyers subjected perhaps the most famous celebrity in attendance – Donald Trump – to a merciless barrage of jokes. It was clear that Obama in particular, after enduring months of Trump's baseless questioning of his birthplace, relished deploying his considerable comedic talent to embarrass Trump in front of the elites whose respect Trump craved. Obama joked:

> Now I know that he's taken some flack lately, but no one is prouder to put this birth certificate matter to rest than 'The Donald'. And that's because he can finally get back to focusing on the issues that matter, like: did we fake the moon landing? [Laughter] What really happened in Roswell? [Laughter] And – where are Biggie and Tupac?! [Laughter]

> [. . .]

> We all know about your credentials and breadth of experience. For example [laughter] – no, seriously – just recently, in an episode of *Celebrity Apprentice* [laughter] – at the steakhouse, the men's cooking team did not impress the judges from Omaha Steaks. And there was a lot of blame to go around. But you, Mr. Trump, recognized that the real problem was a lack of leadership. And so ultimately, you didn't blame Lil Jon or Meatloaf – you fired Gary Busey. [Laughter] And these are the kinds of decisions that would keep me up at night. [Laughter] Well handled, sir. Well handled. (Schulman 2011)

Meyers continued the onslaught:

> Donald Trump has been saying he will run for president as a Republican — which is surprising, since I just assumed he was running as a joke. (Meyers 2011)

The laughter generated by the Obama–Meyers tag team clearly humiliated Trump. He stared ahead stone-faced during their routines and left the dinner quickly after its conclusion. Several Trump confidants claim that Trump decided to run for president that evening (Haberman and Burns 2016; PBS 2016). The laughter Trump suffered at the hands of the Washington establishment (particularly from a Black man whose status as American – let alone president – he resented) had to be avenged.

However, when Trump actually launched his presidential bid in 2015, the laughter only grew louder. Everything from his hair to tacky hotels, racist and sexist remarks, and half-baked policy proposals became fodder for unrelenting mockery by journalists, political opponents and late-night comedians. But in what proved to be an inspired rhetorical manoeuvre, Trump linked the laughter that others enjoyed at his expense to the laughter he claimed America as a whole had been suffering from for years. In his announcement speech, Trump proclaimed, 'When do we beat Mexico at the border? They're laughing at us, at our stupidity!' (Time 2015). A standard line in any 2015–16 Trump speech or interview was 'they [Mexico, China, Iran, ISIS, North Korea, etc.] are laughing at us. They think we're so stupid!' This rhetoric of laughter was so central to his campaign that, after only a few months, the *Washington Post* created a compilation video titled '100-plus times Donald Trump assured us that America is a laughingstock' (Chokshi 2016). Trump successfully depicted the widespread laughter that the political and media establishment directed at him as but a single manifestation of the more general laughter directed at the American people. 'The same people who are laughing at me are laughing at you', Trump seemed to be saying. In an era of elite indifference to persistent joblessness, crippling personal debt and endless foreign wars, Trump's rhetoric – suggestive of a global conspiracy against 'everyday' Americans – proved remarkably effective. By making the real laughter directed at him resonate with the imagined laughter of America's enemies, Trump guaranteed that comedic attacks levelled against him did not – as his liberal opponents expected – undermine his support but rather intensified his followers' devotion.

Curiously enough, Trump himself hardly ever laughs. Seriously: try recalling a single time when you saw or heard Donald Trump laugh.[13] For such a skilled performer, Trump is also remarkably inept at telling jokes. His stand-up routine at the 2016 Al Smith Dinner was painfully awkward (Flegenheimer and Parker 2016) and likely explains his absence from the Correspondents' Dinner as president. Trump has, however, mastered one mode of producing laughter:

insult comedy (Nussbaum 2017; Webber 2019b; Wolcott 2015). Recall the first 2016 Republican debate where Megyn Kelly questioned Trump about his history of misogyny. Trump responded with a sexist quip about Rosie O'Donnell that launched the audience into a fury of laughter. With a single remark, Trump established himself as the party's premier political talent. The cruel quip has proved to be Trump's favourite and perhaps most potent rhetorical weapon. Jeb Bush? 'Low energy'; Elizabeth Warren? 'Pocahontas'; Stormy Daniels? 'Horseface'; John McCain? 'I like people who weren't captured'; Joe Biden? 'Sleepy Joe'; Shooting migrants? 'Only in the Panhandle can you get away with that statement!.'

The right-wing, aspirationally fascist political assemblage that has emerged around (but is in no way limited to) Donald Trump features a fifth form of gelopolitics: an *affective economy* of laughter (Ahmed 2004a, 2004b). Trump conducts a circulation of laughter that produces and sustains his political position. Trump 'conducts' laughter in both senses of the word: he *attracts* the laughter of his liberal opponents and then *directs* this laughter onto his supporters ('they're laughing at *us*'). Trump completes the circuit by directing his supporters' cruel laughter onto his liberal opponents, who are in turn motivated and encouraged to laugh at him some more. In this affective economy, laughter flows towards Trump, through Trump, and away from Trump, but Trump himself does not laugh. Both inside and outside the sphere of circulation, Trump establishes himself as its sovereign (Schmitt 2005: 5). This is a vital source of Trump's political appeal. Only the exceptional figure who knows the joke, can play the joke, *but is not in on the joke* can guarantee that he and his supporters will have the last laugh.

We live in an Age of Hilarity where laughter participates in politics in multiple, overlapping and oftentimes contradictory ways. Laughter is a medium through which subjects learn about and engage with political issues; a stake and weapon in violent political struggles; a site of political disruption and transformation; an escape from politics; and a circulating affect that creates and sustains complex political assemblages. The questions of *who* or *what* people laugh at; *why* they laugh at these targets; *when* they are prompted and encouraged to laugh; *how* they conduct their laughter; and the *effects* of such practices of laughter all reside at the heart of political life today.

In the Age of Hilarity, the theoretical task is not – as the a/gelasty dispute suggests – to gaze down upon this laughter and pronounce 'yea' or 'nay'. Such an approach takes for granted what emerges only through the multifarious activity of laughter itself – namely, a *polis*. Our task is instead to stand amidst this laughter and unpack how it shapes, sustains and transforms the distributions of *logos* and *phōnē* that constitute a political community. In place of the traditional, yet increasingly obsolete question of *whether* (or *to what extent*) laughter belongs in the *polis*, we must pose the more basic question that has nevertheless been sidelined by the history of political thought: *how* does laughter operate politically? To that end, this book engages with the work of Hobbes, Adorno, Ellison, and a collection of theorists of feminist politics and human sexuality like Butler and Freud who eschew the a/gelasty dispute in favour of a study of gelopolitics. These thinkers provide the theoretical resources needed to grasp the politics of laughter in the Age of Hilarity.

But before we can articulate this alternative to the a/gelasty dispute, we need a fuller understanding of the latter's philosophical underpinnings. Although I distinguish sharply between a/gelastic political theory and gelopolitics, all a/gelastic theories advance, at least implicitly, an account of gelopolitics – that is, a view of how laughter shapes and is shaped by political life. These accounts serve as the basis for their positions on laughter as an either positive or negative force in the *polis*. (We saw this with Brand, Paxman and Zelensky: their a/gelastic positions were grounded in different views about how laughter operates politically.) The two most prominent philosophical discourses of gelopolitics – those that supply the conceptual vocabulary and argumentative strategies for contemporary a/gelastic political theory – are *liberalism* and *Nietzscheanism*. In what follows, I describe these approaches and explain why a study of gelopolitics requires turning to a different philosophical tradition, namely critical theory.

Liberal Gelopolitics

> Against the assault of laughter, nothing can stand.
> Mark Twain, *The Mysterious Stranger* (1922: 132)

Most popular debate on the relationship between laughter and politics proceeds within the terms of the *liberal discourse of gelopolitics*. The starting point for this discourse is John Stuart Mill's classic thesis that freedom of individual thought and expression is required to discover the truths that fuel human progress (Mill 2002: 14–16).

Liberal theorists maintain that laughter's place in political life hinges on its epistemic value: insofar as laughter yields truth, the *polis* ought to promote and protect it, but insofar as laughter obstructs or fails to contribute to the production of truth, it should be restricted.[14]

The Third Earl of Shaftesbury provides perhaps the first formulation of the liberal discourse of gelopolitics in his 1709 essay 'Sensus Communis, an Essay on the Freedom of Wit and Humour in a Letter to a Friend'.[15] This piece offers a defence of 'raillery', or the practice whereby 'gentlemen and friends' ridicule and taunt one another's philosophical, moral and political arguments (Shaftesbury 1999: 36). Shaftesbury contends that raillery plays an essential role in enlightened discourse by allowing individuals to distinguish between arguments grounded in reason and those based on opinions, prejudice or 'idolatry':

> Truth, it is supposed, may bear *all* lights, and one of those principal lights, or natural mediums, by which things are to be viewed, in order to a thorough recognition, is ridicule itself, or that manner of proof by which we discern whatever is liable to just raillery in any subject. (29–30)

A claim's susceptibility to laughter when under assault by raillery reveals its absence of rational foundation. Laughter is the test that all good arguments must survive:

> For nothing is ridiculous except what is deformed. [. . .] How therefore can we possibly make a jest of honesty? – To laugh *both* ways is nonsensical. [. . .] A man must be soundly ridiculous who, with all the wit imaginable, would go about to ridicule wisdom or laugh at honesty or good manners. (59–60)

According to Shaftesbury, there exists a necessary connection between laughter and untruth, and laughter contributes to enlightenment by exposing faulty claims.

Shaftesbury insists that this power of laughter flourishes only under conditions of liberty where individuals (like gentlemen of 'the Club') can reason by means of an unregulated give-and-take (36). Under a repressive political or religious regime, laughter assumes pathological forms that are incapable of contributing to enlightenment: 'The natural free spirits of ingenious men, if imprisoned and controlled, will find out other ways of motion to relieve themselves in their constraint [. . .] whether it be in burlesque, mimicry or buffoonery' (34). In the absence of freedom, laughter degenerates into the mere foolishness of what Shaftesbury calls 'the many barbarous and illiterate nations' (38). While enlightening laughter is a felicitous by-product of a liberal political culture, Shaftesbury holds that such a culture in turn *requires* laughter to sustain itself. Individuals will want to participate in the taxing 'habit of reasoning' only if this activity is made more enjoyable by raillery: 'A freedom of raillery [. . .] [is] the only terms which can render such speculative conversations any way agreeable' (33; see also Basu 1999: 386).

Laughter, liberty and truth form a tight, mutually reinforcing conceptual network in Shaftesbury. Under conditions of liberty, laughter helps produce the truths by which individuals can further liberate themselves from false beliefs and repressive authorities. Truth-producing laughter is the essential privilege, right and duty of the liberal subject, while irrational laughter is neither worthy nor fitting of that subject. This conceptual network survives intact in the work of today's foremost liberal philosopher of the emotions, Martha Nussbaum. Nussbaum promotes a 'Stoic laughter' that prompts the subject to 'step back' from irrational attachments and attend to things possessing 'real' value as a capability that a liberal society must guarantee its citizens (Nussbaum 2006: 77; 2009: 87; 2013: 308–13). If we translate these liberal accounts of gelopolitics into the earlier Aristotelian idiom, we find that conditions of liberty allow for, entail and incentivise the conquering of the *phōnē* of laughter by its power of *logos*. From the perspective of the liberal discourse, it is in the nature of laughter not to be a senseless, wasteful activity of the body but rather a productive exercise of human reason that helps secure political freedom (Holm 2017: 28).

Contemporary a/gelastic debate operates largely within the framework established by the liberal discourse. For example, political commentators typically defend the laughter produced by comedians like John Oliver for how it exposes truths about political actors and institutions that were previously concealed by rhetoric, deception or ideology. Freed from false beliefs or ignorance, audiences can make more informed and rational political decisions. As Egan writes in the piece quoted earlier, 'the antidote to a long day of White House lies is a long late night of comedy' (Egan 2019). On the other hand, targets of late-night comedians generally condemn this laughter as grounded in falsehoods. For instance, in 2014 Fox News's Bill O'Reilly responded to a critical *Colbert Report* segment by describing Colbert as an 'ideological fanatic' who 'deceives his audience [. . .] under the guise of comedy' (Thompson 2014). Trump, meanwhile, has accused

Saturday Night Live of being untruthful about him, tweeting that the programme is 'totally biased', 'totally one-sided' and, for that reason, 'not funny' (Trump 2016a, 2016b, 2017, 2019). Both O'Reilly and Trump ironically obey the liberal script by associating laughter with truthfulness and dismissing what they view as biased comedy as not *really* funny. We also see the liberal discourse at work around *Charlie Hebdo*. The cartoons' supporters assert that the laughter they generate exposes the dangerous irrationality of Islamic fundamentalism and in doing so secures the liberty of the French public sphere (Hamburger 2017), while sceptics accuse the magazine of publishing 'childish and unserious' material and 'silly provocations' that do not merit the kind of full-throated defence owed to other forms of speech (Trudeau 2015; Yu 2015).

While the liberal discourse opens the conceptual and argumentative space for a wide range of positions on laughter, a significant blind spot limits its utility for a study of gelopolitics. When Shaftesbury distinguishes between the enlightening laughter of the 'Club' of 'well-bred' gentlemen (Shaftesbury 1999: 31) and the 'buffoonery and burlesque' (35) of 'the many barbarous and illiterate nations' (38), he overlooks how the superiority of the former hinges on the inferiority of the latter. Laughter at faulty arguments presumes – and thus helps create and sustain – the distinction between a civilised (rational) class and a backwards (irrational) class. The enlightening, liberating laughter celebrated by Shaftesbury likewise simultaneously functions to mystify and repress. Along the same lines, when *Charlie Hebdo* uses laughter to combat the alleged irrationality of Islamic fundamentalism, it entrenches the marginalised social position of French Muslims. Meanwhile, the laughter generated by American political comedians liberates and enlightens only by disqualifying its targets (e.g., Trump and his supporters) as repressive (or repressed) and deceptive (or ignorant). This is the core paradox – or dialectic – of liberal gelopolitics: laughter is the natural ally of a liberating *logos* only insofar as it consigns its objects to a state of mere *phōnē*. By conceiving of laughter as properly allied with freedom and enlightenment, the liberal discourse obscures how laughter itself produces and reproduces the social meaning of 'freedom' and 'enlightenment'. As the *Charlie Hebdo* attacks and the Trumpist affective economy of laughter illustrate, such blindness can prove quite costly.

Is it possible to imagine laughter participating in politics in ways that are not reducible to *logos*? The dangers of the dialectic of liberal gelopolitics suggest the need for an approach that casts off the philosophical preoccupation with the presence or absence of truth and freedom and instead attends to how laughter itself helps construct the social and political field in which these concepts acquire their meaning and application.

Nietzschean Gelopolitics

> I didn't imagine that *laughter* would dispose me toward *thought*, but that *laughter*, being in certain respects antecedent to my thought, would carry me further than thought.
>
> Georges Bataille, 'Aphorism for the "System"' (2001a: 153)

The *Nietzschean discourse of gelopolitics* provides such an approach. Nietzsche places laughter at the centre of his philosophical project, announcing that 'I should actually risk an order of rank among philosophers depending on the rank of their laughter – all the way up to those capable of *golden* laughter' (Nietzsche 1989: 231–2). Unlike the instrument of reason imagined by liberal theorists, 'golden' laughter is an experience through which subjects question the value of what reason has become historically. As Nietzsche's alter ego Zarathustra declares:

> I bade [men] laugh at their great masters of virtue and saints and poets and world-redeemers. I bade them laugh at their gloomy sages and at whoever had at any time sat on the tree of life like a black scarecrow. I sat down by their great tomb road among cadavers and vultures, and I laughed at all their past and its rotting, decaying glory. (Nietzsche 1982: 308)

Nietzsche argues that learning to laugh at 'truth' as a product of historically contingent political struggles makes possible the emergence of new, more life-affirming systems of truth that are themselves laughable in the very same way: 'we should call every truth false which was not accompanied by at least one laugh' (322). Dispelling the 'spirit of gravity' (153) typically associated with the pursuit of knowledge, golden laughter infuses free spirits who are armed with historical sense and courage in the face of 'truth' (Nietzsche 1996: 5–6, 12–13). Whereas the liberal discourse subordinates the *phōnē* of laughter to the ends of *logos*, Nietzsche attends to how this *phōnē* historicises *logos* and opens it up to becoming otherwise.

Nietzsche inaugurates what Anca Parvulescu calls 'the laughing twentieth century' (Parvulescu 2010: 3), a century whose most innovative philosophical minds (particularly from France) associate their projects with laughter. Declaring that his is 'a philosophy founded on the experience of laughter' (Bataille 2001b: 138), Georges Bataille holds that rather than yielding greater knowledge about the world, laughter carries the subject to the very limits of knowledge itself, dramatically upending what it means to think and know:

> *The unknown makes us laugh.* [. . .] It makes us laugh to pass very abruptly, all of a sudden, from a world in which each thing is well qualified, in which each thing is given its stability, generally in a stable order, to a world in which our assurance is suddenly overthrown. (2001b: 135)

Jacques Derrida builds on Bataille's account by arguing that only a 'burst of laughter' constitutes a negativity that *logos* (in the form of the Hegelian dialectic) cannot reinscribe as a positive moment in its own coming-to-consciousness: 'Laughter alone exceeds dialectics and the dialectician: it bursts out only on the basis of an absolute renunciation of meaning' (Derrida 1978: 256). Hélène Cixous in turn draws on Derrida to articulate a feminist political vision oriented around laughter (Cixous 1976, 1981). For Cixous, laughter embodies the excessive *eros* of the feminine that undermines the *logo*-centrism of patriarchy. (I discuss Cixous's gelopolitics at length in Chapter 4.) Finally, Michel Foucault describes his archaeology of historical structures of knowledge in *The Order of Things* as originating in laughter at Borges's account of a 'certain Chinese encyclopaedia' that features a strange zoological schema:

> This book first arose out a passage in Borges, out of the laughter that shattered, as I read the passage, all the familiar landmarks of my thought – *our* thought, the thought that bears the stamp of our age and our geography – breaking up all the ordered surfaces and all the planes with which we are accustomed to tame the wild profusion of existing things, and continuing long afterwards to disturb and threaten with collapse our age-old distinction between the Same and the Other. (Foucault 1994: xv)

For these thinkers – and others including Gilles Deleuze and Félix Guattari (1986), Luce Irigaray (1985), Julia Kristeva (1980, 1984), Milan Kundera (1999), Lyotard (1988) and Jean-Luc Nancy (1993) – laughter arises at the limits of the human *logos*, where it confronts itself as foreign, strange and unintelligible – that is, as mere *phōnē*. According to the Nietzschean discourse of gelopolitics, the Aristotelian distinction between *logos* and *phōnē* deconstructs itself in laughter.

The Russian philosopher and literary critic Mikhail Bakhtin was not a student of Nietzsche, but his singularly rich and influential account of laughter in *Rabelais and His World* resonates strongly with the Nietzschean tradition (Weeks 2004) and can be considered in the same vein. Bakhtin argues that the Renaissance novels of François Rabelais demonstrate how laughter 'is the second revelation of the world in play' (Bakhtin 1984: 84). The carnivals, feasts and marketplaces depicted by Rabelais disclose a laughing 'second world' alongside the official, serious world of the medieval Church (5–6). This popular culture of folk humour undermines the sanctioned values of piety, hierarchy and austerity in favour of folly, equality and abundance. But unlike the modern reduction of laughter to a force of 'bare negation' (e.g., Shaftesbury's raillery), medieval and Renaissance laughter renews and regenerates that which it degrades and debases: 'True ambivalent and universal laughter does not deny seriousness but purifies and completes it. [. . .] Laughter does not permit seriousness to atrophy and to be torn away from the one being, forever incomplete. It restores this ambivalent wholeness' (122–3). For Bakhtin, the people overcomes its fear of earthly and divine authority by laughingly reinserting the latter into the messy, material processes of historical becoming (90–5, 255–6). Despite waning in modernity, this popular culture of laughter endures as a means by which humans inhabit and renew their common world (276). Bakhtin holds that the *phōnē* of laughter is the tone through which the people degrades, historicises and hence reinvigorates *logos*. While the Nietzschean theorists identify a similar power in laughter, Bakhtin describes this power in explicitly political terms as belonging to the historically conscious, radically democratic and utopian body of the people as a whole (9–12, 92, 255–6).

Rather than theorising laughter in terms of its contributions to the human *logos*, the Nietzschean discourse of gelopolitics understands laughter as a complex, dialectical play between *logos* and *phōnē*. In laughter, *logos* and *phōnē* unravel their constitutive difference by discovering themselves in one another, thus precipitating the historicisation and transformation of the distinction between them. From a Nietzschean perspective, the laughter produced by political comedians, *Charlie Hebdo* and figures like Trump and Zelensky participates in politics not by delivering truth, but by shaping, disrupting and modifying what counts as rational, truthful speech. The Nietzschean theorists express philosophically what Russell Brand suggests colloquially, namely that laughter can interrupt and recompose the very terms of political life. Their discourse responds to the liberal neglect of the historical contingency of *logos* by identifying laughter as a key experience through which 'truth' itself is constructed.

Scholars influenced by Nietzschean calls to historicise and reinvent *logos* advocate an increased role for laughter in politics. For instance, William Connolly suggests an ethos of agonistic respect infused by ironic laughter (Connolly 2002: 120); Judith Butler recommends a parodic laughter that challenges dominant formations of gender identity and sexual desire (Butler 1990: 139); and Lars Tønder endorses comedy as a way to pluralise identities and viewpoints in a democracy (Tønder 2014). The Nietzschean discourse also supplies the resources for disqualifying certain laughter from the *polis*. Bakhtin condemns modern humour and satire for tearing down its targets without stimulating a corresponding regeneration (Bakhtin 1984: 38); D. Diane Davis rejects both 'angelic' laughter that takes joy in truth and 'devilish' laughter that celebrates meaninglessness in favour of a 'cosmic' laughter that affirms the plurality of systems of human meaning (Davis 2000, 55–6, 64); and Alenka Zupančič objects to 'false' comedy that entrenches universal categories in favour of 'true' comedy that 'short-circuits' them with material social conditions (Zupančič 2008: 30–4).

While liberals and Nietzscheans theorise laughter in dramatically different ways, they converge in providing the conceptual and argumentative resources for the contemporary a/gelasty dispute. Their discourses fuel the a/gelastic question of 'what role should laughter play in the *polis*?' by conceiving of laughter as (a) originating in the human subject[16] and (b) naturally emancipatory. When laughter is understood as emanating from a discrete location and as exerting predictable effects, it becomes something the *polis* can manage, like unemployment or disease. If one fears the emancipatory disruptions of laughter, they can, like Plato, work to restrict comedy; if one welcomes these disruptions, they can, like Lyotard, promote it. Leaving behind the a/gelasty dispute and developing an account of gelopolitics likewise requires new philosophical resources. In particular, it requires abandoning the liberal and Nietzschean view of laughter as an inexhaustible source of freedom enjoyed by the human subject as a natural endowment. Fetishising laughter in this way divorces laughter from the social structures of power and hierarchy from which it arises and exerts effects, and it short-changes laughter's political polyvalence within those structures. Determining *how* laughter operates politically – not *whether* it should do so – calls for a theoretical perspective that (a) accounts for its position within a broader *social order* while (b) avoiding the liberal neglect of laughter's dialectically complex relationship to truth and freedom.

A Critical Theory of Laughter

> Laughter is a condition of ideology. It provides us with the distance, the very space within which ideology can take its full swing. It is only with laughter that we become ideological subjects, withdrawn from the immediate pressure of ideological claims to a free enclave. It is only when we laugh and breathe freely that ideology truly has a hold on us.
>
> Mladen Dolar, 'Strel sredi koncerta' (1986: 307; quoted in Zupančič 2008: 4)

Such a perspective is provided by the early Frankfurt School of critical theory, in particular the work of Theodor Adorno. Adorno and his colleagues like Max Horkheimer understand critical theory as an effort to grasp the modern capitalist social order – the complex economic-political-cultural whole linked together and organised by the circulation and accumulation of capital – in such a way that resists it (Adorno 2000: 30–3; Horkheimer 1999: 206–8).[17] Critical theory responds to the contradiction between the enormous productive capacities mobilised by capitalism and the widespread suffering it has wrought historically: 'The experience of the contradictory character of societal reality is not an arbitrary starting point but rather the motive which first constitutes the possibility of sociology as such' (Adorno 1976: 120). Channelling Walter Benjamin's fascination with the 'dialectical image', Adorno proposes investigating society's 'eccentric phenomena' that embody and reveal its contradictory character (110; Buck-Morss 1977: 69–81). Critical theory, or 'negative dialectics', Adorno writes, aims to 'cause the totality to be illuminated in a partial feature' (Adorno 1991a: 16). By exposing the contradictions that characterise the whole, such eccentric phenomena – what Adorno calls the 'non-identical' – provide occasions for imagining and pursuing less oppressive forms of social organisation (Adorno 1973: 52). Critical theory identifies and dramatises the seemingly minor discontinuities that offer openings for social transformation. 'For the mind,' Adorno concludes, 'is indeed not capable of producing or grasping the totality of the real, but it may be possible to penetrate the detail, to explode in miniature the mass of merely existing reality' (Adorno 1977: 133).

As an alternative to the liberal and Nietzschean approaches, I propose treating laughter as one of the 'eccentric', 'apparently out-of-the-way, obscure phenomena' (Adorno 2000: 17) through which we can both grasp *and* think against the contemporary social order – that is, late neoliberal capitalism. (Indeed, Chapter 2 will argue that this is precisely how Adorno himself theorises laughter.) Conceiving of laughter as a site of social non-identity means attending to how it both (a) occurs within and constitutes a product of the social order and (b) enacts a rupture within the social order and its various structures of power and hierarchy (e.g., class, race and gender). At first glance, the claim that laughter exerts a disruptive and emancipatory effect on society may seem like a rehash of the Nietzschean argument that laughter interrupts and transforms the human *logos*. However, there is a crucial difference here. While experiences of laughter highlight (and thus intensify) weaknesses, fragilities or fractures in the social order, *because laughter is also a product of the social order*, it can work to defend and secure that order against these vulnerabilities. As a site of social non-identity, laughter bolsters the social order's structures of power and hierarchy just as readily as it undermines them. Through laughter, the inside of the social order opens itself up to its outside *and* this outside reinscribes the boundaries of its inside. Whether it is a mindless giggle at a colleague's quip, a deliberate chuckle at a rival's mistake, or a howling eruption at a truly funny joke, laughter can deepen *or* fortify the fissures in social life that it exposes. We will see numerous examples of this everyday social undecidability and political polyvalence of laughter in the chapters that follow.

What the Nietzschean discourse identified as laughter's ability to shape, disrupt and transform *logos* – that is, the foundation of a shared political life – now takes on a new significance. This deconstructive capacity of laughter does not operate in an abstract, subjective vacuum but instead functions continually within a determinate social order with its various structures of power and hierarchy. Considering the Nietzschean *logos/phōnē* dialectic alongside critical theory's inside/outside dialectic reveals that laughter is a key experience through which *logos* – understood as rational, truthful speech *as secured by a social order's structures of power and hierarchy* – constructs and transforms itself on an everyday basis. The question of gelopolitics, in other words, is necessarily also a question of the social order. The liberal and Nietzschean discourses' failure to grasp how laughter could, in its essence, be anything but emancipatory stems from their failure to acknowledge the political importance of the concept of social order.

Until now I have followed the liberal and Nietzschean discourses in describing laughter as an *experience* – that is, as something that originates in and affects the human subject. But the tradition of critical theory suggests that laughter is also an *event* – that is, something that originates in and exerts effects on the level of the social order as a whole.[18] Laughter is simultaneously an experience and an event: the truth-delivering or truth-shattering experience of laughter described by liberals and Nietzscheans respectively arises within and transforms the social order, while the event of laughter described from the perspective of critical theory always proceeds by way of and affects subjects who laugh. Experiences of laughter occur in, proceed through and exert objective effects on the social order, while events of laughter occur in, proceed through and exert effects on laughing subjects.

Gelopolitics, in sum, is characterised by three intersecting dialectics: *logos* and *phōnē*; inside and outside; and experience and event.[19] When we consider these relations together, we find that *laughter constitutes a privileged experience/event wherein the contemporary social order constructs, preserves and transforms itself politically*. This is the core argument of *Laughter as Politics*. In laughter, notions of what counts as rational, truthful speech and who qualifies as a rational, truthful speaker form and entrench themselves (often in oppressive, reactionary, exclusionary ways that bolster and secure a social order's structures of power and hierarchy) *and* overcome and transform themselves (often in more emancipatory, subversive, democratic directions that challenge and undermine those structures). The political life of society takes shape, consolidates itself and is resisted in everyday experiences/events of laughter.

This account of gelopolitics – what I call a *critical theory of laughter* – departs decisively from the a/gelasty dispute that dominates scholarly and popular discourse on laughter. The a/gelasty dispute's narrow focus on the normative question of what role laughter should play in the *polis* forecloses an attention to the much larger critical question of how laughter shapes the *polis* and opens it up to change.[20] More specifically, it obscures how laughter (a) constructs *and* transforms the terrain of truth and falsity constitutive of the *polis* (i.e., the *logos/phōnē* dialectic);[21] (b) troubles *and* fortifies the relationship between the laughing subject and the broader social order (i.e., the experience/event dialectic); and (c) undermines *and* secures the structure of the social order as a whole (i.e., the inside/outside dialectic).²² A critical theory of laughter demonstrates that laughter is not simply a political virtue or vice but an open-ended site of politics itself – one that is pivotal to how the late neoliberal social order produces, sustains and transforms itself. Only a theoretical orientation sensitive to these three dialectics can account for the multiple, overlapping and contradictory ways laughter operates politically in the Age of Hilarity. A study of gelopolitics, in other words, is necessarily a critical theory of laughter.

The Path Ahead

> There is no better start for thinking than laughter.
> Walter Benjamin, 'The Author as Producer' (2007: 236)

The following chapters on Hobbes, Adorno, Ellison and contemporary feminist and queer thought articulate and develop this critical theory of laughter. Before introducing these chapters, two disclaimers are in order. The first concerns the book's subject matter. *Laughter as Politics* is a book about laughter. It is *not* a book about comedy, humour, irony, parody or any other genre or technique that produces laughter. One of the difficulties in writing about laughter is that some of the most important scholarship on the subject tends not to differentiate clearly between laughter and what generates it. (For instance, Henri Bergson's *Laughter* is really, as its subtitle indicates, 'an essay on the meaning of the comic'; Bergson 1999.) To be sure, a rigorous account of gelopolitics is impossible without attending to genres like comedy and humour, and *Laughter as Politics* learns from (and hopefully contributes to) the fields of comedy and humour studies that explore these genres' formal features and techniques, material conditions of production and social functions within modern media economies (Attardo 2014; Lockyer 2016; Marx and Sienkiewicz 2018; Wilkie 2020).²³ But even as a study of laughter overlaps with and may at times seem indistinguishable from a study of comedy or humour, I am keen to insist on drawing an analytical distinction between them. As I have already begun to show, there exists a political logic and efficacy of laughter that exceeds that of the genres that produce it, and it is this specificity of gelopolitics that the book seeks to unpack and bring to bear on the current conjuncture. For that reason, *Laughter as Politics* only tangentially engages with the vast political theoretic and philosophical literature on the politics of comedy,[24] humour,[25] satire,[26] irony[27] and parody.[28] Scholars working in these areas may find much of value in *Laughter as Politics*, but they should expect an intervention that remains relatively aloof (hopefully productively so) from these debates. The book instead finds itself much more at home in – and as making an explicitly *political* contribution to – the loosely organised interdiscipline of laughter studies.[29]

The second disclaimer concerns the book's style of presentation. A striking feature of so much popular and academic literature around laughter is that it tries to be (and often is) quite funny. For example, Terry Eagleton's *Humour* (2019) explores the sources and effects of humour by way of a series of breezy jokes and funny anecdotes. Michael Billig perceptively identifies the view that writing about laughter ought to be funny as consistent with the ideology of optimism, positivity and 'fun' that governs late capitalism: 'only in modern times do analysts of humour regularly include jokes in order to amuse their readers and to display their own good-heartedness. [. . .] Indeed, the critic needs to question seriously the force of that pressure' (Billig 2005: 8; see also Bown 2019: vii). If we subscribe to the liberal and Nietzschean conception of laughter as naturally emancipatory, the imperative to adopt a gelastic style makes sense. If, however, we take issue with this assumption and pursue a critical theory of laughter – one that aims to stimulate greater reflection on the political opportunities *and* dangers laughter presents in contemporary society – then a more reserved, even agelastic style is in order. While the reader may get a chuckle or two out of some of the comedic and humorous sources I treat, those looking for a laugh would be well advised – in the unlikely event they have not done so already – to find a different book.

Laughter as Politics employs the resources of political theory to move beyond the a/gelasty dispute and say something new about laughter. The concept of 'gelopolitics' suggests, however, that an examination of laughter as a site of politics also provides the opportunity to say something new about 'politics' as both a concept and a practice. I likewise approach the accounts of laughter offered by Hobbes, Adorno, Ellison and feminist and queer thought as occasions for (a) identifying and cultivating the incipient and previously unrecognised political (in particular, democratic) possibilities of their texts and/or projects, and (b) shedding light on the political origins, dynamics and effects of recent experiences/events of laughter like the 2010 Jon Stewart and Stephen Colbert 'Rally to Restore Sanity and/or Fear' and the 2017 Jordan Peele film *Get Out*. Endeavouring to emulate the tradition of critical theory at its best, *Laughter as Politics* proceeds through a dialectical, mutually illuminating conversation between theory, text and experience/event.

The book's first two chapters hone the basic analytical tools needed for a critical theory of laughter. Chapter 1, 'The Laughing Body Politic: The Counter/sovereign Politics of Hobbes's Theory of Laughter', unpacks the *political logic of laughter* by turning to a theorist who at first appears to be one of the a/gelasty dispute's leading lights: Thomas Hobbes. Nietzsche famously disparaged Hobbes as an agelast, identifying him as 'that philosopher, who being a real Englishman, tried to bring laughter into ill repute' (Nietzsche 1989: 231). While Hobbes indeed objects to laughter, this is perhaps the least interesting aspect of his theory. Much more consequential is the relationship between his conception of laughter as sudden vainglory – that is, an unjustified feeling of power over someone or something else – and his broader political philosophy. Hobbes holds that because the false feeling of superiority in laughter is nevertheless taken seriously by its audience – those laughed at behave as if the laughing individual actually is superior – laughter is a *counter-sovereign* political enactment that destabilises prevailing hierarchies of power. We find this very same logic of sudden vainglory at work in the social contract's establishment of sovereignty. The Hobbesian body politic is a *laughing body politic* at the moment of its foundation. This notion of a laughing body politic highlights both how laughter is an experience/event through which sovereign authority establishes, exerts and entrenches itself and how sovereignty is constitutively haunted by the threat of counter-sovereign disruption. By analysing laughter's role in the 1980 Lenin Shipyard strike and the 2010 Stewart/Colbert Rally, the chapter concludes that the political logic of laughter is neither simply counter-sovereign nor simply sovereign, but rather *counter/sovereign*. Laughter challenges sovereignty (i.e., that which institutes and sustains a given order of *logos*) only by reinscribing it anew (i.e., by instituting an alternative order of *logos*), and it bolsters sovereignty only by dramatising its own vulnerability to challenge. Hobbes, in sum, illuminates laughter as an unauthorised, fragile feeling of power through which sovereignty is made, undone and made again.

While Hobbes sheds light on the first dialectic of gelopolitics identified above (*logos/phōnē*), his inattention to the question of the social order leaves us ill equipped to make sense of the other two dialectics (inside/outside and experience/event). Chapter 2, 'Beyond A/gelasty:

Adorno's Critical Theory of Laughter', remedies this by providing an account of the *social logic of gelopolitics*. Adorno's aesthetic philosophy and essays on the culture industry, light-hearted art, Samuel Beckett and Charlie Chaplin reveal how laughter is not just an emancipatory experience that originates in the human subject but also an objective event that arises within and can entrench the social order's structures of power and hierarchy. Adorno shows that the fractured, contradictory nature of modern capitalist society means that gelopolitics is irreducibly split against itself. Laughter bolsters the social order (i.e., serves oppressive, reactionary ends) only by prompting the imagination of alternative forms of social organisation, and it escapes the terms of existing social life (i.e., serves subversive, emancipatory ends) only when it embodies the violence of that life. This is the social logic of gelopolitics. The chapter concludes by investigating the different kinds of laughter enjoyed by Black and white audiences of the film *Get Out* to demonstrate how Adorno models a critical theory that resists the a/gelastic imperative to either support or oppose laughter in favour of attending to laughter as a site of non-identity that both secures the social order and opens it up to change.

Having established the main theoretical pillars of a critical theory of laughter – the political logic of laughter and the social logic of gelopolitics – the second half of the book considers laughter's role in two of contemporary society's most important political structures: race and sex/gender. These are, of course, enormously complex systems of power marked by high degrees of internal variation and interlocking influence, and the place and function of laughter within them differs accordingly across time and space.[30] Chapters 3 and 4 therefore do not presume to provide anywhere near an exhaustive account of the relationship between laughter and racial, sexual and gender politics. However, in my view the sources I examine – Ralph Ellison's 1985 essay 'An Extravagance of Laughter' and the recent feminist/queer theoretical discourse on laughter – constitute particularly fruitful sites for interrogating how laughter shapes, sustains and transforms conceptions of and regulations around race, sex and gender today. Chapter 2's exploration of the differential politics of Black and white laughter serves as a helpful transition to this new level of analysis.

Chapter 3, 'Over a Barrel: Ellison and the Democratic Politics of Black Laughter', offers a reading of Ellison's remarkable, yet largely overlooked 1985 essay, 'An Extravagance of Laughter'. In this piece, Ellison tells a joke from African American folklore about 'laughing barrels' – barrels into which Black Southerners were supposedly required to laugh during the Jim Crow era – to illustrate how the distinctive sounds, styles and tonalities of Black laughter in America are shaped by white supremacy and how white supremacy constructs and maintains itself by regulating this laughter. If, as Langston Hughes, Angela Davis and others have suggested, Jim Crow segregation was a form of fascism (Churchwell 2020; Toscano 2020; Whitman 2017), then Ellison's account of Black laughter is a crucial resource for understanding gelopolitics amid contemporary neofascism. Ellison establishes that while the American racial order produces and is sustained by a white supremacist regime of laughter, Black laughter can democratise that order by obeying the white supremacist regime in such a way that generates a dissensus within it. For Ellison, Black laughter is neither the 'irrational', 'primitive' force imagined by white supremacy nor the inherently emancipatory force imagined by other Black thinkers. Its politics are instead intensely dialectical: the racist conception of Black laughter as irrational and primitive provides the resources for its own democratic overcoming, and the democratising power of Black laughter depends paradoxically on its association with these attributes. The chapter concludes by showing how Ellison's reflections on laughter illuminate his distinctive conception of democracy as a mode of political life featuring 'antagonistic cooperation' among individuals, collectivities and the social order as a whole.

Perhaps no scholarly field has found itself as entangled in the a/gelasty dispute as feminist and queer theory. Given the historical monopoly on laughter by men (e.g., the stand-up comedy industry) and laughter's frequent deployment in defence of patriarchy (e.g., sexist jokes), feminists have traditionally eschewed laughter in favour of more 'serious' affects. Chapter 4, 'The Best Medicine? Repoliticising Laughter for Contemporary Feminist and Queer Politics', offers a genealogy of the late twentieth- and early twenty-first-century feminist and queer discourse that resignifies laughter as a source of women's emancipation. This gelastic discourse, inaugurated by Hélène Cixous in the 1970s and continued in diverse forms by feminist and queer theorists like Luce Irigaray, Jack Halberstam and Cynthia Willett, conceives of laughter as an experience that is uniquely capable of undermining the rigid and violent notions of gender identity and sexual desire at the root of patriarchy and heteronormativity. While this discourse has been instrumental in expanding the bounds and possibilities of feminist and queer politics, I argue that it hinges on a curious and ultimately counterproductive depoliticisation of laughter itself. In particular, its conception of laughter as naturally emancipatory obscures the multiplicity of ways laughter participates in sex and gender politics beyond and oftentimes in tension with its capacity to oppose patriarchy and heteronormativity. Judith Butler's *Gender Trouble*, Sigmund Freud's *The Joke* and Hannah Gadsby's *Nanette* provide the basis for a repoliticised feminist/queer account of laughter that attends to how laughter helps produce and sustain conventional conceptions of masculinity and femininity. Neither the nemesis nor saviour of feminist and queer politics, laughter is a privileged site of political contestation over sex and gender – one distinguished only by its peculiar efficacy in creating, enforcing and resisting the formations of gender identity and sexual desire that compose the contemporary social order.

The book's coda, 'The End of Laughter? Gelopolitics and the New Agelasty', uses these theoretical tools and insights to consider a recent shift in scholarly and popular discourse around laughter. Confronted by the rise of neofascist deployments of laughter (e.g., Trump's use of insult comedy and right-wing Internet trolling) and the manifest failures of liberal and leftist laughter to successfully combat reactionary politics, many liberal and Nietzschean thinkers who once celebrated laughter now worry it has run out of political steam. For 'new agelasts' like Emily Nussbaum, Ken Jennings and Nidesh Lawtoo, a world awash with laughter has not turned out to be any freer or more democratic; in fact, by blurring the boundaries between the serious and the comedic, the Age of Hilarity has empowered some of the world's most dangerous political actors and movements. The new agelasts aim to restore laughter's critical and emancipatory power by limiting its role in political life. I argue that this new discourse hinges on the same misunderstanding of the relationship between laughter and politics that the chapters on Hobbes, Adorno, Ellison and feminist and queer theory all seek to remedy. It is impossible to secure the *polis* from laughter because the *polis* does not exist apart from the *gelōs* that helps constitute it. All there is is gelopolitics. Those seeking to resist neofascist deployments of laughter should consequently abandon the illusory and self-defeating goal of policing laughter more effectively and instead engage today's enormous quantity and variety of laughter as a unique, albeit danger-ridden opportunity to imagine and build more democratic institutions and ideologies.

Why Gelopolitics?

Laughter as Politics argues that laughter constitutes a privileged site wherein the contemporary social order constructs, preserves and transforms itself politically. But why study laughter at such length today? Amid an ongoing, yet still inchoate global political crisis featuring viral pandemics, racial violence, glacier meltdowns, misinformation campaigns and renewed nationalisms, the focus on laughter might seem to be misguided or even trivialising. However, as I have already begun to show, laughter plays a key role in the production of and resistance to many of these emergent processes. Indeed, gelopolitics has only become more ubiquitous and consequential as this multifaceted crisis deepens and grows. The predominant pattern of thinking about and reckoning with the Age of Hilarity – the a/gelasty dispute as informed by the liberal and Nietzschean discourses – responds by either endorsing the obvious (promote X liberating practice of laughter); advising the impossible (keep Y oppressive practice of laughter out of politics); or recommending the counterproductive (e.g., defeat Z reactionary politician by laughing at them!). The a/gelasty dispute fails as a political-theoretic paradigm because it treats laughter as something external to the political conjuncture in which it arises and exerts effects. What is needed is an approach that resists the imperative to pronounce 'yea' or 'nay' on laughter and instead grapples with laughter as the highly efficacious and fraught site of politics that it is. When we grasp laughter concretely as pregnant with both democratic potential and fascist danger, we find that its outsized presence in the current moment – so much laughter in such dark times – is a function of the multiplicity of political opportunities and risks this moment affords. The critical theory of laughter advanced in the following chapters aims to enhance our capacity to reflect on and constructively engage with this deeply paradoxical political condition.

Notes

1. For contributions to the debate over laughing at Trump, see Almond (2019), Berlatsky (2020), Bunch (2017), Flanagan (2017), Framke (2017), Kein (2017), Kristof (2020), Nussbaum (2017), Olen (2019) and Schwarz (2017). Similar debates have raged outside the United States as well. See, for instance, the 2019 controversy in the United Kingdom over tossing milkshakes at Brexit Party leader Nigel Farage

and far-right activist Tommy Robinson (Chakrabortty 2019; Rifkind 2019; Shrimsley 2019). Meanwhile, in some countries the liberal and leftist political culture as a whole appears to take a position in this dispute. Compare, for example, the prevalence of laughter at Brazil's Jair Bolsonaro (Christofaro 2019; Genot 2020; *Rolling Stone* 2020) with the dearth of laughter at Germany's Alternative für Deutschland (AfD) Party.
2. See, for instance, Rawls (1971, 1996), Nozick (1974) and Nussbaum (2006).
3. See, for instance, Cohen (2003), Gutmann and Thompson (2004) and Habermas (1984, 1990).
4. See, for instance, Arnold (2009), Euben (2003), McWilliams (1995), Tønder (2014), Willett and Willett (2019) and Zumbrunnen (2012).
5. See, for instance, Bakhtin (1984), Bruner (2005), Eagleton (2019) and Hirschkop (2001).
6. See, for instance, Connolly (2002), Conway and Seery (1992), Rorty (1989) and Seery (1990).
7. See, for instance, Deleuze (1990) and Lombardini (2013, 2018).
8. See, for instance, Butler (1990).
9. For various accounts of the Age of Hilarity, see Jennings (2018), Holm (2017), Martin, Kaye and Harmon (2018) and *The Economist* (2019).
10. See, for instance, Baumgartner and Becker (2018), Baumgartner and Morris (2006, 2008, 2011), Cao (2010), Feldman and Young (2008), Hollander (2005), Lichter, Baumgartner and Morris (2018), Morris (2009) and Xenos and Becker (2009).
11. Even this modest aspiration was quickly dashed as Zelensky became embroiled in the American arms-for-dirt extortion scheme that precipitated Donald Trump's first impeachment. Protests against the new Zelensky government rocked Ukraine in late 2019 (Schwirtz and Kramer 2019).
12. On this point, it is worth reflecting on Russell Brand's comparison of himself to Boris Johnson. Ideology aside, are these two figures – one a comic actor, the other a Prime Minister – *really* all that different from one another?
13. To my knowledge, Trump has been seen laughing on video only three times since 2015. All three incidents came in response to comments shouted by supporters at campaign rallies: the first comparing Hillary Clinton to a dog; the second referring to Bill Clinton as 'Slick Willie"; and the third advocating shooting migrants at the border.
14. The liberal discourse can in a sense be traced back to Plato, who, as we have seen, permits laughter provided that it helps secure the truth. However, the modern liberal discourse articulates laughter's relation to truth not in terms of an objective rational order (like Plato), but in terms of the individual subject's capacity to reason.

15. While Shaftesbury, an eighteenth-century Whig, predates liberal political philosophy in the tradition of Mill, his commitment to human reason and the liberty of thought and expression makes his account of laughter an early – and perhaps for that reason, particularly shrewd and sophisticated – example of the liberal discourse of gelopolitics.
16. In Bakhtin's case, this is the collective subject of 'the people' as a whole.
17. When Adorno and other members of the Frankfurt School refer to 'society', 'the social whole' or 'the social totality', they are referring to roughly the same object that Louis Althusser and his followers identify as 'the social formation' (Althusser 2005; Chambers 2014). However, in order to respect the specificity of the Althusserian discourse and to avoid the positivist Comtean or Durkheimian connotations of the term 'society', I generally employ 'social order' in my discussion of Adorno and the Frankfurt School.
18. By describing laughter as an 'event', I am not invoking the influential accounts of the event advanced by Alain Badiou (2005, 2007) or Gilles Deleuze (1987, 1990). Alfie Bown's recent book, *In the Event of Laughter*, theorises laughter as an event in the Badiouian sense. Rejecting the traditional philosophical quest for the cause of laughter, Bown proposes that laughter's effect is to retroactively modify its causes: the event of laughter 'changes the place into which it erupts, reorganizing the world but making it appear as though things have always been that way, as if laughter was merely a response to what was already there' (Bown 2019: 4). My approach resonates with Bown's (particularly his focus on how laughter 'erects and constructs ideologies and subjectivities, but simultaneously calls these very things into question'; 2–3), but whereas Bown draws on Badiou and Lacan to make these claims, I turn to the (decidedly less metaphysical) Adornian tradition of critical theory. I also do not employ Deleuze's concept of the event. Deleuzean 'event-thinking', as Mariam Fraser helpfully puts it (Fraser 2006: 129), challenges Cartesianism and determinism by viewing all occurrences as open-ended moments within a constitutively creative process of becoming. 'Everything is event' for Deleuze because nothing is reducible to its efficient causes or to being an efficient cause itself (Deleuze 1987: 7). While laughter can certainly qualify as an event in this sense (as the Nietzschean discourse showed, laughter exceeds the determining bounds of discourse), this concept doesn't allow us to grasp laughter's *specificity* as a political enactment or its concrete facticity and materiality within the social order. What my notion of 'event' lacks in philosophical sophistication (at least when compared to Badiou or Deleuze), it hopefully makes up for in theoretical utility by highlighting how laughter originates and exerts objective effects within a determinate social order.

19. To be clear, by 'dialectic', I am referring to the 'consistent sense of non-identity' described by Adorno (Adorno 1973: 5), not the progressive, teleological logic championed by Hegel. Thinking in terms of dialectics means grasping the non-identical in a given situation as an occasion for thinking against and beyond that situation.
20. For more on the difference between a normative and a critical study of laughter, see Giamario (2020).
21. This blind spot only characterises liberal versions of the a/gelasty dispute.
22. A short note on my use of the concepts '*polis*' and 'social order'. As I have already suggested, a *polis* is a community characterised by the specifically *political* divide between those capable of *logos* (rational, intelligible speech) and those capable of mere *phōnē* (irrational, meaningless noise) (Aristotle 1996: 1252b–1253a; Rancière 1999: 21–42). The concept of 'social order' – the complex economic-cultural-political whole that is structured, in our case at least, by the circulation and accumulation of capital – is not interchangeable with, nor meant to replace, that of the '*polis*'. Instead, a critical account of the social order entails an account of the *polis*, that is, of the distribution of *logos* and *phōnē* that governs its various spheres and the relations between them. My use of the concept '*polis*' likewise refers not to a discrete entity inside or outside the social order, but rather to the political articulation of the social order itself (Chambers 2014).
23. For instance, the following chapters examine comedy's role in the social acknowledgement of white supremacy, the patriarchal structure of the comedy industry and the requirements of a successful joke.
24. See, for instance, the work of Lauren Berlant and Sianne Ngai (2017), Peter Euben (2003), Angus Fletcher (2016), Krista Giappone et al. (2018), Todd McGowan (2017), Wilson McWilliams (1995), Lars Tønder (2014), Julie Webber (2019a), Cynthia Willett and Julie Willett (2019), John Zumbrunnen (2012) and Alenka Zupančič (2008).
25. See, for instance, the work of Sammy Basu (1999), Michael Billig (2005), Simon Critchley (2002), Terry Eagleton (2019), Nicholas Holm (2017), John Lombardini (2018) and Kyle Stevens (2021).
26. See, for instance, the work of Jessica Milner Davis (2017), Jessyka Finley (2020) and Mehnaaz Momen (2020).
27. See, for instance, the work of William Connolly (2002), Daniel Conway and John Seery (1992), John Seery (1990) and Cynthia Willett (2008).
28. See, for instance, the work of Judith Butler (1990).
29. For examples of laughter studies scholarship, see the work of Mary Beard (2014), Alfie Bown (2019), Jacqueline Bussie (2007), Albrecht Classen (2010), Ingvild Gilhus (2004), Donna Goldstein (2013), Stephen Halliwell (2008), Anca Parvulescu (2010), Robert Provine (2000), Christopher Rea (2015), Barry Sanders (1995) and Michael Screech (2015).

30. For instance, Vine Deloria, Jr's *Custer Died for Your Sins* asks readers to reflect on the political function of Native American humour in a context that differs fundamentally from that inhabited by Black Americans (Deloria, Jr 1988). Meanwhile, scholars have recently highlighted how the political interventions made by the comedy of Black women are irreducible to those made by Black men or other women (Burrell 2020; Finley 2020; Leng 2019; Wood 2018).

Chapter 1
The Laughing Body Politic: The Counter/sovereign Politics of Hobbes's Theory of Laughter

> [I]t is vain glory, and an argument of little worth, to think the infirmities of another sufficient matter for his triumph.
> Thomas Hobbes, *The Elements of Law* (2008: 55)

> They say truly and properly that say the world is governed by opinion.
> Thomas Hobbes, *The Elements of Law* (2008: 72)

The first step in developing a critical theory of laughter is to determine laughter's *political logic*. What is the relationship between laughter and the distributions of *logos* and *phōnē* – the notions of who counts as a reasonable speaker and what counts as reasonable speech – that constitute a political community? How exactly do experiences/events of laughter shape and reshape the terrain of power in the contemporary social order? The Nietzschean discourse of gelopolitics examined in the Introduction suggests an answer to this question: by exploding the very distinction between *logos* and *phōnē*, laughter disrupts and transforms existing hierarchies of power. However, the Nietzschean discourse's operation on a primarily philosophical register leaves the political implications of laughter's deconstructive activity largely under-theorised.[1] This chapter elucidates the political logic of laughter by turning to a theorist who provides both his own view of the political stakes of the *logos/phōnē* relationship and his own account of laughter: Thomas Hobbes.

Hobbes's goal as a political philosopher is relatively straightforward: to challenge and root out Aristotelianism in all its forms. To that end, he provides an alternative to Aristotle's understanding of the relationship between *logos* ('Reason') and *phōnē* ('insignificant speech', 'meere sound' or 'absurdity') (Hobbes 2012: 60, 64, 68).[2] Although Hobbes agrees with Aristotle that *logos* makes political life possible (48), he rejects the notion that what constitutes *logos* is self-evident or written into the nature of things. 'REASON,' Hobbes writes, 'is nothing but *Reckoning* (that is, Adding and Subtracting) of the Consequences of generall names agreed upon, for the *marking* and *signifying* of our thoughts' (64). The phrase 'agreed upon' here is crucial, as Hobbes believes that the premises that form the object of rational 'reckoning' are products of 'inconstant', highly idiosyncratic individual sense impressions (62). '[F]or want of a right Reason constituted by Nature', Hobbes argues that the decisions of a sovereign power are needed (66). A sovereign – established by the agreement of those subject to its authority – defines what is good and bad, right and wrong, and true and false such that the sound reasoning that characterises a political community is possible. As Hobbes puts it in *De Cive*:

> What is by reason blameable is not to be measured by the reason of one man more than another, because of the equality of human nature; and there are no other reasons in being, but only of those of *particular men*, and that of the *city*: it follows that the *city* is to determine what *with reason is culpable*. So as a *fault*, that is to say, a *sin*, is that which a man does, omits, says, or wills, against the reason of *the city*. (Hobbes 1991: 283)

Whereas for Aristotle *logos* constitutes the unproblematic foundation of a shared political life, for Hobbes *logos* is the site of politics itself – that is, the object of a sovereign decision that delivers humans from the anarchy attendant to the natural indeterminacy of speech.

What is the relationship between laughter and this sovereign decision? How does an experience/event that resides at the intersection of and troubles the distinction between *logos* and *phōnē* affect the determination of what counts as *logos* (and hence the structure of the *polis*)? What, in other words, is the political logic of laughter? To answer these questions, I offer a gelopolitical reading of Hobbes's 'superiority theory' of laughter. Whereas a merely *political* reading of this theory employs the resources of Hobbesian philosophy to examine the political dynamics of laughter, a *gelopolitical* reading goes one step further and takes Hobbes's theory of laughter as an occasion for reimagining elements of his political thought (namely, his concept of sovereignty). Only by moving back and forth between Hobbes's theory of laughter and his political philosophy in this way – that is, only by grasping laughter as both an object of political analysis *and* a site of politics in its own right – can we fully unpack laughter's political logic.

The point of contact between these two facets of Hobbesian thought is the concept of vainglory. Hobbes defines vainglory as a feeling of individual superiority that arises from a false or merely imagined conception of power (Hobbes 2008: 50–1; 2012: 88). Laughter, he argues, is sudden vainglory. When an individual laughs, they unexpectedly experience an unjustified feeling of power over someone or something else. Laughter 'is incident most to them, that are conscious of the fewest abilities in themselves; who are forced to keep themselves in their own favour, by observing the imperfections of other men' (Hobbes 2012: 88).[3] Hobbes holds that because the groundless feeling of superiority in laughter is nevertheless taken seriously by its audience – those laughed at behave *as if* the laughing individual is actually superior – laughter destabilises the hierarchies of power secured by sovereign authority. Laughter, in other words, constitutes a *counter-sovereign* political enactment. This is the chapter's first argument. Next, I contend that the establishment of sovereign power via the social contract is also an experience of sudden vainglory. The Hobbesian body politic is a *laughing body politic* at the moment of its foundation. Third, this concept of a laughing body politic reveals that sovereignty is constitutively haunted by the threat of counter-sovereign disruption and that laughter is an experience/event through which sovereign authority institutes, exerts and entrenches itself. Fourth, I conclude that the political logic of laughter is consequently neither simply counter-sovereign nor simply sovereign, but rather *counter/sovereign*. Laughter challenges sovereignty (i.e., that which institutes and sustains a given order of *logos*) only by reinscribing it anew (i.e., by instituting an alternative order of *logos*), and it bolsters sovereignty only by dramatising its own vulnerability to challenge. A gelopolitical reading of Hobbes's theory of laughter, in short, illuminates laughter as an unauthorised, fragile feeling of power through which sovereignty is made, undone and made again.

The chapter proceeds in four sections. Section I introduces Hobbes's various accounts of laughter, paying particular attention to their gradual depoliticisation over time. Section II investigates laughter's place in Hobbes's discussions of the law of nature to determine whether, as Quentin Skinner (2002c) and others claim, Hobbes views laughter as a moral vice. This requires addressing the question of the authority of the law of nature itself, for which I turn to James Martel's reflections on Hobbes as an author (Martel 2007). Section III explores the intersections between Hobbes's theory of laughter and his more familiar account of the social contract to articulate the concept of a laughing body politic. Section IV concludes by examining two historical laughing bodies politic – one that emerged during the 1980 Lenin shipyard strike in Gdańsk, Poland and the other at the 2010 Jon Stewart and Stephen Colbert Rally to Restore Sanity and/or Fear – that, in light of Jason Frank's arguments about the aesthetic dimensions of popular sovereignty (Frank 2015), illustrate the counter/sovereign political logic of laughter.

I. The Shifting Nature of Hobbesian Gelopolitics

Hobbes discusses laughter at length in three texts: *The Elements of Law* (1640), *Leviathan* (1651) and *De Homine* (1658). (He treats laughter more briefly in *De Cive* and three minor texts, all of which I consider below.) Hobbes's first account of laughter comes in *The Elements of Law*. Chapter IX's inventory of the human passions introduces 'a passion that hath *no name*; but the sign of it is that distortion of the countenance we call *laughter*' (Hobbes 2008: 54). While at this point Hobbes refers to laughter as only 'the sign' of a nameless passion, he goes on to identify 'the passion of laughter' three times in the lines that follow. Here he provides the first formulation of his so-called 'superiority theory': 'the passion of laughter is nothing else but *sudden glory* arising from some sudden *conception* of some *eminency* in ourselves, by *comparison* with the *infirmity* of others, or with our own formerly' (54). Laughter, Hobbes argues, is the passion of sudden glory.

Glory constitutes the linchpin of Hobbes's early theory of the passions. Glory is the first passion Hobbes identifies in *The Elements*, and all the other passions (including laughter) derive from glory in one way or another. Hobbes explains that an individual 'glories' when they imagine they possess more power than someone else: 'GLORY [. . .] is that passion which proceedeth from the imagination or conception of our own power above the power of him that contendeth with us' (50). *Power*, he writes, is an individual's capacity to produce something in the future over and against someone else's will (48). Hobbes conceives of power in strictly relational terms:

> Power simply is no more, but the excess of the power of one above that of another. [. . .] The signs by which we know our own power, are those actions which proceed from the same; and the signs by which other men

know it, are such actions, gesture, countenance and speech, as usually such powers produce [. . .]. (48)

My power is only the power I have in excess of your power, but this same power might be no power at all when compared to that of a third person. Power is identified by its signs, or certain conventional patterns of acting, gesturing and speaking. For Hobbes, passions originate and exert effects within an economy of power relations, or what he describes as a race where 'we must suppose to have no other goal [. . .] but being foremost' (59).

As the passion of sudden glory (or, as Hobbes's initial formulation suggests, 'the sign' of a nameless passion), laughter plays a key role in this race. An individual who laughs feels a sudden excess of power with respect to someone else (or themself formerly). One never laughs in a vacuum: laughter arises out of the power relations that envelop and exceed the individual. As one of the 'countenances' that signifies an excess of power, laughter also modifies these relations by signalling to others that the individual feels more powerful than they did previously. Hobbes theorises laughter in explicitly political terms in *The Elements of Law*: laughter emerges within, makes reference to and transforms a prevailing economy of power relations.

Hobbes returns to laughter in *Leviathan*. In Chapter VI he describes laughter as a bodily motion accompanying the passion of sudden glory:

> *Sudden Glory*, is the passion which maketh those *Grimaces* called LAUGHTER; and is caused either by some sudden act of their own, that pleaseth them; or by the apprehension of some deformed thing in another, by comparison whereof they suddenly applaud themselves. (Hobbes 2012: 88)

One year earlier, Hobbes had advanced a similar formulation in a fragment titled 'Of Passions', writing that 'sudden imagination of a mans owne abilitie, is the passion that moves laughter' (Skinner 2002c: 148). Hobbes in this period takes the position that laughter only signifies the passion of sudden glory, and he makes no mention of the 'passion of laughter' in *Leviathan*. That said, laughter appears as a capitalised entry in the book's inventory of the passions (Hobbes 2012: 88), suggesting that Hobbes remains at least somewhat ambivalent on this question.

Leviathan offers revised accounts of glory and power, the two concepts at the heart of *The Elements*'s theory of laughter. Whereas in *The Elements* all the passions derive from glory, in *Leviathan* glory is a species of joy. 'Joy', Hobbes writes, 'arising from imagination of a mans own power and ability, is that exultation of the mind which is called GLORYING' (88). The Hobbes of the *Leviathan* no longer understands the passions as dependent on an individual's location within an economy of power relations; they instead stem from six 'simple Passions' (appetite, desire, love, aversion, hate and joy) that denote one's relation to objects of sense (84). Hobbes's conception of power reflects this change. In *The Elements* power is analytically prior to glory and the passions, while in *Leviathan* power follows the account of the passions and is understood in narrower, more instrumental terms: 'The POWER *of a Man*, (to take it Universally), is his present means, to obtain some future apparent Good' (132). *Leviathan*'s emphasis on glory as joyful and power as instrumental removes laughter from the economy of power relations that was its home in *The Elements of Law*. Rather than expressing superiority *in relation* to others, laughter now constitutes a private feeling of being able to act *upon* other people and things.

De Homine's examination of laughter entrenches these changes. Hobbes explains that 'when the animal spirits are suddenly transported by the joy arising from any word, deed, or thought of one's own that is seemly, or of a stranger that is unseemly, this passion is laughter' (Hobbes 1991: 59). In a departure from both *The Elements* and *Leviathan*, Hobbes is unequivocal that laughter is a passion, and he makes no mention of glory in relation to laughter.[4] This decoupling of laughter and glory consequently dissociates laughter from the concept of power. Power plays only a minor part in *De Homine*'s chapter on the appetites and aversions (49), and the book's account of the passions makes no mention of power. The universe in which laughter arises and exerts effects shrinks dramatically in *De Homine*. No longer a sign or instance of glory within an economy of power relations, laughter is instead a simple joy associated with an individual's self-image. As Hobbes concludes, 'the passion of laughter is sudden self-commendation resulting from a stranger's unseemliness' (59).

Hobbes's initial conception of laughter as participating in a complex economy of power relations is ultimately supplanted by a view of laughter as an individualised pleasure. From *The Elements of Law* to *De Homine*, Hobbes's theory of laughter is gradually depoliticised. This depoliticisation occurs by way of (a) Hobbes's sidelining of the concepts of glory and power in favour of joy and seemliness, and (b) his elimination of ambiguity about laughter's status as a passion. This second form of depoliticisation requires further explanation. Passions, Hobbes writes, are motions of the body (Hobbes 2012: 78),[5] while signs of passions reflect events that usually, but not always, follow these natural motions: 'A *Signe*, is the Event Antecedent, of the Consequent; and contrarily, the Consequent of the Antecedent, when the like Consequences have been observed, before: And the oftner they have been observed, the lesse uncertain is the Signe' (44; see also Hobbes 2008: 33). If laughter is the sign of the passion of sudden glory, then it typically – but not necessarily – accompanies sudden glory. This distinction between passions and their signs mirrors that between *phōnē* and *logos* that is at the heart of Hobbes's broader political philosophy. Passions – just like the 'meere sound' (Hobbes 2012: 60) of 'senslesse Speech' (68) – are 'natural', while the signs of those passions – just like the rules for what qualifies as 'right Reason' (66) – are conventional. If political life for Hobbes emerges out of a decision about what constitutes *logos* versus *phōnē*, his equivocation about laughter's status as a passion speaks to its political significance. At the intersection of a human's natural and conventional lives, laughter – like the sovereign decision itself – calls that distinction into question. By unambiguously classifying laughter as a passion, *De Homine* dissolves this politically generative tension into a politically trivial theory of an individual's natural motions.

In sum, although the basic thrust of Hobbes's 'superiority theory' of laughter remains more or less the same from *The Elements of Law* to *De Homine*, the *politics* of this theory shifts markedly. Depending on how Hobbes understands and arranges the concepts of the passions, glory and power, laughter is either an intensely political phenomenon (as in *The Elements*) or is liquidated altogether as a political issue (as in *De Homine*). The ostensible consistency of Hobbes's accounts of laughter belies the shifting conceptions of gelopolitics they entail. The following section aims to determine the motivation behind this depoliticisation of laughter.

II. Vainglory and the Counter-sovereign Politics of Laughter

As others have suggested (Heyd 1982; Skinner 1996, 2002c), the standard view that Hobbes advances a 'superiority theory' of laughter suffers from a fatal flaw: Hobbes repeatedly insists that laughter is sudden *vain*glory. While glory is the triumph of the mind proceeding from a 'just and well grounded' conception of superiority, vainglory proceeds from an illusory conception of superiority: 'Further, the *fiction*, which is also imagination, of actions done by ourselves, which never were done, is *glorying*; but because it begetteth no appetite nor endeavour to any further attempt, it is merely *vain* and unprofitable' (Hobbes 2008: 50–1). Vainglory is *vain* in both senses of the word: it betrays an unjustifiably high opinion of one's self and, as a consequence, achieves nothing. To be vainglorious, Hobbes writes, is '[t]o lose ground with looking back' (59). Laughter is vainglorious because it is 'an affection of glory from other men's infirmities, and not from any ability of their own' (59). Hobbes repeats this criticism of laughter in *Leviathan* (Hobbes 2012: 88), *De Homine* (Hobbes 1991: 59), and two other minor pieces, a 1638 letter to Charles Cavendish (Hobbes 1983: 52) and 'The Answer to Sir William Davenant's Preface before Gondibert' (Hobbes 1994b). In the latter essay Hobbes emphasises the absence of laughter from the lives of truly powerful individuals:

> Great persons, that have their minds employed on great designs, have not leisure enough to laugh, and are pleased with the contemplation of their own power and virtues, so as they need not the infirmities and vices of other men to recommend themselves to their own favour by comparison, as all men do when they laugh. (Hobbes 1994b: 454–5)

From Hobbes's perspective, laughter is a passion (or sign of a passion) in which individuals deceive and diminish themselves.

Pointing to passages where Hobbes condemns laughter as not befitting a virtuous individual (e.g., his claim in *De Homine* that 'those who laugh the most are those who collect the fewest arguments for their virtue from their own praiseworthy deeds'; Hobbes 1991: 59), commentators have traditionally interpreted Hobbes as seeing the vaingloriousness of laughter as a moral vice. For instance, John Morreall writes that 'Hobbes was concerned that laughter could be harmful to a person's character. There is something wrong, he felt, with the person who can feel good about himself only by looking down on others' (Morreall 1983: 6). Meanwhile, R. E. Ewin contends that Hobbes views laughter as morally problematic because an individual could instead sympathise with or pity an inferior:

> That nameless passion is but one possible reaction to the perceived calamity of another. Even when the other has been attempting to dishonour one, it is possible (and, on Hobbes's account, desirable) to ignore

it; a great mind will pay no attention to, not glory in its superiority, and compare itself only with other great minds. (Ewin 2001: 40)

Finally, Quentin Skinner argues that Hobbes believes laughter detracts from the moral obligation to be magnanimous: 'Hobbes is clearly in earnest in counseling us to avoid derisive laughter whenever possible' because 'gifted people have in addition a positive moral duty to help others to cultivate similar feelings of magnanimity and respect' (Skinner 2002c: 175–6). In what follows, I turn to *De Cive* – a long neglected source for Hobbes's theory of laughter (Giamario 2016: 312) – to counter that Hobbes's characterisation of laughter as sudden vainglory highlights its specifically *political* stakes that we began to uncover in the previous section. *De Cive*'s treatment of laughter as a violation of the 'law of nature' demonstrates that Hobbes views laughter not as a moral vice but as a political threat to the sovereign interest in social peace.

Hobbes opens *De Cive* by challenging the Aristotelian thesis that humans are 'born fit for society' (Hobbes 1991: 110). He holds that humans seek only the benefits from life in society, namely business profits and honour (111). After noting that the profit motive alone cannot sustain society, Hobbes explains that individuals in the state of nature congregate to inflate their reputations by feigning glory to one another. Laughter plays an important role here:

> [I]f [men meet] for pleasure and recreation of mind, every man is wont to please himself most with those things which stir up laughter, whence he may, according to the nature of that which is ridiculous, by comparison of another man's defects and infirmities, pass the more current in his own opinion. And although this be sometimes innocent and without offense, yet it is manifest they are not so much delighted with the society, as their own vain glory. (111; see also 2008: 78)

Laughter constitutes a public display of vainglory that generates the 'greatest discords' between individuals (114). Although laughter is an illusory conception of superiority, this vanity remains imperceptible to those who are laughed at. As Hobbes reminds his readers, 'men take it heinously to be laughed at or derided, that is, triumphed over' (Hobbes 2008: 55). The objects of laughter believe and behave *as if* the laughing individual is actually superior, and they feel that protecting their reputation requires laughing back. For instance, when John laughs at Susan, Susan finds a reason to laugh at Peter in order to protect her honour in the eyes of John. Peter then does the same to a fourth person, and so on: 'men must declare sometimes some mutual scorn and contempt, either by laughter, or by words, or by gesture, or some sign or other' (Hobbes 1991: 115). An unjustified feeling of power, laughter succeeds in creating a world in its own illusory image. Hobbes concludes that such a self- and publicly deceptive passion (or sign of a passion) forms a wholly inadequate foundation for social life: 'no society can be great or lasting, which begins from vain glory' (113).

The story that follows is familiar to readers of Hobbes. Awash in public displays of vainglory and lacking a natural fitness for life in society, individuals muddle along in a miserable and dangerous condition of fear (118). The 'fundamental law of nature' discoverable by reason instructs man to exit this state of nature and seek peace to the extent possible (123). This law grounds a host of subsidiary laws that direct individuals to enter into agreements with one another and avoid antagonistic conduct. While Hobbes's accounts of the laws of nature in *The Elements* and *Leviathan* proscribe signs, words or actions that declare hatred and contempt (what Hobbes calls 'contumely') (Hobbes 2008: 92; 2012: 234), *De Cive*'s seventh law of nature against reproach prohibits laughter explicitly: '*no man, either by deeds or words, countenance or laughter, do declare himself to hate or scorn another*' (Hobbes 1991: 142–3).[6] According to Hobbes, laughter violates the law of nature because it undermines social peace.

On what grounds, exactly, do the Hobbesian laws of nature obligate individuals? A brief detour into this old and complex debate is necessary to specify the problem Hobbes believes is posed by the vaingloriousness of laughter. On the one hand, Hobbes describes the laws of nature as simple maxims of prudential reason designed to help preserve one's life: 'A LAW OF NATURE, (*Lex Naturalis,*) is a Precept, or generall Rule, found out by Reason, by which a man is forbidden to do, that, which is destructive of his life, or taketh away the means of preserving the same' (Hobbes 2012: 198; see also 1991: 123). The fundamental law of nature instructs one to seek peace because reason dictates that peace is necessary for self-preservation. *De Cive*'s seventh law of nature likewise forbids laughter because it increases the risk of life-threatening social discord.

But Hobbes also describes the laws of nature as moral obligations. 'The laws of nature,' he writes, 'are the sum of *moral* philosophy' (Hobbes 1991: 152; see also 2012: 242). Seeking peace (and avoiding laughter) is not only prudent; it is morally required. As Michael Oakeshott remarks, a subtle 'change of idiom' marks Hobbes's argument: 'The conditions of peace, first offered to us as *rational theorems* concerning the nature of shameful-death-avoiding conduct (that is, as a piece of prudential wisdom), now appear as *moral obligation*' (Oakeshott 1991: 309). Importantly, however, the laws of nature only morally obligate *endeavours* in the state of nature. Blindly conforming one's *actions* to these laws in the absence of an enforcement mechanism that compels universal obedience may inadvertently increase the danger posed to one's life. Hobbes explains this as a difference between *in foro interno* ('internal court') and *in foro externo* ('external court') obligations: 'The Lawes of Nature oblige *in foro interno*; that is to say, they bind to a desire they should take place: but *in foro externo*; that is, to the putting them in act, not alwayes' (Hobbes 2012: 240; see also 1991: 149; 2008: 97). Hobbes concludes that it is *just* for an individual to endeavour to obey the laws of nature: 'He that endeavoureth their performance, fulfilleth them; and he that fulfilleth the Law, is Just' (Hobbes 2012: 240; see also 1991: 150).

Why do reason's prudential maxims take the form of moral obligations? Why is something that reason dictates it is *wise* to do necessarily also something one *ought* to do? The answer to this question resides in Hobbes's distinction between reason and 'appetites and aversions'. Hobbes claims the values 'good' and 'evil' amount to nothing more than individual appetites and aversions, or what one is attracted to or repelled by due to their idiosyncratic sense perceptions (Hobbes 1991: 45–6; 2008: 44; 2012: 78–80). Because no one shares the same sense perceptions, 'scarce two men' can agree 'what is to be called good, and what evil', thus making rigorous moral philosophy impossible (Hobbes 2008: 39; see also 2012: 196; 1991: 47). Hobbes elaborates:

> Every man, for his own part, calleth that which pleaseth, and is delightful to himself, GOOD; and that EVIL which displeaseth him: insomuch that while every man differeth from another in constitution, they differ also from one another concerning the common distinction of good and evil. (Hobbes 2008: 44; see also 2012: 242; Tuck 1989, 1996; Skinner 2002b; Flathman 2002)

Hobbes seeks to save the possibility of moral philosophy by turning to reason. Whereas appetites and aversions refer to hopelessly idiosyncratic *immediate* evaluations, reason involves a 'reckoning' of *future* consequences that admits no such disagreement (Hobbes 2012: 64). In a crucial passage in *De Cive*, Hobbes explains that social peace is a moral good due to its origin in a rational reckoning about the future. I have italicised the key lines of his argument:

> They are, therefore, so long in the state of war, as by reason of the diversity of the present appetites, they mete good and evil by diverse measures. All men easily acknowledge this state, as long as they are in it, to be evil, and by consequence that peace is good. *They therefore who could not agree concerning a present, do agree concerning a future good; which indeed is a work of reason; for things present are obvious to the sense, things to come to our reason only.* Reason, declaring peace to be good, it follows by the same reason, that all the necessary means to peace be good also; and therefore that modesty, equity, trust, humanity, mercy (which we have demonstrated to be necessary to peace), are good manners or habits, that is, virtues. The law therefore, in the means to peace, commands also good manners, or the practice of virtue; and therefore it is called *moral*. (Hobbes 1991: 150–1; see also 2008: 98; 2012: 242)

Because future-oriented reason – not mere appetite or aversion – dictates that peace is good, the laws of nature escape the scepticism plaguing other values. An individual in the state of nature consequently has a moral obligation to seek peace and, as a means to that end, avoid laughter.

Hobbes's appeal to reason raises more problems than it solves, however. First, as noted earlier, the use of reason presupposes an agreement on definitions (Hobbes 2012: 64). But it is precisely such agreement on definitions that is missing in this case. Second, even if such agreement existed, there is no guarantee of consensus on the value of *peace* in particular. Hobbes's reflections on the 'right' use of reason suggest that disagreement is just as likely:

> As in Arithmetique, unpractised men must, and Professors themselves may often erre, and cast up false; so also in any other subject of Reasoning, the ablest, most attentive, and most practised men, may deceive themselves, and inferre false Conclusions; Not but that Reason it selfe is always Right Reason, as well as Arithmetique is a certain and infallible Art. (Hobbes 2012: 66)

The mere possession of reason, in other words, does not ensure its 'right' use. Finally, even if individuals were to somehow all agree that reason dictates that peace is 'good', consensus on the *meaning* of peace remains lacking. As Skinner explains, every individual possesses their own view of the practical requirements of 'peace': 'the contention that a given action will in fact conduce to peace remains a judgement. Who, then, shall be judge?' (Skinner 2002b: 138; see also Tuck 1996: 189). Because an idiosyncratic determination about the meaning of peace cannot yield a moral obligation, individuals remain without a standard for knowing when their endeavours violate the law of nature.

Hobbes suggests that the presence of a sovereign power resolves each of these problems. First, a sovereign establishes the definitions from which rational reckoning proceeds:

> [I]t belongs to the same chief power to make some common rules for all men, and to declare them publicly, by which every man may know what may be called his, what another's, what just, what unjust, what honest, what dishonest, what good, what evil. (Hobbes 1991: 178)

Second, a sovereign determines what constitutes the 'right' use of reason in this reckoning. Hobbes writes: 'Therefore, as when there is a controversy in an account, the parties must by their own accord, set up for right Reason, the Reason of some Arbitrator, or Judge, to whose sentence they will both stand' (Hobbes 2012: 66). If everyone agrees that social peace is good, it is because a sovereign authority has decided that this is what 'right' reason demands. Third, a sovereign determines what 'peace' means and requires in practice. Hobbes explains:

> It is annexed to the Soveraignty, to be Judge of what Opinions and Doctrines are averse, and what conducing to Peace [. . .]. It belongeth therefore to him that hath the Soveraign Power, to be Judge [. . .] as a thing necessary to Peace; thereby to prevent Discord and Civill Warre. (Hobbes 2012: 272)

Hobbes ties all these points together in *Leviathan* when he argues that the laws of nature require the decisions of a sovereign to be effective as moral obligations:

> For it is the Soveraign Power that obliges men to obey [the laws of nature]. For in the difference of private men, to declare, what is Equity, what is Justice, and what is morall Vertue, and to make [the laws of nature] binding, there is need of the Ordinances of Soveraign Power.[7] (Hobbes 2012: 418)

By determining that reason dictates that peace is 'good' and that 'peace' means and requires what the laws of nature stipulate, a sovereign secures the status of the laws of nature as morally obligatory.

But if all of this is true and the laws of nature morally obligate one's endeavours only in the presence of a sovereign, then they presuppose precisely what has not yet occurred: an exit from the state of nature and the establishment of a sovereign power. The obvious question at this point is: *who* is the sovereign that makes Hobbes's laws of nature morally obligatory?[8]

Several scholars have explored the complex issue of the kind of authority Hobbes claims for himself in his texts (Kahn 1985; Martel 2007; Strong 1993). James Martel poses the question in the following terms: if, as Hobbes insists, all authority originates in a sovereign, by what authority does Hobbes write about sovereignty? 'Hobbes seems to be appropriating the sovereign "last word" even while appearing to defer to that sovereign authority. He seems to be surrendering to something that he is in the process of creating or authoring' (Martel 2007: 45). Following Martel, I argue that Hobbes *performs* or *enacts* sovereignty in his accounts of the laws of nature. That is, beyond merely *describing* the origin of sovereignty with these laws, Hobbes himself exercises sovereignty by defining the requirements of social peace. The laws of nature are moral obligations because Hobbes, as textual sovereign, says so: 'The great achievement of *Leviathan*', Martel writes, 'is to enable its readers to catch the author in the act of producing his own textual authority and furthermore, the authority of the sovereign' (38). We 'catch' Hobbes producing his own sovereign authority when he makes the groundless assertions that the right reason of all declares social peace to be good and that 'peace' requires the precise list of do's and don'ts he provides (Hobbes 1991: 150–1; 2012: 242). As we have seen, peace is an undisputed moral value only from the perspective of sovereignty (i.e., from the perspective of an authority whose *raison d'être* is the cessation of moral disagreement), and the practical requirements of peace always involve a sovereign decision. Hobbes's renditions of the laws of nature illustrate the task facing prospective political sovereigns, namely to define and enforce conceptions of what is true and false, good and evil, and right and wrong.

Hobbes's laws of nature are consequently not a mere inventory of natural reason's dictates, but rather a set of rules grounded in a *political* interest in social peace and *political* decision about what peace requires.[9] Interpreting laughter in Hobbes as a simple moral vice (as Morreall, Ewin and Skinner propose) depoliticises his theory of laughter: it reduces a political problem – laughter's capacity to undermine social peace – down to one of individual moral conduct. Laughter

The Laughing Body Politic: Hobbes's Theory of Laughter 53

in Hobbes is a counter-sovereign political enactment: its unjustified feeling of superiority precipitates a self-amplifying upheaval in power relations that endangers the sovereign interest in stable, well-defined hierarchies (Hobbes 2012: 276). To be clear, laughter is not simply immoral for this reason; as we have seen, the determination that it is morally wrong to threaten sovereignty is itself a sovereign decision. Hobbes's objections to laughter are political all the way down: it is wrong to laugh because a sovereign (Hobbes) has determined that laughter threatens sovereignty. Laughter is thus also a counter-sovereign political enactment in a second, larger sense: sudden vainglory undermines attempts by sovereigns (like Hobbes) to naturalise their rule – that is, to present their authority as the product of natural reason rather than the consent of those subject to it.[10]

III. The Laughing Body Politic and the Sovereign Politics of Laughter

Hobbes's accounts of the law of nature reveal that laughter performs a counter-sovereign political enactment. However, the ability of laughter to exert a controlling influence over its targets' conduct suggests that it shares a connection with sovereignty as well. When we read Hobbes's theory of laughter alongside the central passages of his political philosophy, we find that laughter also performs a *sovereign* political enactment. This section completes the gelopolitical reading of Hobbes's theory of laughter begun above by exploring how it prompts the reimagination of a key element of his political thought.

As is well known, Hobbes theorises 'politics' in terms of bodies. Unlike a human's natural body, the political body or 'body politic' is an artificial body that individuals create (or find themselves subject to via conquest) by entering into covenants with one another (Hobbes 2012: 130; 1991: 35; 2008: 107). Individuals establish a body politic by agreeing to 'conferre all their power and strength upon' a sovereign person or assembly (Hobbes 2012: 260). They authorise a sovereign to 'beare their Person' – that is, the person of the body politic (Skinner 2002a) – in order to ensure the latter's benefit and protection (Hobbes 2012: 260). Hobbes spares no superlatives when describing the degree of power that individuals grant a sovereign. 'There is no power on earth that can be compared to him', reads the verse above the sovereign's head on the *Leviathan* frontispiece (Hobbes 1985: 71). Sovereignty, Hobbes writes, is 'so unlimited a Power' and 'as great, as possibly men can be imagined to make it' (Hobbes 2012: 320); it is *'absolute'*, 'the greatest dominion that can be granted' (Hobbes 1991: 181–2). According to Hobbes, individuals inhabit a political body when they grant a sovereign absolute power to compel the obedience of their natural bodies.

Several commentators have questioned Hobbes's grandiose depictions of sovereign power. Sheldon Wolin points out that the person or assembly appointed sovereign does not receive any *new* power from the body politic but simply retains the natural right to do whatever it takes to preserve oneself that is ceded by the other individuals (Wolin 2004: 254–5). As Hobbes explains, sovereignty

> consisteth in the power and the strength, that every of the members have transferred to him from themselves by covenant. And because it is impossible for any man really to transfer his own strength to another, or for that other to receive it; it is to be understood, that to transfer a man's power and strength, is no more but to lay by, or relinquish his own right of resisting him to whom he so transferreth it. (Hobbes 2008: 107)

The power of the sovereign is equal only to that of a natural individual, and its efficacy depends on the willingness of subjects to honour their promises to not interfere. Wolin argues that

> the Hobbesian conception of political power was a grossly oversimplified, even hollow one. The power to act required only the elimination of hindrances rather than the active enlistment of the private power and support of the citizens. The citizens had simply to stand aside and not interfere. (Wolin 2004: 255)

William Connolly, meanwhile, contends that sovereign authority hinges on subjects believing in the binding force of natural reason and its commandment (expressed in the law of nature) to obey. If subjects begin to doubt or contest this faith (as I did in the previous section by tracing 'natural reason' back to an arbitrary sovereign decision), the system's 'principle of sovereignty would be shattered. Order would be based upon command, but sovereign commands would lack the intrinsic, obligatory status Hobbes invested in them' (Connolly 1993: 39). Finally, Martel emphasises how the efficacy of sovereign power requires that subjects believe in the person of the sovereign themself: 'the sovereign is an "object of our Faith"; it really does matter how we think about it; without a sense of trust and "taking their word," sovereign authority disappears' (Martel 2007: 56). Wolin, Connolly and Martel demonstrate that the power

The Laughing Body Politic: Hobbes's Theory of Laughter

of the Hobbesian sovereign depends crucially on the good behaviour and faith of those subject to it.

The political enactment performed by those who establish a body politic is highly analogous to that performed by the laughing individual. I argue that the Hobbesian body politic is a *laughing body politic* at the moment of its foundation for three reasons.

First, laughter and the establishment of a body politic share the same temporality. As the passion (or sign of the passion) of '*Sudden Glory*', the time of laughter is quick, unexpected and singular (Hobbes 2012: 88). The suddenness of laughter – its coming out of nowhere – is a function of the novelty of its cause. As Hobbes writes, 'whatsoever it be that moveth laughter, it must be new and unexpected' (Hobbes 2008: 54). An individual likewise laughs at a given object only once: 'Almost nothing is laughed at again and again by the same people' (Hobbes 1991: 59). The covenant founding a body politic features this same temporality. The social contract instantly modifies the prevailing economy of power relations: where there existed only isolated, warring individuals, there is at once a 'reall Unitie of them all' (Hobbes 2012: 260). The time of the contract is necessarily sudden as an authorisation of sovereign power that is anticipated ahead of time has for all intents and purposes already occurred. The covenant also occurs exactly once. Hobbes writes that individuals who institute a body politic are bound to it forever or 'as long, and no longer, than the power lasteth, by which he is able to protect them' (344). Laughter and the establishment of a body politic are both sudden and singular political enactments.

Second, both enactments are forms of 'glorying'. Like the laughing individual, those who institute a body politic enjoy a feeling of superiority. The quality of life in a commonwealth greatly exceeds that in the state of nature (as Hobbes notes, an individual agrees to the social contract only because it provides 'some *Good to himselfe*'; Hobbes 2012: 202). The glory of establishing a commonwealth is immortalised by the image of the sovereign towering over the town and countryside in the *Leviathan* frontispiece. One can almost hear Hobbes laughing derisively at critics who insist that humans are better off in the state of nature:

> But a man may here object, that the Condition of Subjects is very miserable [. . .] not considering that the estate of Man can never be without some incommodity or other; and that the greatest, that in any forme of Government can possibly happen to the people in generall, is scarce

sensible, in respect of the miseries, and horrible calamities, that accompany a Civill Warre; or that dissolute condition of masterlesse men. (282)

Just like laughter, the 'glorious' political enactment of instituting a body politic modifies the prevailing economy of power relations. The individuals who covenant with one another render themselves powerless with respect to the sovereign they authorise (160), and they enter into a state of war with those outside the commonwealth (268).

As we have seen, the conception of individual superiority at the root of laughter is illusory, and this vainglorious quality is the body politic's third and most significant parallel with laughter. The arguments of Wolin, Connolly and Martel concerning the fragility of Hobbesian sovereignty suggest that the body politic performs a vainglorious political enactment. The individuals who institute a commonwealth feel a sudden abundance of power that the sovereign they authorise can never hope to exercise but that they and others nevertheless take seriously. There are too many sites of sovereign vulnerability to accept Hobbes's claims about its 'unlimited', 'absolute' power at face value, and his repeated declarations about sovereign omnipotence betray the vanity involved in the social contract. Any peace and stability won by the body politic's institution of sovereignty thus always remain tenuous and provisional. (The commonwealth's vanity might, for instance, fuel an ill-considered attack on a foreign power or distract it from domestic discontent.) The establishment of sovereignty does not, as Hobbes promises, bring an end to the war of all against all; as a vainglorious enactment, it simply renews that war by giving it a different shape and cast of characters.

Reading the central scene of Hobbes's political thought alongside his theory of laughter yields two unexpected results. First, if the Hobbesian body politic is a laughing body politic at the moment of its foundation and laughter is a counter-sovereign political enactment, then *the establishment of sovereignty simultaneously constitutes an enactment of counter-sovereignty*. The individuals who form a body politic aim to authorise an omnipotent sovereign to secure permanent social peace, but their covenant is a performance akin to laughter that instead destabilises power relations anew. A gelopolitical reading of Hobbes's theory of laughter reveals that the vaingloriousness of sovereignty means that it is constitutively haunted by the threat of counter-sovereign disruption. Second, whereas the previous section identified the political logic of laughter as counter-sovereign, the concept of a laughing body politic introduced here shows that laughter is also an experience/event through which sovereignty establishes, exerts and entrenches itself. Laughter not only challenges and destabilises sovereign authority; it also helps institute and bolster it.[11] In Adorno's terms, Hobbes's political theory of sovereignty becomes non-identical to itself when brought into contact with his theory of laughter, just as the latter's politics of counter-sovereignty becomes non-identical to itself when brought into contact with his political thought. The next section locates the political logic of laughter at the intersection of these two non-identities.

IV. Feeling Power: Laughing Bodies Politic and the Counter/sovereign Logic of Laughter

Hobbes demonstrates that the political logic of laughter is neither simply sovereign nor simply counter-sovereign, but rather *counter/ sovereign*. I mean two things by this. First, laughter counters sovereign authority only by reinscribing it anew. As described earlier, those targeted by laughter behave as if the laughing individual is actually superior. It is only because laughter exercises this kind of controlling – i.e., sovereign – influence on its audience that it succeeds in undermining the hierarchies of power established by another sovereign authority. Second and conversely, laughter institutes and bolsters sovereignty only by dramatising its weakness. Because laughter stems from an illusory conception of superiority, the sovereignty it establishes always remains vulnerable to challenge. Every exercise of counter-sovereignty in laughter inscribes a new form of sovereignty, while every exercise of sovereignty in laughter opens the door for counter-sovereign resistance.[12] A gelopolitical reading of Hobbes's theory of laughter shows that sovereignty is continually produced, disrupted and reinscribed in laughter.

Two historical laughing bodies politic exemplify this counter/ sovereign political logic of laughter. The first emerged during the August 1980 Lenin shipyard strike in Gdańsk, Poland. Spearheaded by the future Polish president Lech Wałęsa, this strike catalysed the Solidarity trade union movement which ultimately toppled the country's communist dictatorship. Sociologist Colin Barker relates the history of the Lenin shipyard strike as an upheaval in everyday laughter practices (Barker 2001). He explains that prior to the strike, workers regularly joked and laughed quietly among themselves as a means of coping with the regime's violence and oppression: 'a widespread "unofficial consciousness" manifested itself in political jokes about official corruption, privilege, inefficiency, and injustice' (179). Once the workers' occupation of the shipyard began, however, this laughter poured out into the open. Barker describes how '[t]he gates [of the shipyard] were a place to laugh, to be solemn and anxious, to weep, to hope' (187). In the public labour negotiations, the assembled workers reacted to misleading statements by government officials with outbursts of laughter (190). Such laughter indicated their fearlessness and determination but also served the more practical purpose of signalling to the labour leadership how far to push the regime: 'The MKS [Inter-Factory Strike Committee] Praesidium did the actual talking with government, taking its cues from the delegates, whose comments, sarcastic laughter, and applause could be heard throughout' (189). Whereas the shipyard workers previously kept their laughter private and quiet, they now laughed openly and loudly with direct political effects. Celebrating this gelopolitical transformation, a workers' newspaper exclaimed, 'People laugh, laugh more and more, more and more freely!' (191).

The laughing body politic formed by the Lenin shipyard workers exemplifies the counter/sovereign logic of laughter revealed by Hobbes. As sudden vainglory, the workers' laughter originates in an illusory conception of superiority: they feel more powerful than the regime despite their subordinate status in the official hierarchy. This unjustified feeling of superiority undermines the regime's sovereign authority precisely because they and the MKS leadership take it seriously – that is, they behave *as if* the workers are more powerful. The workers' laughter likewise succeeds in exercising sovereignty over the labour negotiations by specifying which statements and proposals the body politic finds acceptable. Meanwhile, the laughter-fuelled MKS organisation engages in all of the activities characteristic of sovereignty. 'Imposing their own collective order' (184), Barker describes how the MKS became its own government of sorts, providing food and shelter, establishing security forces, designing flags, issuing permits and holding formal ceremonies (187). The laughing body politic that materialised at the Lenin shipyard in August 1980 countered the sovereign authority of the Polish government by itself exercising sovereignty.

Jon Stewart and Stephen Colbert's Rally to Restore Sanity and/or Fear is a second example of a laughing body politic. Held on a late October Saturday in 2010, the rally attracted nearly a quarter of a million people to the National Mall in Washington, DC (Montopoli

2010). With Colbert playing the incendiary, divisive foil to Stewart's reasonable and unifying persona, the comedians joined a slate of celebrities in a festival of satire targeting the Great Recession-, Tea Party-era American political culture of partisan polarisation and media fearmongering. The programme concluded with a giant papier mâché of 'Fearzilla' Colbert being 'defeated' by the crowd's chant of unity. Attendees participated by constructing witty, humorous signs promoting tolerance, civility and reason in politics. For example, an older veteran held a sign that read, 'I fought Nazis, and they don't look like Obama', while a young Muslim woman's sign pleaded, 'Please don't call me terrorist' (Funny or Die 2010). Other signs read 'Calm The F*** Down America', 'I Am Moderately Excited For This', and 'You Don't Have To Be Nice, Just Don't Be Mean' (NPR 2010).

Unlike the Polish shipyard workers, the laughing body politic that materialised at the Rally to Restore Sanity and/or Fear was decidedly counter-revolutionary in nature. As its name indicates, the rally aimed to *restore* an imagined past when American politics was 'sane' and unburdened by extreme ideologies. In his concluding monologue ('a moment of sincerity'), Stewart argued that Fox News, talk radio and social media make it increasingly difficult for the American people to recognise a basic truth: that the values uniting them are stronger and more numerous than those dividing them.

> The image of Americans that is reflected back to us by our political and media process is false. [. . .] Where we live, our values and principles form the foundation that sustains us while we get things done, not the barriers that prevent us from getting things done. (Stewart 2010)

Stewart illustrated his point with an analogy of vehicles merging to enter a New York City tunnel. No one knows or cares about other drivers' political beliefs; everyone simply takes turns so they can get on with their day: 'You go, then I'll go'. Stewart hopes that the laughter he and Colbert generate will help deflate the arrogance of ideology so that the values of tolerance, civility and rationality that govern citizens' everyday lives can re-establish themselves in the political realm. As Nicholas Holm explains:

> This is indeed the arch-liberal message espoused by Stewart – the 'hero' of the Rally – against the villainously ideological and therefore unreasonable Colbert: ideology hurts. Consequently, in the liberal moment, the reasonable subject must aspire to escape ideology and emerge into the light of a pragmatic, reasonable and tolerant world. (Holm 2017: 33)

This laughing body politic also exemplifies the counter/sovereign logic uncovered in Hobbes. The rally's crowds enjoy a feeling of superiority over Fox News pundits, talk radio hosts and Tea Party politicians stemming from the recognition of the falsity of ideological worldviews. Their laughter consequently bolsters the prevailing order of sovereignty – namely, the liberal centrism of the Obama administration. However, because the conception of superiority at the root of this laughter is illusory, it supports that sovereign order only at the cost of exposing its weakness. The fact that Stewart, Colbert and their fans believed that a massive comedy show was needed to defend liberal centrism highlights the tenuousness of the latter's political position. (Indeed, three days after the rally, the Tea Party-fuelled Republican Party stormed to massive gains in the midterm elections. Watching the Stewart/Colbert rally ten years and a Trump presidency later, it looks less like a celebration of liberal strength and more like a cry for help.) Whereas the laughing body politic in the Lenin shipyard challenges a sovereign order only by itself exercising sovereignty, the laughing body politic at the Stewart/Colbert rally bolsters a sovereign order only by revealing its own vulnerability to challenge. The former illuminates the sovereign dimensions of laughter's counter-sovereign enactment, while the latter illustrates the counter-sovereign possibilities opened up by laughter's enactment of sovereignty.

Jason Frank's reflections on the aesthetic dimensions of sovereignty help explain the political efficacy of such a paradoxically self-undermining experience/event. According to Frank, the early modern transition from royal to popular sovereignty – a shift captured theoretically by Hobbes's arguments about the popular foundations of monarchical rule – poses not only legal and institutional challenges, but aesthetic ones as well (Frank 2015). In particular, images of popular power are necessary for 'the people' – an entity that, unlike a monarch, never exists in its full presence – to recognise itself as a unified body capable of enacting its will: 'Images of peoplehood mediate the people's relationship to their own political empowerment – how they understand themselves to be a part of and act *as* a people' (3). The people, in other words, 'must see themselves assembled in order to feel their power' (5). The bodies politic reviewed above demonstrate that one way the people 'feel their power' and manifest their sovereignty to themselves is by laughing together. In laughter, a shared lack of power becomes the occasion for a shared feeling of power. The political efficacy of this feeling – either counter-sovereign or sovereign – hinges decisively on its vanity – that is, on its disregard for its own lack of objective foundation. In laughter, a body politic aesthetically conjures itself into being by enjoying the pleasures of an unauthorised feeling of power that remains blind to its own fraudulence and fragility.

V. Hobbes and the Critical Theory of Laughter

This chapter has identified the political logic of laughter by providing a gelopolitical reading of Hobbes's 'superiority theory'. Moving back and forth between Hobbes's account of laughter and his political philosophy reveals the complex dialectic at work between sovereignty and counter-sovereignty in laughter. Laughter resists sovereignty only by inscribing it anew, and it bolsters sovereignty only by dramatising its vulnerability to challenge. If, as Hobbes contends, sovereignty is that which establishes the rules and bounds of a shared political life – that is, what counts as *logos* versus *phōnē* – then as a counter/sovereign political enactment, laughter plays a central role in determining what the *polis* looks and sounds like on an everyday basis. This political efficacy of laughter stems from how its vainglorious quality prompts both its subject and object to behave as if it were 'glory well grounded' (Hobbes 2008: 58). Hobbes, in short, illuminates laughter as an unauthorised, fragile feeling of superiority through which sovereignty is continually made, undone and made again.

Hobbes's account of the counter/sovereign political logic of laughter supplies the first analytical tool needed for a critical theory of laughter. But this tool cannot get the job done on its own. A philosophical framework that conceives of laughter as emanating spontaneously from discrete subjects (either individual or collective) does not do justice to the full range of laughter practices in circulation today. As we have already begun to see, laughter is oftentimes deliberately encouraged, produced and regulated on the level of society as a whole. The Hobbesian approach explored in this chapter remains too subject-centric and consequently too amenable to the a/gelastic preoccupation with determining laughter's proper place in the *polis*. A critical theory that grasps laughter as a site of politics in its own right requires an additional element: an account of the *social logic of gelopolitics*. For this, I turn to the thinker whose critical vision orients this entire study, but whose own account of laughter we have not yet examined: Theodor Adorno.

Notes

1. At most, we have Derrida's attempt to link laughter to the highly idiosyncratic notion of sovereignty offered by Bataille (Derrida 1978).
2. For Hobbes, the ability to speak distinguishes humans from other animals because it facilitates both reason *and* absurdity: 'But this priviledge [Reason], is allayed by another; and that is, by the priviledge of Absurdity; to which no living creature is subject, but man only' (Hobbes 2012: 68). Hobbes believes that while it is impossible for speechless animals to lapse into absurdity, when humans speak absurdly, they descend to the level of animals and emit 'insignificant sounds' or 'meere sound' (60).
3. Laughter's roots in vainglory belie the conventional wisdom that Hobbes advances a superiority theory of laughter (Billig 2005: 50–6; Critchley 2002: 2; Morreall 1983: 5–6; Provine 2000: 4). I likewise put 'superiority theory' in quotes throughout this chapter.
4. Hobbes discusses glory two paragraphs before laughter but draws no direct connection between them (Hobbes 1991: 58–9).
5. As is well known, Hobbes divides his philosophical system into three parts: the philosophy of natural bodies, the philosophy of man and civil philosophy (Hobbes 1991: 102–3; 1994a: 11–12; Sorell 1996; Tuck 1996). Hobbes's philosophical trilogy (*De Corpore*, *De Homine*, *De Cive*) reflects this organisational schema. Although the passions clearly belong to the philosophy of man, Hobbes describes them as man's *natural* motions. In *De Corpore* and the 'Epistle Dedicatory' to *De Homine*, Hobbes proposes studying man as a natural body in terms of physics (Hobbes 1994a: 72–3; 1991: 35), and in *Leviathan* he classifies the passions as part of natural philosophy (Hobbes 2012: 130–1; Strong 1993: 140). While Hobbes's philosophy of man occupies a somewhat ambiguous position between his more cleanly delineated natural and civil philosophies, the narrow issue of man's passions (versus the broader subject of his morality) belongs to natural philosophy.
6. Two brief notes about this law. First, Hobbes here appears to prohibit laughter only insofar as it functions to declare hatred or scorn. Does *De Cive* open the door to less divisive, more affirmative forms of laughter? This is unlikely as Hobbes provides no indication elsewhere that laughter can play such a role; as sudden vainglory, laughter is always a declaration of scornful superiority. Second, and somewhat interestingly, a discussion of the strong laughing at the weak follows *De Cive*'s statement of the law against reproach: 'But although nothing be more frequent than the scoffs and jeers of the powerful against the weak [. . .] yet these kind of men do act against the law of nature' (Hobbes 1991: 143). Given Hobbes's repeated claims that laughter stems from an illusory conception of superiority, one can only assume

that the 'powerful' identified here are only apparently so. (Along these lines, Section IV of this chapter considers the laughter of newly vulnerable sovereigns.)
7. While Hobbes in this quotation is almost certainly describing how the laws of nature require a sovereign in order to obligate *in foro externo* (i.e., in action), the same logic also applies to *in foro interno* obligations (i.e., to endeavours). The laws of nature cannot obligate individual consciences unless and until there exists an authority who establishes the meaning and requirements of these laws. As Hobbes notes, the laws of nature 'cannot be observed save through pre-existing civil laws and the power of coercion' (Hobbes 1991: 85).
8. Hobbes appears to have a simple answer to this question: God. He writes: 'These dictates of Reason, men use to call by the name of Lawes; but improperly: for they are but Conclusions, or Theoremes concerning what conduceth to the conservation and defence of themselves; whereas Law, properly is the word of him, that by right hath command over others. But yet if we consider the same Theoremes, as delivered in the word of God, that by right commandeth all things; then are they properly called Lawes' (Hobbes 2012: 242). The decisive phrase in this quote is 'if we consider'. Hobbes understands 'God' as nothing more than a figure to whom individuals can imaginatively attribute the dictates of reason so that they take on the quality of commands. Indeed, for Hobbes the 'word of God' is just a synonym for 'what reason requires': '*Natural* [law] is that which God hath declared to all men by his *eternal word* born with them, to wit, their natural reason' (Hobbes 1991: 275). While the laws of nature are *consistent with* scripture and can be *treated as* the word of God, their authority does not derive *from* a God whose word can be known independent of human reason. As Hobbes notes in *The Elements of Law*, the laws of nature must do nothing more than 'to agree, or at least, not to be repugnant to the word of God' (Hobbes 2008: 99). So, the question remains: by what authority does Hobbes claim that reason requires what he says it does?
9. Hobbesian moral philosophy is, in other words, a function of Hobbesian politics. This position departs from several other prominent readings of Hobbes's laws of nature. A first group understands the laws of nature as forming a self-sufficient theory of moral obligation (Boonin-Vail 1994; Taylor 1938; Warrender 1961). These accounts neglect how the laws of nature 'onely concern the doctrine of Civill Society' and avoid more general ethical issues (Hobbes 2012: 238). Hobbes is a moral theorist only insofar as he is a political theorist. A second group acknowledges the links between Hobbes's moral and political philosophy but interprets Hobbes's moral views as enjoying analytic priority (in one way or another) over the arguments made in his political thought

(Connolly 1993; Martinich 2005; Sorell 2007; Strauss 1984). My approach reverses this order of priority and emphasises how Hobbes's political investments determine the contours of his moral philosophy. Oakeshott's argument that the laws of nature constitute moral obligations only by virtue of a sovereign command comes closest to my view. He writes: 'the sole cause of moral obligation is the will of this Sovereign authority; the only sort of action to which the term moral obligation is applicable is obedience to the commands of an authority authorised by the voluntary act of him who is bound. [. . .] Natural law is morally binding, but it consists of those theorems of reasoning that have been commanded by the Sovereign; until the Sovereign has willed them, they are not laws and therefore create no moral obligation' (Oakeshott 1965: lx–lxi). While Oakeshott correctly identifies the priority of the political over the moral, he neglects how the laws of nature owe their moral authority to Hobbes's textual performance of sovereignty.

10. We can speculate that the gradual depoliticisation of laughter from *The Elements of Law* to *De Homine* reviewed earlier reflects an attempt by Hobbes to excise this counter-sovereign experience/event from the domain of politics.
11. Zachariah Black's study of Hobbesian humour shows that Hobbes himself deployed laughter on behalf of the sovereign goals of social peace and stability (Black 2020).
12. What Foucault says about power in sexual politics – 'where there is power, there is resistance' (Foucault 1990: 95) – applies just as well to sovereignty in gelopolitics: 'where there is sovereignty, there is counter-sovereignty (and vice versa)'.

Chapter 2
Beyond A/gelasty:
Adorno's Critical Theory of Laughter

> Fun is a medicinal bath which the entertainment industry never ceases to prescribe. It makes laughter the instrument for cheating happiness. [...] In wrong society laughter is a sickness infecting happiness and drawing it into society's worthless totality.
>
> Max Horkheimer and Theodor Adorno,
> *Dialectic of Enlightenment* (2002: 112)

> Our capitalist foresaw this situation, and that was the cause of his laughter.
>
> Karl Marx, *Capital, Volume 1* (1990: 301)

That Theodor Adorno objects to laughter is not at all surprising: perhaps no twentieth-century philosopher is more closely associated with a melancholic ethos (Rose 2014). But as is the case with almost any topic treated by Adorno, his views on laughter are not as simple and straightforward as they might initially appear. Adorno exhibits an unyielding commitment to dialectical thinking, and while he certainly criticises laughter – especially that manufactured by the capitalist culture industry – he also grants laughter a privileged role in his account of the freedom offered by aesthetic experience. This chapter explores how Adorno resists the a/gelastic imperative to either support or oppose laughter in favour of practising a critical theory that conceives of laughter as a site of politics replete with both emancipatory potential and fascistic danger. In doing so, Adorno uncovers the social logic of gelopolitics and provides a model for the critical study of laughter today.

As described in the Introduction, contemporary scholarly and popular sources generally identify the human subject as the locus of laughter. The liberal discourse highlights laughter's capacity to emancipate the individual from falsehoods, while the Nietzschean discourse emphasises how laughter transforms *logos* itself. However, the subject-centrism of both approaches leaves us with an incomplete and inadequate picture of gelopolitics. In particular, it obscures how laughter arises within and exerts political effects on social structures of power and hierarchy that exceed and indeed constitute the human subject as a political animal. For instance, when I find myself laughing mindlessly along with the laugh-track of a mediocre sitcom (think *The Big Bang Theory*), can I really describe my laughter as a spontaneous eruption originating entirely within myself? Or is this laughter better understood as the product of an entertainment and advertising apparatus with interests of its own? Meanwhile, can we really explain the audience's laughter at Donald Trump's sexist jokes solely in terms of processes occurring within individual subjects? And does this laughter really resemble the emancipatory or deconstructive experience depicted by liberal and Nietzschean theorists? Or do we instead need a conception of a social order historically structured along patriarchal lines to make sense of this laughter's political origins and efficacy? While subject-centric discourses (a category in which I include Hobbes's theory, despite its subtlety and insightfulness) illuminate many key aspects of laughter's relation to politics, they do not provide a full understanding of gelopolitics in the Age of Hilarity. What remains necessary is an account of the *social logic of gelopolitics*, or of laughter's relation to the social order in which it operates politically.

The main innovation Adorno introduces to the study of gelopolitics is an attention to the question of social order. Originating in a Benjamin-inflected reading of Marx (Buck-Morss 1977), Adorno's conception of social order[1] critically negates both empiricist and idealist modes of social theory. Against empiricism, Adorno theorises society as *a whole*. Knowledge of specific empirical phenomena requires attending to their mediation by a larger social order that develops historically. In a 1961 essay, 'On the Logic of the Social Sciences', Adorno writes that 'the usual empirical asceticism with regard to theory cannot be sustained. Without the anticipation of that structural moment of the whole, which in individual observations can hardly ever be adequately realised, no individual observation would find its relative place' (Adorno 1976: 107). But against idealism, Adorno resists the epistemological presumption that the subject can grasp society as an entirely determinable system: 'societal totality does not lead a life of its own over and above that which it unites and of which it, in its turn, is composed. It produces and reproduces itself through its individual moments. Many of these moments preserve a relative independence' (107). Adorno conceives of the social order as a 'fractured totality' (Jay 1984: 94) that can only be known by studying the concrete, material events (earlier referred to as 'eccentric phenomena') that embody, express and point the way to overcoming its contradictory character (Adorno 1977: 133). Adorno's accounts of the laughter produced by the culture industry, 'lighthearted art', Samuel Beckett and Charlie Chaplin provide just such analyses of the modern social order. For Adorno, a critical study of society and a critical study of laughter proceed in and through one another: we understand society by grasping laughter's place and function within it, and we understand how laughter operates politically by way of an account of the social order.

I argue that Adorno offers three critical insights for studying gelopolitics. First, while the subject-centric liberal and Nietzschean discourses insist on laughter's properly emancipatory character, Adorno's conception of laughter as both a subjective experience and an objective event reveals that laughter just as readily entrenches forms of power in society. Because laughter does not originate in a subject who exists independent of the social order, there is nothing intrinsically liberatory or subversive about it. Laughter's political valence is always dependent on its place and function within society.[2] Second, this is not a straightforward claim that 'context matters' when determining the politics of laughter. Adorno shows that because the modern capitalist social order is fractured and self-contradictory, laughter's political efficacy hinges crucially on its own 'impurity'. Laughter serves oppressive, reactionary ends only by making possible an escape from social power, and it serves subversive, emancipatory ends only when it bears traces of that power within itself. This is the social logic of gelopolitics. Third and finally, Adorno models a critical theoretical practice that dwells in and accentuates this dialectical complexity of laughter. Eschewing the a/gelastic imperative to either promote or object to specific practices of laughter, an Adorno-inspired critical theory attends to how concrete experiences/events of laughter both shape the political life of society and open it up to change. It grasps, in other words, laughter as a privileged site of politics in the social order.

In keeping with the densely layered and oftentimes circuitous composition of Adorno's texts, this chapter proceeds by way of several close engagements with his analyses of modern society, laughter and aesthetics, and my arguments emerge in their full form only in the final section. Section I introduces Adorno's account of the violent, proto-fascistic logic of identity that governs life in the capitalist social order. Section II describes his critique of laughter manufactured by the culture industry and less familiar objections to 'polemical' laughter directed against sites of social power. Section III turns to Adorno's *Aesthetic Theory* and essays on light-hearted art, Beckett and Chaplin in order to explain how his conception of aesthetic experience illuminates the possibility of a 'reconciled' form of laughter. Section IV considers the controversial laughter produced by Jordan Peele's 2017 horror film *Get Out* to illustrate how Adorno does not advocate 'reconciled' or 'critical' laughter as an emancipatory political strategy, but instead employs these concepts as part of a critical theory that aims to make the political dangers and possibilities of laughter both thinkable and urgent.

I. The 'Systematized Horror' of Modern Society

Understanding Adorno's views on laughter requires a familiarity with his broader critique of the modern capitalist social order. *Dialectic of Enlightenment* (*DoE*), Adorno's famous 1944 joint venture with Max Horkheimer, provides the clearest and most forceful statement of this critique. The authors explain that the 'advance of thought' known as enlightenment begins when archaic humans seek to disenchant the fearsome and chaotic forces of nature to control them for their own benefit (Horkheimer and Adorno 2002: 2). Enlightenment entails an idealist epistemology wherein human reason (*logos*) is held to be constitutive of and capable of comprehending objects in the natural world. In enlightenment, 'the single distinction between man's own existence and reality swallows up all others. Without regard for difference, the world is made subject to man' (5). Adorno characterises enlightenment as a philosophy of *identity*: the objective world is – or can be made – identical with the concepts the subject employs to navigate and exploit it (Adorno 1973: 146–8). This belief in the qualitative equivalence of all natural objects from the perspective of the human subject finds expression in the methodological priority that modernity affords to mathematics, quantification and formal logic and its piety to the principles of self-preservation and utility-maximisation (Horkheimer and Adorno 2002: 4). For Horkheimer and Adorno, enlightenment is a set of material exercises of power that yields an idealist epistemology wherein a knowing human subject rules over a known, objective world.

The emergence of the capitalist mode of production extends the enlightenment philosophy of identity across the entire social field. The commodity form reduces all qualitative differences between objects into mere differences in price. Everything in the world – including human labour (Adorno 1973: 146) – becomes exchangeable with everything else because everything is ultimately for-man (Horkheimer and Adorno 2002: 4). Horkheimer and Adorno contend that 'enlightenment is totalitarian' because it constitutes an insatiable historical demand that everything submit to human calculation and control: 'For enlightenment, anything which does not conform to the standard of calculability and utility must be viewed with suspicion. Once the movement is able to develop unhampered by external oppression, there is no holding it back' (3–4). Enlightenment begins with human exercises of power over nature, and it culminates historically in the domination of human beings over themselves in capitalism.

Horkheimer and Adorno conclude that enlightenment betrays its own promise of securing human freedom. By transforming itself into a tool of self-preservation, utility-maximisation and value-creation, reason abjures its critical and imaginative capacities and instead functions to bind humans to their prevailing conditions of existence ever more tightly: 'what appears as the triumph of subjectivity, the subjection of all existing things to logical formalism, is bought with the obedient subordination of reason to what is immediately at hand' (20). The apparatuses of mass control developed in twentieth-century capitalist societies exemplify these reactionary and repressive tendencies of enlightenment.[3] Whatever escapes, resists or simply remains outside the system of profit-based exchange must be incorporated, disciplined or eliminated (21–2). Fascism, or the social institutionalisation of practices of violence that enforce existing notions of identity, represents this logic's natural endpoint. Adorno explains how the Holocaust married enlightenment's antipathy to the non-identical with its most technologically advanced systems of control and destruction. 'Genocide is the absolute integration', he writes in *Negative Dialectics*. 'Auschwitz confirmed the philosopheme of pure identity as death' (Adorno 1973: 362). Horkheimer and Adorno find that attempts to deliver humanity from the violence of nature by installing the human subject as sovereign culminate in the unleashing of even greater violence by humans against themselves: 'humanity, instead of entering a truly human state, is sinking into a new kind of barbarism' (Horkheimer and Adorno 2002: xiv). This is the dialectic of enlightenment.

It is crucial to note that Horkheimer and Adorno do not conceive of enlightenment as a 'motor' of history à la Hegelian idealism; rather, they trace modern society's historical development *as* a process of enlightenment. Categories of thought are functions of material social conditions (Adorno 1973: 11), and the concept of identity only becomes thinkable as such when a social system based on exchange-value has levelled the differences between qualitatively distinct use-values (Jameson 1990: 23–4). Capitalism is thus not a product of the enlightenment logic of identity; the logic of identity is a product of capitalist historical development. Modern society obeys the logic that its own material conditions make possible. *DoE* likewise must not be read – as it so often is – as a free-standing, 'pessimistic' philosophy of history. The speculative history sketched by Horkheimer and Adorno instead reflects a critical negation of capitalist society's conception of its own historical development as natural, idyllic and preordained (Buck-Morss 1977: 61). The Adornian narrative about enlightenment is always already a critique of the modern capitalist social order.

The stark and unyielding force of *DoE* corresponds to what the authors consider to be the inescapably dreadful reality of life in that order. 'The world is systematized horror' because literally every thought or action predicated on the dichotomy between knowing human subject and known objective world reinscribes the violent and potentially fascistic logic of identity governing society as a whole (Adorno 2005c: 113). Adorno's 1951 text *Minima Moralia* (2005c) illustrates just how thoroughly enlightenment principles have penetrated spheres of life that are conventionally thought to resist or escape their influence. One such sphere is laughter.

II. Adorno's Critique of Laughter

Adorno offers a two-pronged critique of laughter. First, laughter manufactured by the capitalist culture industry entrenches social power[4] by cruelly attacking sites of difference in such a way that becomes enjoyable second nature to subjects. Second, polemical laughter, or laughter directed against sites of social power, forecloses the imagination of alternative forms of social organisation by assuring subjects of their own political innocence. Adorno finds that despite taking diametrically opposed positions with respect to power, both laughter manufactured by the culture industry and polemical laughter bolster the violent logic of the capitalist social order.

Laughter in the Culture Industry

DoE's essay on the culture industry features Adorno's most frequently discussed (though by no means most extensive) reflections on laughter.[5] Rejecting the Durkheimian thesis that the shattering of traditional social ties in modernity leads to cultural chaos, Horkheimer and Adorno argue that modern culture is homogeneous and homogenising because it has become an industry (Horkheimer and Adorno 2002: 94). Having ceded the autonomy it once enjoyed with respect to the economy, culture subordinates itself to the capitalist imperatives of profit, efficiency and mass production (128). Hollywood films, television programmes and radio shows (today we could add YouTube and Netflix) promise subjects a pleasurable escape from the toils and miseries of the daily work process even as they impose the terms of existing social life ever more forcefully (100). The pleasures provided by the culture industry are ephemeral and hollow (and, of course, always for profit), and they secure the power of capital by repeatedly diffusing the subject's dissatisfactions in a way that leaves the social order responsible for them essentially unchanged. Horkheimer and Adorno conclude that the culture industry is a continuous bait-and-switch that 'endlessly cheats its consumers out of what it endlessly promises' (111).

Horkheimer and Adorno target the laughter generated by newspaper comics and cartoon and stunt films as a pseudo-pleasure that is particularly effective at enforcing subjects' domination by capital (110–14).[6] Miriam Hansen notes that their focus on laughter constitutes a direct response to Walter Benjamin's arguments in the second version of his 'Work of Art in the Age of Mechanical Reproduction' essay (Hansen 2012: 163–82). Here Benjamin asserts that the collective laughter generated by Disney films like *Mickey Mouse* can have positive – perhaps even revolutionary – political effects by diffusing the violent, proto-fascistic energies that accumulate and fester in modern audiences. He writes:

> If one considers the dangerous tensions which technology and its consequences have engendered in the masses at large – tendencies which at critical stages take on a psychotic character – one also has to recognize

> that this same technologization has created the possibility of psychic immunization against such mass psychoses. It does so by means of certain films in which the forced development of sadistic fantasies or masochistic delusions can prevent their natural and dangerous maturation in the masses. Collective laughter is one such preemptive and healing outbreak of mass psychoses. [. . .] American slapstick comedies and Disney films trigger a therapeutic release of unconscious energies. (Benjamin 2002: 118)

For Benjamin, the collective laughter generated by Disney films can help forestall outbreaks of fascist violence. Hansen explains that 'by activating individually based mass-psychotic tendencies in the space of collective sensory experience and, above all, in the mode of play, the cinema might prevent them from being acted out in reality' (Hansen 2012: 165).

Adorno disagrees. In a 1936 letter to Benjamin, he expresses doubts about the therapeutic and subversive powers of laughter. 'The laughter of a cinema audience', Adorno writes, 'is anything but salutary and revolutionary; it is full of the worst bourgeois sadism instead' (Adorno 1999: 130). He and Horkheimer make this dispute with Benjamin a major theme in 'The Culture Industry', insisting that the collective laughter generated by Disney films *intensifies* (rather than reduces) the public's fascistic tendencies under capitalism. When an audience laughs at the mishaps of a Mickey Mouse or a Donald Duck, they engage in an act of cruelty that embodies and reinscribes capitalist society's hostility to non-conformity and non-instrumental activity:

> Cartoon and stunt films were once exponents of fantasy against rationalism. They allowed justice to be done to the animals and things electrified by their technology, by granting the mutilated beings a second life. Today they merely confirm the victory of technological reason over truth. [. . .] The quantity of organized amusement is converted into the quality of organized cruelty. (Horkheimer and Adorno 2002: 110)

Adorno repeats this argument in *Minima Moralia* when he describes 'the collective of laughers' at newspaper comics as those 'who have cruel things on their side' (Adorno 2005c: 141). The audience that laughs at cartoon characters disciplines itself by publicly reaffirming that non-instrumental, 'silly' behaviour will be met with collective cruelty:

> To the extent that cartoons do more than accustom the senses to the new tempo, they hammer into every brain the old lesson that continuous

attrition, the breaking of all individual resistance, is the condition of life in this society. Donald Duck in the cartoons and the unfortunate victim in real life receive their beatings so that the spectators can accustom themselves to theirs. (Horkheimer and Adorno 2002: 110)

Rejecting Benjamin's rosy assessment of the laughter generated by popular films, Horkheimer and Adorno contend that this laughter constitutes a micro-performance of fascism that reinscribes the social order's brutality and primes subjects for future acts of violence. The manufacturing of laughter epitomises the culture industry's broader political strategy of fusing individual pleasure with social cruelty. Industrialised laughter makes fascism fun, carefree and second nature.

Before considering Adorno's critique of polemical laughter, we should take stock of just how far we have departed from the dominant liberal and Nietzschean conceptions of laughter as an experience that spontaneously emancipates the subject from either falsehoods or truth itself. Adorno demonstrates that laughter is often anything but spontaneous, emancipatory or centred in the subject; it is instead *manufactured* by society's apparatuses of control. While laughter passes through human subjects, the latter are not the primary loci of laughter. Laughter is not only a subjective *experience*, but also an objective *event*.[7] Treating laughter as beginning and ending in the human subject leads theorists like Benjamin to overstate its emancipatory efficacy and overlook how it operates as a mechanism of fascistic violence. For Adorno, philosophical conceptions of laughter as naturally spontaneous, emancipatory and centred in the subject are myths born of an inattention to the question of social order.

Polemical Laughter

Given Adorno's antipathy to the culture industry, one might expect that he favours 'polemical' forms of laughter that target institutions and mechanisms of social power. Surely Adorno supports laughing *at* capitalism, the culture industry and fascism, right? Not so fast. According to Adorno, laughter that imagines or positions itself as subversive paradoxically reinscribes the violent logic of identity that governs the social order as a whole. It is not enough to oppose social power; one must do so in such a way that resists the very *form* that power takes.

Adorno first raises the issue of polemical laughter in a *Minima Moralia* aphorism titled 'Juvenal's error.' Citing the Roman poet's remark that 'it is difficult not to write satire', Adorno questions the politics of irony (particularly satiric irony) in modern society (Adorno 2005b: 209). Satire, Adorno explains, works by exposing the distance between a society's ideological justification of itself and actual material conditions:

> Irony convicts its object by presenting it as what it purports to be; and without passing judgment, as if leaving a blank for the observing subject, measures it against its being-in-itself. [...] In this it presupposes the idea of the self-evident, originally of social resonance. He who has laughter on his side has no need of proof. (210)

Adorno argues that while modern society could certainly benefit from satiric criticism, its saturation by the imperatives of self-preservation, utility-maximisation and value-creation has transformed existing reality into its own justification such that the gap between reality and ideology upon which satire depends has closed. He writes:

> The impossibility of satire today should not be blamed, as sentimentality is apt to do, on the relativism of values, the absence of binding norms. Rather, agreement itself, the formal *a priori* of irony, has given way to universal agreement of content. As such it presents the only fitting target for irony and at the same time pulls the ground from under its feet. Irony's medium, the difference between ideology and reality, has disappeared. [...] There is not a crevice in the cliff of the established order into which the ironist might hook a fingernail. (211)

Modern society makes polemical laughter – laughter directed at sites of social power – both necessary and impossible. (Adorno's argument remains highly relevant today. For instance, what good does satirical laughter at the Trump administration's cruelty, corruption and incompetence do when the administration embraces these qualities as virtues?)

Adorno elaborates on *Minima Moralia*'s claim about the impossibility of polemical laughter in a 1958 essay, 'Trying to Understand Endgame'. I examine Adorno's reading of Beckett's play *Endgame* more closely in the following section, but for now I want to note how Adorno enlists Beckett to question the value of polemical laughter. He writes:

> the laughter [*Endgame*] arouses ought to suffocate the ones who laugh. This is what has become of humor now that it has become obsolete as

an aesthetic medium and repulsive, without a canon for what should be laughed about, without a place of reconciliation from which one could laugh, and without anything harmless on the face of the earth that would allow itself to be laughed at. (Adorno 1991b: 257)

Adorno holds that humour has become 'obsolete' because the all-encompassing nature of the capitalist social order makes it impossible for the subject to inhabit a 'place of reconciliation' from which to laugh at it in a critical manner. The standpoint we saw Shaftesbury occupy with respect to social irrationality is not available to the modern subject because the latter remains inextricably entangled with their object of laughter. Laughter that presumes to originate from a privileged, external position is 'repulsive' because in attacking an object deemed to be anomalous or irrational, the subject exhibits the same hostility to difference that characterises laughter manufactured by the culture industry. When Adorno contends that satire has become impossible and that humour is obsolete, he does not mean that these genres cease to exist in the twentieth century but that they no longer perform their intended emancipatory function and instead operate as ideological supports for the social order. Laughter that aims to resist social power ultimately reinforces it by entrenching the violent idealist logic of identity.

Adorno crystallises his objections to polemical laughter in a 1967 essay, 'Is Art Lighthearted?'. Here Adorno assesses the political value of comedies or parodies (like Brecht's *The Resistible Rise of Arturo Ui* and Chaplin's *The Great Dictator*) that target fascistic leaders and political assemblages (Adorno 1992: 251; 1974: 81). Adorno rejects the belief that laughing at fascism constitutes a viable emancipatory political strategy:

> By now the polemical form of humor has become questionable as well. [. . .] One cannot laugh at [fascism]. [. . .] Comedies about fascism would become accomplices of the silly mode of thinking that considered fascism beaten in advance because the strongest battalions in world history were against it. (Adorno 1992: 251–2)

Comedies about fascism disrespect its victims not because they violate some code of moral decency, but because the laughter they generate presumes to originate from a position external to the social order responsible for the emergence of fascism in the first place. (Once again, Adorno speaks to us today: how would the laughter generated by Stephen Colbert's nightly anti-Trump jokes sound to the detained migrant parent whose child has been taken from them?) By reinscribing the viewer's identity as wholly distinct from that of their object of laughter, such comedies absolve the viewer of responsibility for resisting the fascistic energies that continue to circulate in society. Adorno explains how

> the historical forces that produced the horror [of fascism] derive from the inherent nature of the social structure. They are not superficial forces, and they are much too powerful for anyone to have the prerogative of treating them as though he had world history behind him and the Führers actually were the clowns whose nonsense their murderous talk came to resemble only afterwards. (Adorno 1992: 252; see also 1974: 81; 1991a: 148)

Adorno believes that laughter directed at fascism obeys and thus strengthens the logic of identity that governs the capitalist social order as a whole.

Despite important differences in their mode of production and intentional structure, both laughter manufactured by the culture industry and polemical laughter bolster the social order and its systems of power and hierarchy. Industrialised laughter distracts subjects from their domination by capital, while polemical laughter distracts subjects from their entanglement in social irrationality and from any thought of resistance. Although the first form of laughter emerges from society's apparatuses of control and the second takes aim at these very same mechanisms, both enact a cruelty that diverts subjects from the oppressive conditions of the whole. From Adorno's perspective, laughter manufactured by the culture industry and polemical laughter are two sides of the same proto-fascistic coin.

III. Reconciled Laughter: The Suffocating Shock of Aesthetic Experience

This is not the end of the story when it comes to Adorno's views on laughter, however. Adorno envisions an alternative, genuinely antifascist practice of laughter called 'reconciled laughter' that resists social power and prompts the imagination and pursuit of alternative forms of social organisation. In this section I turn to Adorno's aesthetic philosophy and essays on light-hearted art, Beckett and Chaplin to elaborate the meaning and possibility of reconciled laughter.

Reconciled Laughter

Following their critique of industrialised laughter in 'The Culture Industry', Horkheimer and Adorno introduce a decisive distinction between 'wrong' and 'reconciled' laughter. Wrong laughter, such as polemical laughter or laughter manufactured by the culture industry, embodies and entrenches social power. It succeeds in doing so, the authors explain, because it *convincingly parodies* a more 'reconciled' social condition: '[t]he collective of those who laugh parodies humanity. [. . .] Their harmony presents a caricature of solidarity. What is infernal about wrong laughter is that it compellingly parodies what is best, reconciliation' (Horkheimer and Adorno 2002: 112). What does Adorno mean by reconciliation and, by extension, reconciled laughter? Adorno's notion of reconciliation is notoriously complex,[8] and while I cannot unpack its intricacies here, a brief excursus can clarify the basics.

Adorno rejects the traditional Hegelian conception of reconciliation as a social state wherein the difference between subject and object has been overcome. This, he believes, is a fantasy of idealist philosophies of identity that functions to suppress the object's innumerable and inexhaustible differences with the subject (Adorno 1973: 142–3). Adorno instead envisions reconciliation as a fleeting moment wherein an object's non-identity with the subject exists and is allowed to affect the subject *as* non-identical. In *Negative Dialectics* he writes that 'reconcilement would release the non-identical, would rid it of coercion [. . .]. Reconcilement would be the thought of the many as no longer inimical, a thought that is anathema to subjective reason' (Adorno 1973: 6; see also 2005c: 247). As Mort Schoolman explains, Adornian reconciliation amounts to the momentary overcoming of the enlightenment construction of difference as an 'otherness' to be conquered or incorporated by the subject (Schoolman 2020: 152–3). While non-identity might seem to constitute the very opposite of 'reconciliation', Adorno believes that it is only under such conditions that both subject and object escape from the intrinsically violent logic of identity. Reconciliation, in other words, *abolishes the hierarchy* between subject and object, allowing each to freely encounter and affect the other on its own terms (Adorno 1973: 181). Reconciliation as non-identity necessarily takes the form of a fleeting moment because any sustained experience of the non-identical risks becoming identical to itself. 'The idea of reconcilement', Adorno insists, 'forbids the positive positing of reconcilement as a concept'

(Adorno 1973: 145). Schoolman concludes that reconciliation for Adorno is this 'twofold endless striving to realize, once and for all, the achievement of the all-inclusiveness of difference, while reflexively recognizing there always remain differences belonging to the object to be included' (Schoolman 2020: 161).

With this notion of reconciliation in place, we can now make sense of 'reconciled laughter'. According to Horkheimer and Adorno, 'wrong laughter' succeeds at entrenching social power because it 'compellingly parodies' an experience of reconciliation (Horkheimer and Adorno 2002: 112). Consumers are drawn to Disney films and *The Daily Show* because the laughter produced by these sources creates the illusion of an escape from or resistance to social power (i.e., the illusion that the non-identical is speaking on its own terms). For the reasons described earlier, this is not actually what happens. But Horkheimer and Adorno insist that when wrong laughter parodies reconciliation, it parodies an achievement that laughter *actually makes possible*. 'Reconciled laughter' is an experience that generates a fleeting moment of reconciliation: 'Reconciled laughter resounds with the echo of escape from power; wrong laughter copes with fear by defecting to the agencies which inspire it' (112). Wrong laughter bolsters social power only because subjects have a familiarity with its ability to deliver reconciliation. This is what the authors mean when they claim that 'there is laughter because there is nothing to laugh about' (112). Wrong laughter makes reference to – and its political efficacy depends on – the possibility of a reconciled laughter that resists social power.

Adorno's concept of reconciled laughter transforms how we understand his broader critique of laughter. Contrary to what a cursory reading of 'The Culture Industry' or *Minima Moralia* might suggest, Adorno does not simply reject Benjamin's claim that collective laughter serves liberatory ends. His critique of 'wrong' laughter in fact *requires* the possibility of such a reconciled laughter. Earlier in *DoE* Horkheimer and Adorno describe just how tightly bound these opposed political valences of laughter are:

> If laughter [throughout class history] has been a sign of violence, an outbreak of blind, obdurate nature, it nevertheless contains its opposite element, in that through laughter blind nature becomes aware of itself as such and thus abjures its destructive violence. [. . .] Laughter is in league with the guilt of subjectivity, but in the suspension of law which it announces it also points beyond that complicity. It promises a passage to the homeland.[9] (60)

Adorno likewise *agrees* with Benjamin about the emancipatory potential of laughter, but he believes that Benjamin takes a too one-sided (i.e., non-dialectical) view of gelopolitics under mid-twentieth-century capitalism.[10] Grasping how laughter functions in the modern social order requires distinguishing between its opposed political tendencies and carefully tracing their relation. We have already seen how laughter's capacity to oppress hinges on its ability to emancipate, but how does this emancipatory power of laughter itself come into being? To understand the possibility of reconciled laughter, I turn to Adorno's *Aesthetic Theory*, particularly his notion of aesthetic experience. Reconciled laughter, we will find, is a self-shattering aesthetic experience that prompts the subject to imagine and pursue alternative modes of social organisation.

The Impure Autonomy of Art and Aesthetic Experience

The central thesis of *Aesthetic Theory* is that art alone achieves autonomy in modern society. In a world where 'wrong life cannot be lived rightly' (Adorno 2005c: 39), art has the power to separate itself and its audience from prevailing social conditions: 'artworks detach themselves from the empirical world and bring forth another world, one opposed to the empirical world as if this other world too were an autonomous reality. Thus, however tragic they appear, artworks tend a priori toward affirmation' (Adorno 1997: 1). Art is autonomous because a subject cannot comprehend it with the concepts they employ in everyday life. What makes art *art* is its ability to make the subject feel something utterly new and inexpressible in existing language. One's experience of an artwork – or 'aesthetic experience' – is consequently an experience of the non-identical. Adorno writes: 'Aesthetic identity seeks to aid the nonidentical, which in reality is repressed by reality's compulsion to identity. Only by virtue of separation from empirical reality [. . .] does the artwork achieve a heightened order of existence' (4). In aesthetic experience, the subject comes face to face with the falseness of the idealist principle that the objective world is or can be made identical to their concepts. Owen Hulatt explains that art 'delivers an experience in which nonidentity is made palpable and the falsity of our way of reasoning (and derivative way of life) is made apparent' (Hulatt 2016: xix). As an encounter with a difference that exceeds the subject's capacity to conceive of it, aesthetic experience challenges – even *undoes* – the subject, making them non-identical to their own self-conception as an autonomous, world-constituting entity (Adorno 1997: 244–5). 'Aesthetic experience', Adorno concludes, 'is a countermovement to the subject. It demands something on the order of the self-denial of the observer, his capacity to address or recognize what aesthetic objects themselves enunciate and what they conceal' (346).

By opening the subject up to a non-identitarian and hence non-violent relation with the objective world, art provides a fleeting moment of reconciliation. Adorno writes: 'the shock aroused by important works [...] is the moment in which recipients forget themselves and disappear into the work; it is the moment of being shaken' (244). In aesthetic experience, the subject becomes receptive to difference and allows it to exist and affect them on its own terms. Aesthetic experience is an explosive 'shock' or 'shudder' (Adorno 1997: 244–6) because an anticipated or sustained experience of the non-identical is impossible lest the non-identical become identical to itself (Adorno 1973: 154–5). Aesthetic experience testifies to the possibility – indeed, imperative – of constructing alternative, less oppressive and violent forms of social organisation: 'By emphatically separating themselves from the empirical world, their other, [artworks] bear witness that the world should be other than it is; they are the unconscious schemata of that world's transformation' (177).

Adorno's account of artistic autonomy breaks with conventional liberal notions of autonomy as individual freedom or escape from society, and its focus on self-overcoming and transformation resonates strongly with Nietzschean conceptions of autonomy. However, Adorno adds a crucial (and characteristic) dialectical twist. Although art is non-identical to the social order, it always remains a 'social fact' (5). Art is produced in a determinate historical situation (43) with the socially available materials, instruments and techniques of production (34); it takes social material for its thematic content (225); and it generally offers itself for sale in the marketplace (236). Adorno writes that 'art is related to its other [i.e., society] as is a magnet to a field of iron fillings. Not only art's elements, but their constellation as well, that which is specifically aesthetic and to which its spirit is usually chalked up, refer back to its other' (7). The autonomy art achieves with respect to society is thus thoroughly mediated by society: 'Art negates the categorial determinations stamped on the empirical world and yet harbors what is empirically existing in its own substance' (5; see also Zuidervaart 1991: 88). Aesthetic experience likewise cannot be understood simply as an escape from or transcendence of the social order; it is simultaneously an *event* that unfolds *within* the social order. As Adorno notes, '[t]he share of subjectivity in the artwork is itself a piece of objectivity' (Adorno 1997: 41). The subject-undoing shock provided by aesthetic experience proceeds within and by way of the very same social order whose transformation it heralds.

Adorno insists that this impure quality of art's autonomy is not cause for despair but is rather the source of its distinctive political efficacy (Adorno 1974: 89). Were art to achieve absolute (i.e., liberal) autonomy, it would fail to critically engage the social order. Like polemical laughter, art that imagines itself as having completely escaped the terms of social life would leave the latter unchanged and perhaps even strengthened. Conversely, were art to shed its claim to autonomy, it would devolve into the mere entertainment and pleasure-peddling of the culture industry (Adorno 1997: 138). From Adorno's perspective, art's impurity paradoxically empowers it to resist prevailing social conditions: 'only by its double character, which provokes permanent conflict, does art succeed at escaping the spell by even the slightest degree' (138). In art, an object tainted by the horrors of society nevertheless becomes an occasion for transforming society.

Adorno, in sum, holds that reconciliation in the capitalist social order is provided by a constitutively impure, fleeting and self-shattering aesthetic experience/event – one wherein the subject encounters and opens themselves up to the non-identical. The Nietzschean self-transcendence delivered by art is dialectically tempered by its emergence and operation within a contradictory social order. Adorno's essays on light-hearted art, Beckett and Chaplin show that a certain type of laughter is just this kind of aesthetic experience/event.

Laughter as Aesthetic Experience/Event

Let's return to 'Is Art Lighthearted?'. Here Adorno considers Friedrich Schiller's thesis that art provides a 'lighthearted' escape from the miseries of 'serious' life (Adorno 1992: 247). While Adorno rejects this argument as prefiguring the culture industry's view of art as mere entertainment and consolation, he acknowledges that a light-hearted quality is essential to all art:

> The thesis of art's lightheartedness is to be taken in a very precise way. It holds for art as a whole, not for individual works. [. . .] A priori, prior

to its works, art is a critique of the brute seriousness that reality imposes upon human beings. (248)

Art is light-hearted – even playful (Adorno 1997: 39) – in its refusal to take the terms of existing social life too seriously. Previewing his claim about the impurity of artistic autonomy, Adorno explains that an artwork's political efficacy consists in how it embodies a dialectical tension between serious life and light-hearted escape. Art is serious because it emerges from, bears the traces of and critically engages with the social order, but it is light-hearted in its resistance to the terms governing that order. Adorno concludes that 'as something that has escaped from reality and is nevertheless permeated with it, art vibrates between this seriousness and lightheartedness. It is this tension that constitutes art' (Adorno 1992: 249).

Adorno leverages this conception of art to restate the critique of laughter he and Horkheimer levelled in 'The Culture Industry' and to elaborate on the possibility of reconciled laughter. Adorno argues that laughter that functions solely as a light-hearted diversion from oppressive social conditions inevitably becomes an ally of the social order: 'laughter, once the image of humanness, becomes a regression to inhumanity' (251). On the other hand, laughter that is an 'image of humanness' (i.e., reconciled laughter) maintains a dialectical tension between its light-hearted and serious qualities. Such laughter is light-hearted in that it pokes fun at existing social reality, but it is serious in how it acknowledges its own embeddedness in and takes aim at that reality: 'the moment of lightheartedness or humor is not simply expelled from [artworks] in the course of history. It survives in their self-critique, as humor about humor' (252). Eschewing the detached innocence of polemical laughter, reconciled laughter finds itself to be just as laughable as that at which it laughs. Hardly the exuberant laughter of the Nietzschean free spirit, the 'seriousness' of reconciled laughter implicates and in turn undermines the laughing subject. Again invoking Beckett, Adorno claims that 'humor is salvaged in Beckett's plays because they infect the spectator with laughter about the absurdity of laughter and laughter about despair' (253). For Adorno, reconciled laughter embodies the serious/light-hearted dialectic constitutive of art and aesthetic experience.

'Trying to Understand *Endgame*' further elucidates Adorno's conception of reconciled laughter. Set in a barren, depopulated world, *Endgame* features a series of dark, absurd dialogues and interactions between three family members and their servant who are all waiting to die (Beckett 1978). Adorno interprets Beckett's play as depicting the 'general disaster' in which the enlightenment logic of identity culminates historically (Adorno 1991b: 266). Having depleted and destroyed the natural world, humans descend into a state of complete meaninglessness and alienation:

> The Beckettian situations of which his drama is composed are the photographic negative of a reality referred to meaning. They have as their model the situations of empirical existence, situations which, once isolated and deprived of their instrumental and psychological context through the loss of personal unity, spontaneously assume a specific and compelling expression – that of horror. (253)

Laughter is the experience/event that Adorno associates with *Endgame*. Beckett's 'schizoid situations are comical [. . .] [b]ut the laughter it arouses ought to suffocate the ones who laugh' (257). The subject literally cannot survive the laughter generated by *Endgame* because by confronting them with a world where there is nothing left to grasp or control, Beckett's play calls into question the idealist logic of identity that governs the social order as a whole. Rendering the subject non-identical to themselves, such laughter prompts the imagination of alternative forms of social organisation. Adorno writes: 'the immanent contradiction of the absurd, the nonsense in which reason terminates, opens up the emphatic possibility of something true that cannot even be conceived of anymore. It undermines the absolute claim of the status quo' (273). Beckett's work gives rise to a dark, self-reflexive laughter that delivers a fleeting moment of reconciliation.

Adorno's reflections on clowns and clowning provide a final and particularly illuminating account of reconciled laughter. According to Adorno, clown performances recall a primitive, mimetic rationality distinct from the instrumental rationality that predominates in modernity. Clowns embody an 'anarchistic and archaic immediacy [that] cannot be adapted to the reified bourgeois life, and becomes ridiculous before it – fragmentary, but at the same time allowing it to appear ridiculous' (Adorno 2002a: 489). By playfully parodying the routinised and neurotic dimensions of everyday social life (e.g., labourers working in a factory or police officers patrolling a neighbourhood), clowns highlight the irrationality of enlightenment reason.

Given this fascination with clowning, it is not surprising that Adorno admires his era's most famous clown-like actor, Charlie Chaplin. In a short but important 1964 essay, 'In Malibu', Adorno recalls meeting Chaplin at a California dinner party (Adorno 1996; Habermas 1983: 99). Adorno writes that Chaplin strikes him as embodying two opposed tendencies. On the one hand, Chaplin's insatiable will to parody evokes the violence of enlightenment reason:

> His powerful, explosive, and quick-witted agility recalls a predator ready to pounce. [...] There is something about the empirical Chaplin that suggests not that he is the victim but rather, menacingly, that he would seek victims, pounce on them, tear them apart. (Adorno 1996: 59–60).

As Jarno Hietalahti notes, for Adorno, clowns 'bring violent humour right before the eyes of the spectators, and the audience laughs with the violent performance' (Hietalahti 2020: 38). But on the other hand, Adorno holds that Chaplin employs a mimetic rationality that playfully subverts this violence: 'it is as though he, using mimetic behavior, caused purposeful, grown-up life to recede, and indeed the principle of reason itself, thereby placating it' (Adorno 1996: 60). Adorno argues that Chaplin's aesthetic genius consists in how he embodies these two opposed tendencies without resolving their antinomy. Chaplin is 'a vegetarian Bengal tiger' who 'projects upon the environment his own violence and dominating instinct, and through this projection of his own culpability produces that innocence which endows him with more power than all power possesses' (59–60). Rather than offering hollow entertainment *or* detached polemical indictment,[11] Chaplin's clownish performances turn the violence of the social order against itself.

'In Malibu' concludes by recounting how Chaplin parodied Adorno himself. At one point during the dinner party, an absent-minded Adorno extended his hand to say goodbye to Harold Russell, an actor who lost his hands in the Second World War. Upon gripping Russell's iron prosthetic, Adorno was startled and 'sensed immediately that I could not reveal my shock to the injured man at any price. In a split second I transformed my frightened expression into an obliging grimace that must have been far ghastlier' (59). Chaplin, of course, witnessed the entire encounter, and before long he was mimicking Adorno's reaction in front of the entire party.

Adorno's description of the laughter Chaplin generated is decisive for understanding his conception of reconciled laughter. Adorno writes: 'all the laughter he brings about is so near to cruelty; solely in such proximity to cruelty does it find its legitimation and its element of the salvational' (60–1). The salvational power of laughter –

its capacity to reconcile – depends, paradoxically, on its 'proximity' to its opposed political tendency: cruelty. By parodying Adorno, Chaplin reveals the philosopher – exactly the kind of figure who supposedly exemplifies life at its most serious, sober and high-brow – to be just as ridiculous as anyone else. Because Chaplin's performance exposes the absurdity of Adorno in such a way that exposes the absurdity of the larger social order, it ensures that the cruelty directed at Adorno redounds back on those who laugh. Adorno believes that without this self-suffocating element, laughter lacks the seriousness necessary to avoid lapsing into mere entertainment. As he notes in *Aesthetic Theory*, 'only by the strength of its deadliness do artworks participate in reconciliation' (Adorno 1997: 134). For Adorno, laughter contributes to reconciliation only when it embodies and displaces the violence of the social order in which it arises.

IV. A Theory of Critical Laughter vs. A Critical Theory of Laughter: The Case of *Get Out*

At first glance, Adorno's reflections on laughter look awfully like an intervention in the a/gelasty dispute. To the question of 'to laugh or not to laugh?' Adorno seems to have a clear answer: laughter that channels and entrenches the violence of capitalist society (wrong laughter) is a political vice, while laughter that resists this violence (reconciled laughter) is a political virtue. Adorno appears to be an agelast when it comes to wrong laughter, but a gelast when it comes to reconciled laughter. Along these lines, Shea Coulson argues that Adorno offers a 'theory of critical laughter' (Coulson 2007: 142–3). Seeking to rescue Adorno from charges that he simply dislikes laughter, Coulson claims that Adorno only disapproves of uncritical practices of laughter (i.e., wrong laughter) and finds significant aesthetic, ethical and political value in more critical, subject-undoing forms of laughter (i.e., reconciled laughter). 'Adorno's apparent mirthlessness is actually disdain for an uncritical use of laughter that simply concretizes social repression', Coulson writes. 'Laughter, for Adorno, should act violently against reified structures and unhinge the subject from reification' (143). According to Coulson, Adorno distinguishes between uncritical and critical laughter and endorses the latter as an 'art of laughter' that helps achieve social reconciliation (141).

While this a/gelastic reading of Adorno is tempting, it fundamentally misunderstands both his accounts of laughter and his broader theoretical project. Adorno refuses to reify wrong and reconciled laughter into determinate practices that one can either support or oppose. He instead sees wrong and reconciled laughter as richly dialectical concepts through which one can identify and grapple with the dangers and opportunities of gelopolitics in modern society. Adorno does not promote a specific *type* of laughter – a 'theory of critical laughter' – that resists the terms of life in the capitalist social order; he models a *theoretical practice* – a critical theory of laughter – that attends to concrete experiences/events of laughter as complex, unstable sites of emancipatory possibility and fascistic danger. In keeping with the culturally engaged nature of Adorno's work, I will elucidate the contours of this critical theory by considering the laughter produced by *Get Out*, a 2017 film by comedian Jordan Peele.

Theorising Laughter Critically: Get Out

Get Out tells the story of Chris Washington, an African American man in his mid-twenties who accompanies his white girlfriend, Rose Armitage, to meet her well-to-do family at their countryside estate in upstate New York. Despite Rose's and her family's earnest assurances of their liberal attitudes about race, Chris becomes uneasy upon meeting the family's two mysteriously stilted and obsequious Black housekeepers, Georgina and Walter. Chris's suspicions (and those of Rod, his Black friend with whom he communicates by phone) are confirmed when Dean – Rose's neurosurgeon father – uses Chris's temporary absence while on a walk with Rose to auction off his body to implant it with the brain of the highest white bidder – the same operation he has already performed on the bodies of Georgina and Walter. After being hypnotised by Rose's psychiatrist mother Missy, Chris manages to evade the planned lobotomy by outwitting and outmuscling the Armitage family, killing them all before escaping from the estate with Rod.

Peele's film raises a host of timely and subtle questions about the modalities of white supremacy, the tenability of white liberalism and the prospects of Black political solidarity. For now, however, I would like to focus on a dispute surrounding the film's genre. In November 2017, the Hollywood Press Association announced that *Get Out* would compete as a comedy in the annual Golden Globes award contest (Desta 2017). An uproar ensued over how the Association could possibly categorise *Get Out* – a horror film featuring only a few lines of comic relief – as a comedy. Although this uproar was itself somewhat frivolous – Peele's production company had strategically submitted the film for consideration in the Globes' notoriously capacious 'comedy/musical' category – it drew attention to a more interesting set of questions about the laughter *Get Out* was in fact producing in its audiences. Following the film's release, Black moviegoers reported white audiences laughing at seemingly inappropriate moments (e.g., the lobotomy scene), while white viewers were perplexed by Black audiences laughing during other key scenes (e.g., Chris killing Rose) (Benjamin 2017; Ngangura 2017; Yuan and Harris 2018). When Stephen Colbert asked Peele about the film's classification as a comedy, Peele responded, 'The real question is, what are you laughing at? Are you laughing at the horror, the suffering? It is the kind of movie that Black people can laugh at, but white people, not so much' (Desta 2017). How can Adorno – a theorist uniquely attuned to the intersections of laughter and social horror – help elucidate this differential racial politics of laughing at *Get Out*?

We can begin by following Peele's lead and considering the laughter of white audiences to be a form of 'wrong' laughter, or laughter that participates in and strengthens social power – in this case, the institutions and mechanisms of white supremacy. *New Yorker* critic Rich Benjamin (2017) helpfully explains how *Get Out* performs the 'death of white racial innocence', or the collapse of the rhetorical posture of shocked disbelief adopted by white liberals when confronted with evidence of racism in American society. The character of Rose – the epitome of white millennial sophistication and progressivism – exposes white racial innocence to be a ruse that functions to insulate white supremacy from political efforts to identify and dismantle it. Benjamin writes:

> What a juicy moment when Rose, on the phone with Chris's black friend [Rod], realizes that the jig is up; her caper is about to be exposed. Rose drops her sweet face and hardens it into a stare. Her stony eyes reveal her about-face from liberal ingénue to calculating racial predator. [. . .] Her family's bloody antics, like this country's recent racial politics, had careened to that moment when everybody knows what's what, and all bets are off.

Vice contributor Tari Ngangura contends that white audiences use laughter to secure their sense of innocence against this challenge posed by the film. By laughing along with the Armitages' scheme, white audiences seek to redraw the lines of racial innocence that divide 'good' (i.e., non-racist) whites from 'bad' (i.e., racist) whites

(Ngangura 2017). 'The Armitages are obviously bad, racist people', white audiences seem to be saying, 'and we can laugh at Chris's travails because we're *good* white people who would *never* do anything like that.' The laughter of white audiences signals and performatively reinscribes their own distance from the Armitages' racism. Ngangura argues that this reaction reflects a fundamental, yet utterly predictable failure by white viewers to grasp how the film challenges their place in the racial hierarchy: 'The white liberals I saw knee slapping themselves into hysterical oblivion clearly missed the mark and seemingly saw the film as only a comedy and not a commentary of their actual faults . . . You are Rose. All of you.'

From this perspective, white laughter at *Get Out* reflects a microperformance of white supremacy that fuses the logics of polemical laughter and laughter manufactured by the culture industry. Such laughter identifies a target (the Armitages) as the source of racial wrongdoing in a way that assures the subject of their own political innocence and distracts them from the ways they participate in and benefit from white supremacy. Arising within the context of a Hollywood film, this self-distracting laughter converts the horrors that befall Chris and the Armitages' other victims into mere material for entertainment. By diverting the subject from both their own cruelty and that of the racialised social order, white laughter at *Get Out* primes them for future involvement in and/or indifference towards more extreme acts of racial violence.

Meanwhile, we can understand the laughter of Black audiences at the film as a form of 'reconciled' laughter, or laughter that resists social power. Like Beckett's *Endgame*, Peele's *Get Out* portrays existing society in a horrific form that exposes its absurdity. Ngangura explains that by depicting white supremacy as the horror show that Black subjects live every day, the film renders that reality laughable: 'I'm allowed to laugh during *Get Out*, because the awkward situations Chris had to extricate himself from are regular scenarios in my everyday life. Incredulous laughter is what makes them bearable' (Ngangura 2017). *Get Out* is a liberating film for many Black audiences because it vindicates their experiences in a social order that sustains itself in no small part by denying the validity of those experiences. Tinged with horror – the horror of white supremacy – laughter at the film troubles and transforms how a Black subject conceives of their place in the social order, offering a rare glimpse of a form of social life that acknowledges and responds to the trauma of white supremacy. In Adornian terms, this laughter renders the

Black subject non-identical to the non-identical status they occupy in white supremacist society. This non-non-identity is not a consolidation of the terms of identity under white supremacy, but rather a displacement that gestures towards a more egalitarian mode of social organisation.

But do Peele's rules for laughing at *Get Out* capture the full range of this laughter's political possibilities? In particular, can white audiences laugh at *Get Out* in a 'reconciled' way? And can Black audiences laugh at the film in a 'wrong' way? Is the political valence of laughter (i.e., its capacity to either entrench or resist social power) determined simply by the laughing subject's position within a given structure of domination – in this case, white supremacy? It is on these questions that Adorno's approach proves especially fruitful. As described earlier, laughter that participates in and entrenches social power (i.e., wrong laughter) necessarily contains the seeds of possible emancipation. Wrong laughter 'nevertheless contains its opposite element, in that through laughter blind nature becomes aware of itself as such and thus abjures its destructive violence' (Horkheimer and Adorno 2002: 60). If wrong laughter did not make reference to this reconciling ability, it would sacrifice its oppressive efficacy as subjects would no longer believe it provides an escape from power. Conversely, laughter that actually resists social power (i.e., reconciled laughter) always emerges out of and bears traces of that power's violence: 'solely in such proximity to cruelty does it find its legitimation and its element of the salvational' (Adorno 1996: 60–1). If reconciled laughter were not contaminated by serious life in this way, it would sacrifice its critical relation to society and risk becoming an ideological support for it. Adorno shows that in a fractured social order, experiences/events of laughter are dialectically complex and contain their opposed political tendencies within themselves. Laughter serves oppressive, reactionary ends only by making possible an escape from power, and it serves subversive, emancipatory ends only by bearing the social order's violence within itself. This is the social logic of gelopolitics.

The wrong laughter enjoyed by many white audiences of *Get Out* likewise contains the seeds of a reconciled laughter that would undermine white supremacy. Indeed, white laughter at *Get Out* is so unnerving precisely because it stems from an otherwise noble opposition to racism ('we can laugh at this film because its plot is so obviously racist that it could never – and should never – actually occur') that has been (mis-)deployed to secure the subject's own racial innocence. A reconciled white laughter would allow this anti-racist commitment to exceed its myopic parochialism and call into question the self-assurance of the laughing subject. Reconciled white laughter would spring from a horror-tinged recognition among white subjects that they too are Rose, Dean, Missy and even Jeremy, Rose's younger brother who fetishises Chris's body.[12] This laughter would motivate a reckoning with their participation in and benefiting from the racial terror depicted by the film and with white supremacy more generally. However, as Adorno's treatment of Chaplin suggests, because reconciled laughter always emerges out of and bears the traces of social power, it is never politically pure. White laughter at *Get Out* that rests content with its own enlightened anti-racism (i.e., its own 'wokeness') or enjoys itself a bit too much thus risks backsliding into a wrong laughter that is complicit with white supremacy.

Meanwhile, Black laughter at *Get Out* also risks devolving into a form of wrong laughter. Wrong Black laughter would enjoy the film's depiction of white terror as a merely entertaining registering of an essentially untransformable social reality. In this way, it would obey the logic identified by 'The Culture Industry' in its discussion of how laughter at the suffering of cartoon characters leads audiences to identify with their own oppression. Chris and the Armitage family's other victims would, to paraphrase Adorno, 'receive their beatings so that the spectators can accustom themselves to theirs' (Horkheimer and Adorno 2002: 110). Wrong Black laughter would resonate with the cynical, dismissive guffaws enjoyed by Detective Latoya, the middle-aged Black policewoman who invites her co-workers to laugh along at Rod's attempt to file a missing person report for Chris, whom he speculates (not all that inaccurately) is a victim of 'this family [that] is abducting Black people and brainwashing them to work for them as sex slaves and shit'. Wrong Black laughter would reflect a celebration of one's own transient or relative privileges (e.g., enjoying a movie or working in law enforcement) amid wider social suffering. Such laughter, despite its 'origin' in a Black subject, follows the script written by white supremacy by silencing and discrediting Black trauma.

Bringing Adorno to bear on the laughter generated by *Get Out* demonstrates that his reflections on laughter are not, as Coulson recommends, best read as a 'theory of critical laughter'. If Adorno were merely promoting an art of critical laughter, he would not have much to say about *Get Out*. Black laughter at the film would be praised as reconciled (critical) laughter, white laughter would be condemned as wrong (uncritical) laughter, and that would be that. Drained of their dialectical energy, the concepts of wrong and reconciled laughter would be unable to illuminate how the different forms of laughter produced by *Get Out* constitute dynamic, open-ended sites of politics capable of both bolstering and undermining the racial order. Adorno instead practises a critical theory of laughter. A critical theory of laughter differentiates between wrong laughter (e.g., white laughter at *Get Out*) and reconciled laughter (e.g., Black laughter at the film), but it refuses to reify these concepts. Rather, it uses them as tools to unearth the non-identical within concrete experiences/events of laughter. A critical theory of laughter cultivates the possibilities for reconciliation in oppressive laughter (e.g., the incipient anti-racism in white laughter at *Get Out*) and warns against the violent tendencies of emancipatory laughter (e.g., the risk of resigned cynicism posed by Black laughter at the film). It grasps laughter's intensely dialectical quality as embodying, expressing and offering a means for overcoming the political contradictions of the modern social order.

What explains Adorno's refusal to take a position in the a/gelasty dispute is precisely what makes him such an astute theorist of gelopolitics – namely, his steadfast commitment to dialectical thinking. Adorno consistently declines – often to his critics' great consternation (Benhabib 1986; Buck-Morss 1977; Habermas 1990; Honneth 2009) – to make ontological or programmatic arguments. *Minima Moralia*, *Negative Dialectics* and *Aesthetic Theory* read less like treatises that advance 'theories *of*' anything than they do densely layered critical engagements with concrete elements of modern social life. Adorno insists that theory's political value consists in its autonomy from practical politics (Adorno 2005a, 2005d; Marasco 2015: 109–13). Theory is autonomous in the same mediated sense that art is autonomous: it transcends social reality not by offering recommendations for practice but by assimilating itself to that reality to such an extreme degree that it displaces and transforms the very terms of practice (Adorno 2005a: 276). By avoiding the trap of either uncritically accepting or pretending to escape the terms of social life, negative dialectics bears witness to the non-identical and helps achieve reconciliation more effectively than theoretical interventions that take reconciliation as their explicit subject matter or objective (Adorno 2005a: 277–8; 2005e: 292–3).

Adorno's gelopolitical reflections likewise should not be read as attempts to promote a particular type or art of laughter ('reconciled' or 'critical' laughter) for its salutary political effects. Such an approach inevitably fails to contribute to reconciliation because it sketches in advance what emerges only within a concrete political situation: an experience/event of the non-identical. Reconciled laughter, in other words, is not a political *programme*; it is a *concept* that, like all concepts, is necessarily incomplete (Adorno 1973: 5) and whose incompleteness prompts subjects to think about, unearth and cultivate possibilities for social transformation. Instead of offering a necessarily illusory theory of critical laughter, Adorno models a critical theory of laughter that intervenes in the social order by making laughter's political dangers and opportunities thinkable and urgent. Following the dictum that 'we are not to philosophize above concrete things; we are to philosophize, rather, out of these things' (Adorno 1973: 33), this theoretical practice grasps laughter as a fraught and dynamic site of politics wherein the social order produces, sustains and becomes otherwise to itself.

These chapters on Hobbes and Adorno have crafted the basic analytical tools needed for a critical theory of laughter: first, an account of laughter's political logic, and second, an account of the social logic of gelopolitics. Hobbes showed that laughter shapes, disrupts and reshapes the conceptions of *logos* and *phōnē* that constitute a political community, and Adorno demonstrated how this political activity of laughter unfolds within in a modern capitalist society. Both theorists are uniquely attentive to the dialectical complexity of gelopolitics, and they each address blind spots in the other's approach. Adorno reveals the necessity of abandoning subject-centrism and studying laughter on the level of the social order, while Hobbes highlights the importance of conceiving of laughter's operation in society in explicitly political terms – that is, with respect to how it modifies notions of who counts as a reasonable speaker and what counts as reasonable speech. Taken together, Hobbes and Adorno illustrate that a critical theory of laughter studies laughter as a privileged site of politics wherein the social order constructs, preserves and transforms itself. The next chapters deploy this framework to investigate laughter's place in two of contemporary society's most important and entrenched political structures: race and sex/gender.

Notes

1. As explained in the Introduction, I use the term 'social order' to refer to what Adorno typically identifies as 'society' (Adorno 1969), the 'social

whole' (Adorno 1973: 37; 1997: 68; 2005c: 153; Horkheimer and Adorno 2002: xviii) or the 'social totality' (Adorno 1973: 47; 1997: 55, 234; 2005c: 17).
2. Liberal and Nietzschean theorists of laughter might object to my claim that they neglect the question of social order. In particular, these theorists often emphasise how laughter arises in concrete social situations and frequently targets conventional modes of speech and action. However, as Sam Chambers notes, identifying a relation to broader social factors (that is, using 'the word *social* mainly as a descriptor to indicate relationality, to mark contextuality, and to suggest a basic sense of plurality') is not the same as analysing something in light of *an account* of social order (Chambers 2014: 56; see also Adorno 1969: 148). An account of social order explains how the various spheres of human and non-human life (e.g., the economy, culture and ocean currents) interact with one another to form a whole (Chambers 2014, 11). Adorno and other Frankfurt School theorists and students of Marx like Louis Althusser provide such accounts. Only when we attend to the question of social order in this way do we overcome subject-centric approaches and their faith in laughter's properly emancipatory character. Mary Beard (2014), Michael Billig (2005), Alfie Bown (2019), Nicholas Holm (2017) and Alenka Zupančič (2008) offer other studies of laughter that take the question of social order seriously.
3. Horkheimer and Adorno's critique of enlightenment is aimed at Western capitalism, but it also implicates the twentieth century's putatively socialist societies. The horrors of Stalinism demonstrate that a commitment to the enlightened human subject as the source of freedom makes the *logos* of central planning just as potentially violent as that of the capitalist marketplace. As Adorno remarks, 'authoritarian personalities are altogether misunderstood when they are construed from the vantage point of a particular political-economic ideology' (Adorno 2005f: 94).
4. The following sections make frequent reference to 'power' and 'social power'. Consistent with the above account of enlightenment, Adorno believes that subjects exercise 'power' when they make nature or other humans into objects for their use or control. In modern capitalism, such exercises of power congeal into various relations of domination (e.g., capital over labour; monopolies over consumers; humans over nature) whereby the social order as a whole reproduces itself. I call these relations of domination 'social power'.
5. As Gunzelin Noerr notes, and as any reader familiar with the different styles of Adorno and Horkheimer would surmise, 'The Culture Industry' was originally drafted by Adorno (Noerr 2002: 222–4).
6. Perhaps today we could add 'laughter yoga clubs' to the list of sources that produce laughter as a pseudo-pleasure. Laughter clubs first emerged

in India in the 1990s, and they are now popular all over the world. Laughter yoga aims to reap the physiological and psychological benefits of laughter (Cousins 1976; Mora-Ripoll 2010) by generating it in a controlled setting (Alvarez 2010). From an Adornian perspective, laughter yoga distracts and consoles subjects from the suffering inflicted by the capitalist social order while doing virtually nothing at all to call that order into question.

7. See note 18 in the Introduction.
8. For more on Adorno's notion of reconciliation, see Doxtader (2003), Feola (2014), Schoolman (2020), Stone (2014) and Zuidervaart (1991: 164–9).
9. This passage comes from the 'Odysseus or Myth and Enlightenment' essay in *DoE*, another piece that is believed to have been written primarily by Adorno (Noerr 2002: 221, 224). Adorno's likely authorship of these lines and 'The Culture Industry', along with the absence of any sustained treatment of laughter in Horkheimer's sole-authored works, suggests that the source of *DoE*'s fascination with laughter is Adorno, not Horkheimer.
10. Adorno in fact overstates the extent to which Benjamin ignores the political dangers associated with laughter manufactured by the culture industry. In a footnote to the 'Work of Art' essay quoted above, Benjamin writes that 'a comprehensive analysis of these films should not overlook their double meaning. It should start from the ambiguity of situations which have both a comic and a horrifying effect. [. . .] What is revealed in recent Disney films was latent in some of the earlier ones: the cozy acceptance of bestiality and violence as inevitable concomitants of existence' (Benjamin 2002: 130n30).
11. Chaplin's film *The Great Dictator* (which concludes with Chaplin pleading with his audience to resist authoritarianism) is the obvious exception here, and Adorno takes issue with this turn in Chaplin's style (Adorno 1974: 81).
12. Along these lines, Bradley Whitford, the actor who plays Dean Armitage, acknowledges how the laughter produced by his character challenged his own white liberalism: 'Dean was a delicious opportunity for self-parody. I mean, I say lines like, "I would have voted for Obama for a third term." In my defense, I say them to white people as often as I say them to African-Americans. I didn't realize how much of a laugh line that was' (Yuan and Harris 2018).

Chapter 3
Over a Barrel:
Ellison and the Democratic Politics of Black Laughter

> That must be the reason, thought Sandy, why poverty-stricken old Negroes like Uncle Dan Givens lived so long – because to them, no matter how hard life might be, it was not without laughter.
>
> Langston Hughes, *Not Without Laughter* (1995: 249)

> This race has the greatest of the gifts of God, laughter. It dances and sings; it is humble; it longs to learn; it loves men; it loves women. It is frankly, baldly, deliciously human in an artificial and hypocritical land. [. . .] The white world has its gibes and cruel caricatures; it has its loud guffaws; but to the black world alone belongs the delicious chuckle.
>
> W. E. B. Du Bois, *Dusk of Dawn* (1968: 148)

> Somebody on the set that was white laughed in such a way – I know the difference of people laughing with me and people laughing at me – and it was the first time I had ever gotten a laugh that I was uncomfortable with. Not just uncomfortable, but like, should I fire this person?
>
> Dave Chappelle, *The Oprah Winfrey Show* (2006)

On 22 August 2015, California police removed ten Black women from the Napa Valley Wine Train (Rocha 2015). The Wine Train company, which offers luxury dining along historic rail routes in California wine country, accused the women – members of a book club – of disturbing their fellow passengers by 'laughing too loudly'. This incident generated international media attention and inspired the Twitter hashtag #laughingwhileblack that highlighted other incidents of white hostility towards Black laughter.[1] Such a preoccupation with the styles, patterns and volumes of Black laughter is not new, as the laughter of Black Americans has long constituted a site of intense white anxiety and attempts at regulation (Chasar 2008; Parvulescu 2010: 59–77). Indeed, as scholar of American popular culture Mike Chasar notes, 'we must recognize the extent to which race relations in the United States have been conducted via African American laughter' (Chasar 2008: 60).

In light of this history, the current chapter seeks to determine how a critical theory of laughter can speak to and illuminate laughter's role in racial politics (particularly American racial politics). I will argue that the critical theory developed in the previous chapters identifies white supremacy as a social structure of power and hierarchy that is produced, sustained and transformed by experiences/events of laughter and that laughter in turn is a key site of political contestation around white supremacy. However, in keeping with the Adornian conception of critique this book has sought to emulate, I do not simply *apply* the critical theory sketched earlier to the case of race in the United States. It is impossible to understand the contemporary social order and laughter's political function within it without attending to the structuring role of race, and a critical theory of laughter remains essentially incomplete *until* it has grappled with race. The present chapter, along with the next one on sex and gender, likewise marks the *continued articulation* of the critical theory of laughter whose basic analytical tools were crafted in the preceding engagements with Hobbes and Adorno.

This chapter examines one specific account of racial gelopolitics – that provided by Ralph Ellison in his masterful, yet largely overlooked 1985 essay 'An Extravagance of Laughter'. Thinkers from many different backgrounds and traditions have studied the politics of laughter in the American racial order,[2] but in my view Ellison – the African American novelist and essayist most famous for his Cold War classic *Invisible Man* – offers an especially powerful and productive intervention. 'An Extravagance of Laughter' carefully weaves together American racial history, African American folklore and personal anecdotes to elucidate the political origins, effects and possibilities of Black laughter. Through a remarkable joke about 'laughing barrels' – barrels into which Black Southerners were supposedly required to laugh during Jim Crow – Ellison demonstrates that the distinctive sounds, styles and strategies of Black laughter are shaped by white supremacy and that white supremacy maintains itself in part by regulating this laughter. Despite the central role Black laughter plays in the construction of the racialised social order, Ellison insists that it can also function to radically undermine and democratise that order. Echoing the theme of laughter's dialectical complexity articulated in the previous chapters, Ellison identifies Black laughter as a privileged site of politics in which white supremacy is both produced and resisted. Ellison's reflections on Black laughter in turn illuminate his unique conception of democracy amid white supremacy.

Like Adorno, Ellison theorises laughter as an experience that emerges from and exerts political effects on the level of the social order as a whole. But whereas Adorno attends to gelopolitics within the mid-twentieth-century Western *capitalist* social order, Ellison explores gelopolitics within the nineteenth- and twentieth-century American *racialised* social order.[3] The latter is characterised by *white supremacy*, or what Ellison describes as the 'myth' that white Americans, 'by the mere fact of race, color, and tradition alone were superior to the Black masses below them' (Ellison 1986: 176–7). White supremacy is an ideology of racial difference that entails a programme of systematic political domination: 'Whiteness was a form of manifest destiny which designated Negroes as its territory and challenge. Whiteness struck at signs, at coloration, hair texture, and speech idiom [. . .]. It thrived on violence and sought endlessly for victims' (172). In concrete terms, white supremacy operates by way of a denial of political rights (e.g., slavery and segregation), rituals of physical violence (e.g., lynchings and beatings) and the production and circulation of cultural stereotypes (e.g., the lazy or hyper-sexualised Black male) (174–8). While the 'geopolitical center of white supremacy' was the antebellum and Jim Crow South, Ellison holds that the inextricability of white supremacy from the social, political and economic development of the United States as a whole means that it continues to haunt subjects and institutions far removed from those times and places (Ellison 1986: 173, 175–6; see also Coates 2015; Mills 1997; Olson 2004). Ellison argues that the structuring 'myth' of white supremacy cuts against the democratic principles of freedom and equality enshrined in the country's foundational political documents and espoused by leaders of nearly all eras and ideologies: 'democratic ideals [. . .] were rendered absurd by the prevailing mystique of race and color' (Ellison 1995: xiii; see also 1986: 172–6). This contradiction between white supremacy and democracy motivates Ellison's broader literary project (Ellison 1995, 2003c, 2003g, 2003l) and forms the backdrop to his examination of Black laughter.

This chapter proceeds in four sections. Section I reconstructs Ellison's claim that the distinctive sounds, styles and strategies of Black laughter are shaped by a history of racial oppression and that white supremacy sustains itself by treating these differences in laughter as evidence of natural racial difference. Ellison shows how the American racial order produces and is in turn reproduced by a white supremacist *regime of laughter*. Section II turns to Ellison's rendition of the laughing barrel joke to contend that the politics of Black laughter are intensely dialectical. Black laughter is neither the 'irrational', 'primitive' force imagined by white supremacy nor an inherently emancipatory, democratic force opposed to racial hierarchy. Black laughter democratises the American racial order only when its so-called 'irrationality' and 'primitiveness' exceed the terms set by white supremacy to reveal the very same characteristics in the laughter of whites. The racist conception of Black laughter thus contains the resources for its own democratic overcoming, and the democratising power of Black laughter depends paradoxically on its association with these attributes. Section III contends that these democratising effects materialise not when the laughter of Black subjects disobeys or targets the white supremacist regime of laughter but rather when it generates a dissensus within that regime. Section IV concludes by considering what Ellison's account of Black laughter reveals about his vision of democracy. Challenging scholarship that focuses on Ellison's exploration of the paradoxes of democratic government or ethics of democratic individuality, I contend that Ellison advances a unique theory of democracy as a mode of political life characterised by 'antagonistic cooperation' (Ellison 2003b: 850; 2003c: 602; 2003k: 496) among individuals, collectivities and the social order as a whole.

I. The White Supremacist Regime of Laughter

The year was 1936, and 22-year-old Ralph Ellison had just arrived in New York City after a long bus trip from the Tuskegee Institute in Alabama. Thanks to some lucky timing and a prior connection, Ellison quickly befriended the famous Black poet Langston Hughes (Jackson 2002: 161–4). Within weeks, Ellison was Hughes's guest at the Broadway adaptation of Erskine Caldwell's novel *Tobacco Road* (Ellison 1986: 146–7). *Tobacco Road* was a comedy about a poor Southern white family (the Lesters) that paradoxically embodied the era's worst anti-Black stereotypes about criminality and promiscuity (181, 186). Ellison recalls falling victim to a fit of laughter during a scene where the Lesters' daughter sexually seduces her older sister's husband at the encouragement of their father who

Ellison and the Democratic Politics of Black Laughter 99

wants to steal the poor man's bag of turnips: 'I was reduced to such helpless laughter that I distracted the entire balcony and embarrassed both myself and my host' (186). Ellison describes his laughter as 'an extravagance of laughter, [. . .] a virtual uncontrollable cloud-and-dam-burst of laughter, a self-immolation of laughter over which I had no control' (186). As his seemingly unquenchable laughter angered other theatregoers and even distracted the actors on stage, a mortified Ellison worried about the impression he was making on his famous host. Recalling an old joke from African American folklore, Ellison writes that he imagined Hughes thinking, 'Damn, if I'd known this would be his reaction, I would have picked a theater with laughing-barrels!' (186–7). According to the laughing barrel joke (I will explain why it is a joke in the next section), Southern towns placed barrels marked 'FOR COLORED' in their central squares into which Black citizens were required to stick their heads if they 'felt a laugh coming on' (187). The barrels were designed to 'protect' the town from the disruptive sounds of Black laughter. This memory of laughing barrels prompts Ellison to reflect more closely on laughter's role in the American racial order.

According to Ellison, the United States' history of white supremacy finds expression not only in the differences in social status, wealth and political representation afforded to Black and white subjects, but also in the ways they laugh. The sounds, styles and strategies of Black and white laughter reflect and in turn reproduce distinct historical-political experiences. Ellison recalls an incident from his youth that illustrates these dynamics. When visiting a New York City bookstore, Ellison struck up a conversation about T. S. Eliot with a Jewish college student. The student responded to one of Ellison's comments with a racial slur that he intended to be humorous (160). Ellison writes:

> I didn't like it, but there it was – I had been hit in mid-flight; and so, brought down to earth, I joined in his laughter. But while he laughed in bright major chords I responded darkly in minor-sevenths and flatted-fifths, and I doubted that he was attuned to the deeper source of our inharmonic harmony. (161)

Ellison and the student do not make the same sounds when they laugh, and their respective laughs 'do' different things. The 'bright major chords' of the Jewish student's laughter claim and assert the power of whiteness over Ellison. Meanwhile, Ellison's 'dark', 'minor' laughter reflects an uneasy acknowledgement of and attempt to safely navigate his subordinate position in the racial hierarchy. In this way Ellison participates in a long tradition of Black subjects employing laughter to dissemble in (and thus survive) encounters with whites (Chasar 2008: 71).[4] Ellison's remark about the 'deeper source of our inharmonic harmony' speaks to the contestable and ever-shifting nature of the power of whiteness claimed by his interlocutor: at a different time and place (maybe just the next store down), the Jewish student could be subject to the same kind of laughter he now directs at Ellison. A history marked by oppression and struggle manifests and reproduces itself in how Black and white subjects laugh.[5]

Ellison argues that a white supremacist social order interprets the distinctive sounds, styles and strategies of Black laughter not as products of a history of oppression but as evidence of the Black subject's intrinsic inferiority. While white laughter is considered to be 'rational' and always directed at what Ellison calls a 'discernible target' (e.g., a Black man like Ellison in the bookstore), Black laughter is understood to be fundamentally irrational and without object (Ellison 1986: 188, 193). Black laughter is not heard as fully human (i.e., it is mere *phōnē*), and its 'primitive', uncontrollable sound is understood as threatening civilised society. As Chasar remarks,

> scholars and laughter 'theorists' took great pains to show either that black laughter was different from white laughter by virtue of its childishness and innocence or that laughter itself had behavioral or physiological roots in Africa and was thus a primitive, immature, or uncivilized element in the Western world. (Chasar 2008: 63; see also Parvulescu 2010: 61–6)

Ellison writes that there exists an '*unnatural* and corrupting blackness of Negro laughter' that constitutes a 'confounding, persistent, and embarrassing mystery' to white society (Ellison 1986: 190–1). The distinctive sounds of Black laughter mark one *as Black* – that is, as an inferior, dangerous being. The construction of a racialised social order thus proceeds not only through practices of *seeing* black skin, but also through practices of *hearing* the sounds made by black bodies. For Ellison, laughter constitutes a privileged site of politics wherein 'race' as a naturalised relation of social inequality establishes and entrenches itself.

'Laughing barrels' are the mechanism by which the Jim Crow South defends itself from the mysteriously menacing force of Black laughter. Ellison traces the perverse logic by which the very conditions of slavery, segregation and discrimination that give rise to the distinctive sounds of Black laughter are offered as justifications for regulating it:

> The barrels were considered a civic necessity and had been improvised as a means of protecting the sensibilities of whites from a peculiar form of insanity suffered exclusively by Negroes, who in light of their social status and past condition of servitude were regarded as having absolutely *nothing* in their daily experience which could possibly inspire *rational* laughter. (188)

Crucially, laughing barrels do not *eliminate* Black laughter from public space. Passers-by (white and Black) know exactly why the person's head is buried in the barrel, and they can likely hear muffled laughter through the barrel. Laughing barrels instead *segregate* Black laughter; they localise and contain it such that it poses no significant threat to the *polis*. Laughing barrels teach spectators of all skin tones that the sounds of Black laughter belong to bodies not fit for full and equal participation in public life. Black subjects in particular learn the cruel truth that while failure to segregate their laughter will result in violent police action, obeying the laughing barrel policy affirms their inferior social and political status just as effectively. Laughing barrels ensure that the supposedly disruptive sounds of Black laughter function to secure white supremacy.

The laughing barrel is a common trope in African American folklore (Bercaw and Amon 2016; Dundes 1973: xv–xvi), and it serves as a metaphor for the various mechanisms employed by a white supremacist social order to segregate Black laughter.[6] Sterling Brown's 1932 poem 'Slim in Atlanta' provides an example of another laughing barrel:

> Down in Atlanta,
> De whitefolks got laws
> For to keep all de niggers
> From laughin' outdoors.
> Hope to Gawd I may die
> If I ain't speakin' truth
> Make de niggers do deir laughin
> In a telefoam booth. (Brown 2000: 81)

The police who removed the Black book club from the Napa Valley Wine Train also functioned as a laughing barrel. Another, more widespread twenty-first-century laughing barrel might be Tyler Perry films and television shows. Perry's comedies about middle-class Black life provide African Americans a space to laugh in virtual isolation from whites.[7] Although this laughing barrel lacks the compulsory quality of the Jim Crow barrels or Brown's 'telefoam booth', in light of Perry's trafficking in elements of minstrelsy (Kopano and Ball 2014) that bolster white conceptions of Black laughter as childlike, it functions to segregate Black laughter such that it does not disrupt white society. Ellison demonstrates that laughing barrels operate wherever and whenever Black laughter is segregated in a way that preserves a conception of citizenship premised on white supremacy.

The laughing barrels identified by Ellison constitute a key mechanism of the broader white supremacist *regime of laughter*. This concept of a 'regime of laughter' draws on Foucault's influential notion of 'regime of truth' that describes how the rules and procedures governing the production of knowledge rely on and sustain historically contingent subject positions and relations of power (Foucault 1984: 73–4). A regime of laughter thus refers to the set of rules and mechanisms governing laughter that emerges from and in turn reproduces a historically specific constellation of subject positions and power relations.[8] The regime of laughter operative in Ellison's essay (and which, as the Wine Train and other recent incidents suggest, remains operative today) presumes an essential difference in the origins, meanings and effects of the laughter of Black and white subjects and seeks to police Black laughter in order to secure white supremacy. Through instruments like laughing barrels, the white supremacist regime reproduces the 'Black' and 'white' subject positions that compose the racialised social order.

Theorising laughter in terms of *regimes* highlights how there exists no such thing as laughter 'pure and simple' that can form the object of a study of gelopolitics. Laughter is always produced, understood and regulated within the context of a determinate social order featuring concrete structures of power such as race. This is why I said earlier that my reading of Ellison represents the *continued articulation* of the critical theory developed in Chapters 1 and 2. The philosophical concepts (e.g., *logos* and *phōnē*) and arguments (e.g., the liberal claim that 'civilised' laughter speaks the truth) that we use to theorise laughter have deep historical roots in systems of racial subjugation like slavery, colonialism and imperialism. (Consider, for instance, the metaphorical proximity between the common expression 'a barrel of laughs' and white supremacist representations of Black subjects as simian-like; Boskin 1986: 38; Ellison 1995: 431–4; Gates 1988: 52.) A critical theory of laughter must acknowledge how laughter is always experienced and understood in the terms provided by histories of racial oppression and insist that any account of laughter's emancipatory power explain how it challenges their legacies.

II. Upside Down and Inside Out: The Dialectics of Black Laughter

While laughing barrels are designed to build and defend a white supremacist social order, Ellison explains that they do not always achieve their objective. The barrels can fail – and this is the source of the 'joke' – because they risk generating an even greater social and political disturbance than that posed by Black laughter itself. Ellison claims that the laughing barrels fail when white spectators find themselves laughing along with the Black subjects whose heads are buried in the barrels. He describes how

> the uproar from laughing-barrels could become so loud and raucous that it not only disturbed the serenity of the entire square, but shook up the whites' fierce faith in the stability of their most cherished traditions. For on such occasions the uproar from the laughing-barrels could become so contagious and irresistible that any whites who were so unfortunate as to be caught near the explosions of laughter would find themselves compelled to join in [. . .]. It was an appalling state of affairs, for despite their sternest resistance, even such distinguished whites literally cracked up and roared! (Ellison 1986: 191)

The scene of laughter that results from Black subjects laughing in the barrels generates a scandal within the Southern town. Black laughter – maligned as an irrational force that threatens civilised society – gains control over the public behaviour of the white citizenry. And it does so precisely by way of the mechanism designed to regulate it! Ellison continues:

> The whites assumed that in some mysterious fashion the Negro involved was not only laughing at *himself* laughing, but was also laughing at *them* laughing at his laughing against their own most determined wills. And if such was the truth, it suggested that somehow a Negro (and this meant *any* Negro) could become with a single hoot-and-cackle both the source and master of an outrageous and untenable situation. (191)

Obeying the laughing barrel policy unexpectedly allows even the lowliest Black Southerner to take charge of public (i.e., white) space. Rather than securing white supremacy against Black laughter, the laughing barrels threaten to undermine the racial hierarchy.[9]

Why, exactly, does this scene of laughter precipitate such a grave political crisis? As the minstrel tradition illustrates (and Ellison's bookstore encounter confirms), Black bodies are common objects of white laughter (Chasar 2008: 62; Fauset 1994), and the white laughter at the body in the barrel likely begins as a chuckle of superiority. However, it remains unclear why white laughter proliferates so wildly and persists for such an extended period. Ellison writes:

> For since it was an undisputed fact that whites and blacks were of different species, it followed that they could by no means be expected to laugh at the same things. Therefore, when whites found themselves joining in with the coarse merriment issuing from the laughing-barrels, they suffered the double embarrassment of laughing against their own God-given nature while being unsure of exactly why, or at what, specifically, they were laughing. Which meant that somehow the Negro in the barrel had them *over* a barrel. (Ellison 1986: 192)

Recall that whereas the laughter of Black subjects is considered to be irrational, uncontrollable and without purpose, white laughter is thought to always have a rational motivation and discernible target (193). By putting the white spectators 'over a barrel' – that is, by prompting them to laugh uncontrollably for no apparent reason – the laughing barrel scene *dissolves the distinction between Black and white laughter*. All laughter is now (so-called) 'Black': wild, mysterious and disruptive. The laughing barrels undermine the white supremacist regime's presumption of an essential difference between the laughter of Black and white subjects. Ellison concludes:

> A Negro laughing in a laughing-barrel simply turned the world upside down and inside out. And in doing so, he *in*-verted (and thus *sub*-verted) tradition and thus the preordained and cherished scheme of Southern racial relationships was blasted asunder. Therefore, it was feared that if such unhappy instances of interracial laughter occurred with any frequency, it would create a crisis in which social order would be fatally undermined by something as un-political as a bunch of Negroes with their laughing heads stuck into the interiors of a batch of old whitewashed whiskey barrels. (192)

Rather than functioning as a site wherein white supremacy reproduces and entrenches itself, laughter becomes an experience/event wherein Black and white subjects share public space together on an equal footing. Through their laughter, Black subjects dismantle the racial hierarchy and make themselves count as members of the *polis*; their laughter precipitates a *democratisation* of the Southern town. In Jacques Rancière's terms, the laughing barrel scene enacts a dissensus, or a break in the aesthetic organisation of society wherein the 'part of those who have no part' are now seen and heard as intelligible beings (Rancière 1999: 9; Giamario 2020).[10] This is the source of the crisis generated by the laughing barrels.

The genius of the laughing barrel joke is how it provisionally accepts the white supremacist conception of Black laughter as 'irrational', 'primitive' and 'wild' in order to reveal the very same qualities in the laughter of whites. This revelation occurs at the precise moment when white supremacy aims to spotlight the supposedly essential difference between Black and white laughter (i.e., when the Black subject has their head buried in the barrel). By deconstructing the distinction between Black and white laughter at the foundation of the white supremacist regime, the laughing barrel scene reveals Ellison's intensely dialectical conception of Black gelopolitics. For Ellison, the sounds of Black laughter are neither simply the echoes of an oppressive history nor democratising forces opposed to white supremacy. Both political valences depend on – even as they exceed and undermine – one another. Black laughter's status as a product of racial oppression and sign of racial inferiority hinges on attributes like 'irrationality', 'primitiveness' and 'wildness' that, when taken to their extremes, make possible a democratic transformation of the white supremacist social order. Conversely, the capacity of Black laughter to undermine the racial order depends not on any revolutionary trait intrinsic to such laughter (Chasar 2008; Fauset 1994), but on how white supremacy defines it in racist terms as 'irrational', 'primitive', etc. Ellison shows that the politics of Black laughter are constitutively complex and double-sided, and it is this unstable, dialectical[11] quality that accounts for its enduring saliency in political struggles over white supremacy today.

Similar dynamics characterise Ellison's own outbreak of laughter during *Tobacco Road*. Although there is no formal segregation of laughter in the Broadway theatre (i.e., there are no laughing barrels[12]), the space remains governed by the white supremacist regime. Ellison describes how the theatre's unwritten rules that (a) encourage polite laughter that emanates from the audience as a whole and lasts for a determinate period and (b) prohibit unruly laughter that originates from a single audience member and persists indefinitely are racially coded:

> Things were getting so out of control that Northern white folk in balcony and loge were now catching fire and beginning to howl and cheer the disgraceful loss of self-control being exhibited by a young Negro [. . .]; a young man who was so gross as to demonstrate his social unacceptability by violating a whole *encyclopedia* of codes that regulated proper conduct no less in the theater than in society at large. [. . .] [P]erhaps, in shock and dismay, they too were thinking of laughing-barrels. (Ellison 1986: 187–8)

Ellison's laughter marks him as a Black man in the predominantly white space of the theatre. While the absence of laughing barrels puts the onus on Black subjects to police their own laughter, such self-regulation fails Ellison in this situation:

> It was as though I had plunged into a nightmare in which my personality was split in twain, with the lucid side looking on in wonder while the manic side convulsed my body as thought a drunken accordionist were using it [. . .]. And while I wheezed and choked with laughter, my disgusted lucid self dramatized its cool detachment. (187)

The laughter suffered by Ellison is so remarkable and 'extravagant' because it eludes control by his 'lucid' half that normally enforces obedience to the rules of the white supremacist regime.

Just as the laughter of the Black subject in the barrel democratises the Southern town, Ellison's extravagance of laughter democratises the Broadway theatre. Ellison recounts how his fit of laughter divides the overwhelmingly white audience. Some angrily insist on upholding the rules of decorum, while others allow themselves to laugh along with Ellison:

> But now as I continued to roar at the weird play-without-a-play in which part of me was involved, my sober self marked the fact that the entire audience was being torn in twain. Most of the audience was white, but now many who occupied seats down in the orchestra were beginning to protest the unscheduled disruption taking place above them. Leaping to their feet, they were shaking their fists at those in the balcony, and they in turn were shouting their disdain for those so lacking in an appreciation for the impromptu broadening of the expected comedy. (189)

When white audience members join Ellison in laughing, the distinction between permissible (i.e., white) and impermissible (i.e., Black) laughter breaks down. Black and white audience members now share a prohibited and disorienting laughter together in common. No longer an occasion for reinscribing racial hierarchy, laughter instead becomes an experience/event that enacts equality in the space of the theatre. Ellison remarks on the effects of this scene of laughter:

> Caldwell told me something important about who I was. And by easing the conflict that I was having with my Southern experience (yes, and with my South-Southwestern identity), he helped initiate me into becoming, if not a 'New Yorker,' at least a more tolerant American. (197)

As was the case in the Southern town, the democratising power of Ellison's laughter depends paradoxically on its status as a product of racial oppression and signifier of racial inferiority. It is only by means of the social order's racist conception of Black laughter that the latter succeeds in revealing and affirming the equality of Black subjects. Grateful to Caldwell for creating an occasion where his laughter could yield 'an interracial situation without the threat of physical violence', Ellison concludes by praising the novelist as a 'mighty destroyer of laughing-barrels' (197).

III. How to Destroy Laughing Barrels

Ellison's celebration of Caldwell as a 'mighty destroyer of laughing-barrels' makes clear his commitment to abolishing the white supremacist regime of laughter. However, a crucial passage in 'An Extravagance of Laughter' complicates this straightforward reading of Ellison's attitude towards the regulation of Black laughter. Speculating on the best course of action for one who is about to laugh, Ellison writes: 'Negroes who were wise – or at least fast on their feet – took off *posthaste* for a laughing-barrel. (Just as I, in my present predicament, would gladly have done.)' (188–9). This view of laughing barrels as a resource that Black subjects *actively seek out* accords with other historical accounts of laughing barrels. Folklorist Alan Dundes writes that

> in slavery times and afterward [. . .] if a Negro wished to laugh out loud at his master, he might do so only at considerable risk. So he suppressed the desire to laugh and went instead to the 'laughing barrel', where he could laugh to his heart's content without fear of being heard. (Dundes 1973: xv)

Historians have identified various analogues of laughing barrels in African American folklore such as wash kettles, 'prayer bells' and 'shouting barrels' that were used by Black worshippers as safe outlets to pray and sing in the antebellum and Jim Crow South (Bercaw and Amon 2016; Dundes 1973: xv–xvi). While laughing barrels exist only in a white supremacist society, Ellison suggests that we look beyond their status as instruments of racial subordination and attend to their capacity to protect and even empower Black subjects.

If the relationship between Black subjects and the mechanisms of white supremacy is not simply or strictly antagonistic, then under what conditions does Black laughter democratise the racial order? Two episodes from Ellison's essay suggest a way to answer this question. The first concerns Ellison's experience as a newcomer to the New York City public bus system in the 1930s. Ellison writes that after assuring himself that – unlike in the South – he could sit wherever he likes on the bus, he finds himself considering an unexpected and uncomfortable question:

> I asked myself whether a seat at the back of the bus wasn't actually more desirable than one at the front. For not only did it provide more leg room, it offered a more inclusive perspective on both the interior and exterior scenes. I found the answer obvious and quite amusing [. . .]. Now that I was no longer forced by law and compelled by custom to ride at the back [. . .], what was more desirable – the possibility of exercising what was routinely accepted in the North as an abstract, highly symbolic (even trivial) form of democratic freedom, or the creature comfort which was to be had by occupying a spot from which more of the passing scene could be observed? (Ellison 1986: 153)

For Ellison, Northern buses raise a 'troublesome question' and a 'certain unease' about the meaning of freedom in a country with a deep and enduring history of racial subjugation (156). Does freedom for Black Americans consist in the enjoyment of previously denied rights? Or does freedom instead consist in the pursuit of one's individual preferences, even when these preferences align – at least superficially – with historical practices of oppression?

Digging even deeper, Ellison wonders whether he and others had ignored possibilities for freedom in the segregated South. He describes how his experiences on the Northern buses

> were raising the even more troublesome question of to what extent had I failed to grasp a certain degree of freedom that had always existed in

my group's state of unfreedom? Of what had I neglected to avail myself through fear or lack of interest while sitting silently behind jim-crow signs? [. . .] to what extent had I overlooked similar opportunities for self-discovery while accepting a definition of possibility laid down by those who would deny me freedom? (156)

While in no way criticising the civil rights movement (Ellison 2003d: 433; Warren 1965), Ellison worries that an exclusive focus on securing and enjoying the rights refused to Black Americans confirms the total power of white supremacy and denies them the capacity for acting freely on their own terms. Freedom for Ellison involves a 'play upon life's possibilities' (Ellison 1986: 180) – that is, *critical engagement with* (rather than mere *removal of*) mechanisms of racial oppression. As Lucas Morel notes, Ellison found that 'there was no need to get all of his instruction in liberty from a racist society' (Morel 2004: 58). Ellison believes that actions like voluntarily sitting at the back of the Northern bus affirm that his capacity to determine how to be free is equal to that exercised by whites.[13]

The second episode that explains Ellison's apparent ambivalence towards laughing barrels concerns his memories of Alabama police harassing Tuskegee students on the highway to the university. Ellison describes how students coped with this abuse by laughing together:

Back on campus we were compelled to buffer the pain and negate the humiliation by making grotesque comedy out of the extremes to which whites would go to keep us in what they considered to be our 'place.' Once safe at Tuskegee, we'd become fairly hysterical as we recounted our adventures and laughed as much at ourselves as at the cops. We mocked their modes of speech and styles of intimidation, and teased one another as we parodied our various modes of feigning fear when telling them who we were and where we were headed. It was a wild, he-man schoolboy silliness but the only way we knew for dealing with the inescapable conjunction of laughter and pain. (Ellison 1986: 171–2)

Although Ellison appreciates the therapeutic benefits of this shared laughter, he believes it is an inadequate response to the police violence. He continues:

Thus was violence transcended with cruel but homeopathic laughter, and racial cruelty transformed by a traditional form of folk art. It did nothing to change the Phenix City police, and probably wouldn't have even if they heard the recitation. [. . .] My problem was that I couldn't completely dismiss such experiences with laughter. (171–2)

Unlike the white supremacy-subverting extravagances of laughter emanating from the laughing barrels or the Broadway theatre, the Tuskegee students' 'cruel' laughter merely salves their pain by assuring them of their moral superiority to the racist police. For Ellison, Black laughter that targets mechanisms of white supremacy may be valuable as a survival strategy, but it falls short as a democratic strategy due to its failure to challenge the terms of the racial hierarchy.

These two episodes shed light on the conditions under which Ellison believes Black laughter democratises the white supremacist social order. Just as Ellison eschews a preoccupation with the rights denied to Black subjects and rejects a strategy of laughing at racist whites, he does not believe that Black laughter undermines the white supremacist regime of laughter when it merely violates or targets that regime. Indeed, the Black Southerner in the laughing barrel joke actually *obeys* the laughing barrel policy (even as his laughter functions to undermine that policy). Meanwhile, Ellison's 'lucid side' in the Broadway theatre does not encourage or restrain his laughing 'manic side'; it simply observes the scandalous laughter in 'cool detachment' (187).

An extravagance of laughter likewise does not constitute a deliberate political strategy on the part of Black subjects. Ellison writes that he '*was reduced to* such helpless laughter' by the play and that the Black Southerner was '*taken over* by a form of schizophrenia' (186, 190; italics added). An extravagance of laughter is as much an *event* that happens *to* a subject as it is an *experience* that originates *in* a subject. This laughter takes neither the active nor passive voice, but rather what Parvulescu calls the middle voice, wherein 'the subject [. . .] is not the agent of an action exterior to it, but has an "interest" in the action' (Parvulescu 2010: 14–15). While the extravagance of laughter may begin in Ellison, and he may take an interest in and subtly direct its flow, he is not its sole locus or agent. Emerging from deep within a context where Black laughter is heavily policed, an extravagance of laughter is a collective experience/event that overtakes Black and white subjects alike and in doing so challenges their constitution as 'Black' and 'white'. In contrast to the morally superior laugh Ellison and his Tuskegee classmates deliberately enjoyed at the expense of the police, the laughter that erupts in the Broadway theatre reveals to Ellison that white subjects are not – in their essence at least – the monsters that white supremacy has made them to be. He writes:

> On one side of my mind I had thought of my life as being of a whole, segregated but in many ways superior to that of the Lesters. On the

other side, I thought of the Lester type as being, in the Negro folk phrase, 'a heap of whiteness gone to waste' and therefore a gross caricature of anything that was viable in the idea of white superiority. But now Caldwell had highlighted the warp and woof of my own ragtag American pattern. [. . .] I laughed and I trembled, and gained thereby a certain wisdom. (Ellison 1986: 197)

The scene precipitated by Ellison's laughter affirms equality not just to the white audience, but to Ellison as well. Black laughter exerts democratising effects when its subversion of the white supremacist regime of laughter puts the entire racial order – that is, both white *and* Black subjects (or more precisely, the very concept of 'race' itself) – 'over a barrel'.

IV. Democracy as Antagonistic Cooperation

What do Ellison's reflections on Black laughter reveal about his broader understanding of democracy within a racialised social order? Democracy is a central theme in Ellison's oeuvre (Ellison 1995: vii–xxiii; 2003c; 2003g; 2003k), and political theorists in recent years have found his most famous text, *Invisible Man*, to be a valuable resource for grasping the relationship between democratic politics and white supremacy. For example, Danielle Allen contends that Ellison dramatises the constitutive tensions of democracy as a form of political life. According to Allen, Ellison explores how democratic self-government paradoxically requires citizens to make painful (and in the case of white supremacy, non-reciprocal) sacrifices for one another. 'The politics in [*Invisible Man*]', she writes, 'lies in the novel's account of what it is like, psychologically speaking, to be an individual in a democratic world of strangers, where large scale events are supposed to arise somehow out of one's own consent and yet never really do' (Allen 2004a: 38; see also 2004b: 25–49). Meanwhile, Jack Turner and Lucas Morel argue that Ellison sketches an ethics of democratic individualism. Situating Ellison within the Emersonian tradition that articulates a liberal democratic sensibility capable of challenging unjust social and political conditions, Turner claims that Ellison brings a much-needed attention to white supremacy: 'In *Invisible Man*, Ellison gives us a picture of democratic individuality in black, and in his essays, displays a democratic individualist sensibility that confronts rather than evades race' (Turner 2008: 657). Finally, Morel describes the Ellisonian democratic individual as one who resists white supremacy by pursuing opportunities for creative self-expression and influence within the racial order. 'For [Ellison]', Morel writes, 'the politics of the American regime, despite the segregation he experienced, left sufficient room for aspiring Negro individuals to make their mark. [...] Ellison wrote as an individual striving to contribute to a community of diverse individuals' (Morel 2004: 60–2).[13]

Ellison's exploration of Black laughter suggests an alternative interpretation of his democratic theory. I argue that Ellison conceives of democracy as a distinct mode of political life. By 'mode of political life', I am describing the pattern or structure of everyday political interactions among subjects and between subjects and the broader social order. A 'mode' of political life differs from what I identified above in Allen as a 'form' of political life in that the latter refers to a given structure (e.g., a formally democratic system of government) and how it conditions and constrains everyday political interactions, while the former denotes the everyday interactions themselves and how they give rise to and sustain formal governing structures. Ellison's account of Black laughter reveals that in a democracy the ordinary political interactions among subjects and between subjects and the social order assume a pattern he calls 'antagonistic cooperation' (Ellison 2003b: 850; 2003c: 602; 2003k: 496). Ellison unpacks the notion of antagonistic cooperation most fully in his essays on jazz, and it is to this work that I now turn.

Antagonistic Cooperation in Jazz

Before finding success as a writer, Ellison studied classical music and sought to become a symphony composer (Ellison 2003e, 2003h; Jackson 2002; Rampersad 2007). Ellison's interest in classical music was heavily influenced by his familiarity with the early twentieth-century American jazz scene, and he wrote extensively on the relationship between the two genres (Ellison 2002). Ellison argues that jazz is a product of 'antagonistic cooperation' in at least two ways. First, Black jazz musicians work with and against the classical music tradition which has historically excluded their contributions. Ellison describes how jazz musicians bring their distinctive historical experiences to bear on classical instruments, techniques and styles:

> There is a conflict between what the Negro American musician feels in the community around him and the given (or classical) techniques of his instrument. He feels a tension between his desire to master the classical

style of playing and his compulsion to express those sounds which form a musical definition of Negro American experience. [. . .] This desire to master the classical technique was linked with the struggle for recognition in the larger society [. . .]. It was the tension between these two bodies of technique which led to many of the technical discoveries of jazz. (Ellison 2003i: 271; see also 2003h: 68–71)

According to Ellison, jazz musicians affirm their status as artistic equals to (white) classical musicians without sacrificing what is uniquely 'Black' about their productions. He writes:

[T]he end of all this discipline and technical mastery was the desire to express an affirmative way of life through its musical tradition, and [. . .] this tradition insisted that each artist achieve his creativity within its frame. He must learn the best of the past, and add to it his personal vision. (Ellison 2003e: 229)

For Ellison, the political significance of jazz does not consist in any overt political message it conveys, but in how its antagonistic cooperation with classical music reveals and affirms the capacity of Black artists to make music on their own terms as equals.[15]

Jazz also features a second, internal form of antagonistic cooperation. Ellison describes a jazz jam session as a 'contest' (Ellison 2003i: 267) or 'ordeal' (Ellison 2003j: 247) wherein each musician seeks to prove their 'power to express an individuality in tone' (246). The quality of the group performance depends on how successfully each individual musician articulates their own distinctive talents, feelings or voice against those of the others. Ellison writes:

True jazz is an art of individual assertion within and against the group. Each true jazz moment [. . .] springs from a contest in which each artist challenges all the rest; each solo flight, or improvisation, represents [. . .] a definition of his identity as individual, as member of the collectivity and as a link in the chain of tradition. Thus, because jazz finds its very life in an endless improvisation upon traditional materials, the jazzman must lose his identity even as he finds it. (Ellison 2003i: 267; see also 2003c: 602–3)

The individual jazz musician proves themselves a worthy member of the group by developing and mastering a unique musical identity, yet the latter emerges only fleetingly in response to the play of others and is thus never truly one's 'own'. Ellison admires jazz for how it establishes and sustains a dialectical tension between individual and group that simultaneously advances and undermines the interests of both. 'The delicate balance struck between strong individual personality and the group during those early jam sessions was a marvel of social organization', he writes (Ellison 2003e: 229). Ellison conceives of jazz as a dynamic artistic process wherein Black musicians antagonistically cooperate with the classical music tradition by antagonistically cooperating with one another. Jazz involves the establishment of an intensely dialectical relationship between individual, group and tradition.[16]

Grasping the richness of Ellison's notion of antagonistic cooperation and its significance for his conception of democracy requires analysing the relationship between jazz and classical music more closely. (We could perform a similar analysis on the internal dynamics of the jazz jam session, but I will limit my focus here.) This relationship is one of antagonistic cooperation in at least eight distinct senses. First, jazz *cooperates* with the classical tradition (by employing its instruments, techniques and styles) in such a way that *antagonises* it (i.e., that resists its musical hegemony). Second, jazz *cooperates* with the classical tradition (by employing its instruments, techniques and styles) in order to reveal the classical tradition's *antagonism* with itself (i.e., to reveal that classical music does not, as it claims, exhaust itself in its own instruments, techniques and styles). Third, jazz *cooperates* with the classical tradition (i.e., it reveals new musical possibilities allowed by classical instruments, techniques and styles) by *antagonising* it (i.e., by resisting that tradition's musical hegemony). Fourth, jazz *cooperates* with the classical tradition (i.e., it reveals new musical possibilities allowed by classical instruments, techniques and styles) by revealing that tradition's *antagonism* with itself (i.e., by showing that classical music does not exhaust itself in its own instruments, techniques and styles). Each of these modes of cooperation can in turn be inverted into practices of antagonism. For instance, jazz *antagonises* the classical tradition (i.e., it resists its musical hegemony) by *cooperating* with it (i.e., by employing classical instruments, techniques and styles). And so on.

Despite the dizzyingly contradictory directions in which these permutations run, they are all implied by Ellison's account. This is not a flaw in his reasoning, but rather its decisive feature. Ellison imagines antagonism and cooperation as dialectically intertwined to such an extreme extent that it is impossible to tell for certain where one begins and the other ends. Antagonism is never *simply* antagonistic, and cooperation is never *simply* cooperative; there is an irreducible duplicity to each. The opposite of 'antagonistic cooperation' is not some third term but rather 'antagonism' and 'cooperation' considered separately. An antagonism not keyed towards cooperation forsakes critical engagement with the whole it resists and risks slipping into idle protest, while cooperation lacking an antagonistic element forsakes critical energy and risks devolving into quietism. According to Ellison, the political significance of jazz consists in how it establishes a dynamic, dialectically complex, even Janus-faced relationship of antagonistic cooperation between Black artists and the classical music tradition.[17]

Black Laughter, Antagonistic Cooperation and Democracy

Ellison's account of jazz provides the key for unlocking the distinctive conception of democracy that emerges in 'An Extravagance of Laughter'. When Ellison suggests that the democratising power of Black laughter consists in how it subverts the white supremacist regime of laughter, he describes a process of antagonistic cooperation that resembles the one at work in jazz. Consider once again the case of the laughing barrels in the fictional Southern town. First, Black laughter *cooperates* with the white supremacist social order (i.e., it obeys the laughing barrel policy) in such a way that *antagonises* that order (i.e., in a way that resists the subordination of Black subjects). Second, Black laughter *cooperates* with the white supremacist social order (i.e., it obeys the laughing barrel policy) in such a way that reveals that order's *antagonism* with itself (i.e., it reveals the social order's failure to live up to its stated democratic ideals). Third, Black laughter *cooperates* with the white supremacist social order (i.e., it helps the latter achieve its stated democratic ideals) by *antagonising* it (i.e., by resisting the subordination of Black subjects). Fourth, Black laughter *cooperates* with the white supremacist social order (i.e., it helps the latter achieve its stated democratic ideals) by revealing that order's *antagonism* with itself (i.e., its failure to live up to these ideals). Once again, each of these modes of cooperation can be inverted into practices of antagonism. For instance, Black laughter *antagonises* the white supremacist social order (i.e., it resists the subordination of Black subjects) by *cooperating* with that order (i.e., by obeying the laughing barrel policy). And so on.[18]

As if this relationship between the laughing Black subject and the white supremacist social order were not complex enough, it is actually only part of the story. Ellison describes the Southern town as featuring *multiple* laughing barrels (Ellison 1986: 190–1). The laughter of a single Black subject likewise competes to be heard with – even as it resonates with and intensifies – the laughter emanating from the other barrels. So in addition to antagonistically cooperating with the racialised social order, one's laughter antagonistically cooperates with that of other Black subjects, and this collective laughter in turn antagonistically cooperates with the racialised social order. Ellison shows that the democratising power of Black laughter consists in how it enters into processes of antagonistic cooperation – or cooperative antagonism – with the laughter of other Black subjects and the white supremacist social order more generally.

There is, however, one important way in which the concept of antagonistic cooperation that emerges in 'An Extravagance of Laughter' departs from that articulated in Ellison's jazz essays. Whereas the jazz musician requires special artistic training or talent to antagonistically cooperate with other musicians and the classical tradition, there exist no such qualifications when it comes to laughter (besides, of course, the Black subject's inevitable social training in the rules and regulations governing their laughter). According to Ellison, the laughing barrel joke 'suggested that somehow a Negro (and this meant *any* Negro) could become with a single hoot-and-cackle both the source and master of an outrageous and untenable situation' (191). The laughter emanating from a laughing barrel discloses the equality of even the lowliest Black subject with their white counterparts. As noted in the Introduction, this ordinary, everyday quality of laughter is the source of its distinctive political efficacy in both entrenching and resisting social structures of power and hierarchy.

Ellison's account of Black laughter exhibits his conception of democracy as a mode of political life wherein subjects antagonistically cooperate with one another and the social order as a whole. In the context of white supremacy (the system of political domination from which Ellison writes and that continues to structure American society today), democracy involves antagonistic cooperation by Black subjects and their allies with the various subjects, mechanisms and institutions of the racial order. Neither blind protest of nor quiet acquiescence to racial oppression, antagonistic cooperation is critical – and in a certain sense, duplicitous – work against *and* on behalf of a social whole that oppresses Black Americans. For Ellison, this whole is worth saving because there is literally no other option. Resisting the arguments of Black nationalists who (like racist whites, he believes) conceive of American democracy as irreparably tied to racial oppression (Ellison 2003m: 583), Ellison insists that the futures of Black Americans, white Americans and American democracy in general are bound up with one another. 'American life is of a whole', Ellison writes (Ellison 1986: 185), and 'the nation could not survive being deprived of [Black Americans'] presence because, by the irony implicit in the dynamics of American democracy, they symbolise its most stringent testing and the possibility of its greatest human freedom' (Ellison 2003m: 588). Through antagonistic cooperation, Black subjects affirm their capacity to contribute to public life on their own terms as equals, and only through such actions does the social order overcome its white supremacist roots and realise its stated democratic ideals. Ellison understands democracy, particularly in the context of persistent racial hierarchy, as an intensely dialectical mode of political life that pursues cooperation through antagonism and antagonism through cooperation.

This account builds on but ultimately departs from the interpretations of Ellison's democratic theory offered by Allen, Turner and Morel. (In this sense, it models the process of antagonistic cooperation described by Ellison.) For her part, Allen rightly highlights the importance of contradiction and paradox to Ellison's conception of democracy. But whereas Allen understands the form of democracy as the source of contradictions that citizens must navigate and negotiate, Ellison conceives of democracy *itself* as a contradictory mode of life by which subjects work with and against one another and the larger social order. Meanwhile, Turner's identification of a liberal individualist sensibility in Ellison helpfully demonstrates how democracy involves critical confrontations with white supremacy. But liberalism's core belief in the self-identical individual as the basic unit of social and political life remains at odds with Ellison's understanding of the individual as an ever-evolving product of processes of antagonistic cooperation with other subjects and society as a whole. Ellisonian democracy, in other words, is not a form of liberalism (cf. Foley 2010; Rampersad 2007). Finally, while Morel correctly emphasises Ellison's refusal to allow white supremacy to dictate an individual's experience of freedom, he neglects Ellison's attention to the dialectical interplay between individuals, collectivities and society. This point is crucial because Ellison has often been accused of fetishising individual self-expression at the expense of racial solidarity or a realistic account of white supremacy (Ellison 2003h: 76–80; Warren 1965: 346; Watts 1994). 'An Extravagance of Laughter' shows that Ellison does not theorise democracy simply as a form of government or individual ethic but as a mode of political life involving antagonistic cooperation among individuals, collectivities and the broader social order. His writings reflect an effort to articulate a genuinely dialectical – and thus genuinely radical – account of democratic politics: one wherein individuals and collectivities work with and against one another and the larger social order to overcome white supremacy. This is the political vision that emerges in Ellison's account of Black laughter, and it stands as his most important contribution to democratic theory.

V. Putting White Supremacy 'Over a Barrel'

The preceding chapters on Hobbes and Adorno developed a critical theory that understands laughter as a privileged site of politics wherein the social order constructs, preserves and transforms itself. Ellison demonstrates the centrality of race to this critical theory of laughter. His reflections on the so-called '*rational* laughter' of whites (Ellison 1986: 188) and '*unnatural* and corrupting blackness of Negro laughter' (191) illustrate how the *logos/phōnē* distinction that is continually thematised and reworked by laughter is always already highly racialised. The ways we determine what counts as laughable, the social rules governing laughter and the benefits and harms associated with laughter obey and reinscribe the racial logics stemming from the social order's enduring histories of slavery, colonialism and imperialism. Ellison's essay challenges a critical theory of laughter to recognise, attend to and directly confront this structuring role of race in contemporary gelopolitics.

Conversely, Ellison shows how a critical theory of laughter can illuminate laughter's political dangers and possibilities amid white supremacy. According to Ellison, the white supremacist regime of laughter regulates, and in some cases segregates, Black laughter in order to produce and reproduce ideas of essential racial difference. However, as the laughing barrel joke illustrates, the so-called 'primitive' and 'irrational' sounds of Black laughter can exceed the terms of this regime and democratise the racial order by exposing the very same qualities in the laughter of whites. Through their laughter, Black subjects can make themselves count as members of the *polis*.

Ellison reveals that democracy amid white supremacy does not consist merely in protesting mechanisms of racial oppression or seeking equal rights, nor does it entail rejecting the social order as irreparably racist. Democracy instead involves Black subjects and their allies antagonistically cooperating with one another and the social order as a whole in order to affirm their status as equals. In this way, everyday Black Americans – like the women on the Napa Valley Wine Train – who are forced to stifle or segregate their laughter can nevertheless succeed in putting white supremacy 'over a barrel'. That, at least, is Ellison's democratic hope.

Notes

1. For instance, in 2018 police beat a Black man from Ohio for allegedly laughing at them (the man was ultimately awarded an $80,000 settlement) (Perez 2018), and in 2019 four 12-year-old Black girls from New York were strip searched for drugs after school officials found them to be 'hyper and giddy' during lunch (AP 2019).
2. Luvell Anderson (2015, 2020), Glenda Carpio (2008), Vine Deloria, Jr (1988, 146–67), Caroline Hong (2019) and Kenneth Lincoln (1993) offer some particularly insightful accounts of American racial gelopolitics.
3. To be sure, race plays an important role in Adorno's work (see, for example, *Dialectic of Enlightenment*'s essay on anti-Semitism; Horkheimer and Adorno 2002: 137–72), just as capitalism is a key theme for Ellison (see, for example, his extensive involvement in and subsequent critique of Communist Party politics; Ellison 1995; Foley 2010; Jackson 2002; Rampersad 2007). However, capitalism constitutes the theoretical centre of gravity of Adorno's project, while race occupies a similar position in Ellison's oeuvre.
4. Ellison's laughter thus recalls the advice offered by the Invisible Man's grandfather: 'I want you to overcome 'em with yeses, undermine 'em with grins, agree 'em to death and destruction, let 'em swoller you till they vomit or bust wide open' (Ellison 1995: 16).
5. This connection between the sounds, styles and strategies of Black laughter and a history of oppression recalls W. E. B. Du Bois's description of slave sorrow songs as 'the music of an unhappy people, of the children of disappointment; they tell of death and suffering and unvoiced longing toward a truer world, of misty wanderings and hidden ways' (Du Bois 2003: 255). Ellison's laughing barrel joke (examined in the next section) shows how Black laughter, like the sorrow songs, also resists being reduced to its origins in oppression by 'longing toward a truer world'.
6. Despite the enduring role of the laughing barrel tale in African American thought and folklore (Dundes 1973: xv–xvi), the historical record remains

unclear about whether laughing barrels *actually* existed in the antebellum and Jim Crow South. Because such barrels likely would have been used for multiple purposes (Ellison suggests that most were 'old whitewashed whiskey barrels'; Ellison 1986: 192), historians have been unable to identify specific barrels employed to segregate the sounds of Black laughter (Bercaw and Amon 2016).

7. As the introduction to a recent scholarly anthology on Tyler Perry notes, '[Perry] has unapologetically made it clear that he is principally speaking to, for, and about African Americans' (Bell and Jackson II 2014: 6).
8. While Mary Beard makes passing reference to a 'regime of laughter' in her study of ancient Roman laughter (Beard 2014: 142), she does not define this concept or articulate its significance for the broader study of gelopolitics.
9. Such a hijacking of public (i.e., white) space is unlikely to materialise in the case of the Tyler Perry laughing barrel discussed earlier. In contrast to the highly visible and audible segregation of Black laughter enforced in the Southern town, Perry's comedies move Black laughter almost entirely out of view and earshot of whites. Despite Perry recently being the highest paid male entertainer in the United States (Bell and Jackson II 2014: 1), many whites have never seen (or even heard of) his shows. The segregation of the Tyler Perry laughing barrel *itself* means that the Black laughter emanating from it cannot disrupt the *polis* in the same way Black laughter does in Ellison's story.
10. The logic of democratisation at work in Ellison's laughing barrel joke resonates strongly with that articulated by Rancière over a decade later (Rancière 1999, 2001). That is, Ellison describes how a police order (white supremacy) entails a particular partition of the perceptible (the white supremacist regime of laughter) that the *demos*, or 'part without a part' (the Black citizenry), interrupts to reveal 'the equality of anyone at all with anyone else' (i.e., the equality of Black and white subjects) (Rancière 1999: 15). But whereas for Rancière the *demos* reveals its equality by demonstrating its possession of *logos*, for Ellison the revelation of equality works in the opposite direction: those who possess *logos* (the white Southerners) are reduced to the mere *phōnē* belonging to the *demos* (i.e., to Black laughter). Ellison thus goes further than Rancière by dramatising not only the 'sheer contingency' of the differential allocation of *logos* and *phōnē* in a police order, but also the radical fragility and contingency of *logos* itself (15).
11. Once again, by 'dialectical' I do not mean the progressive, teleological dialectics of Hegel, but rather the negative dialectics of Adorno that emphasises how unruly non-identities (e.g., Black laughter emanating from a laughing barrel) can illuminate and transform the whole (e.g., the white supremacist social order). Achille Mbembe employs a similar notion of dialectics with his conception of 'blackness' as a relation of

social subjection that paradoxically empowers emancipatory political projects (Mbembe 2017).
12. Here I disagree with Parvulescu's otherwise brilliant reading of Ellison's essay. She notes that 'there are rules as to when one laughs and how one laughs in the theater [. . .]. All theaters have their laughing barrels' (Parvulescu 2010: 74). While the Broadway theatre certainly *regulates* laughter according to the terms of the white supremacist regime, it does not *segregate* Black laughter and thus does not have laughing barrels.
13. This focus on the possibilities for freedom amid conditions of unfreedom is a recurring theme in Ellison's oeuvre. For example, in 'Blues People' he writes that slavery 'was a most vicious system, and those who endured and survived it a tough people, but it was *not* (and this is important for Negroes to remember for the sake of their own sense of who and what their grandparents were) a state of absolute repression' (Ellison 2003a: 284).
14. Timothy Parrish (1995) and Meili Steele (1996) also offer incisive analyses of Ellison's contributions to democratic theory.
15. In 'Going to the Territory', Ellison describes the 'vernacular' style characteristic of American artistic production in similar terms. He writes: 'I see the vernacular as a dynamic *process* in which the most refined styles from the past are continually merged with the play-it-by-eye-and-by-ear improvisations which we invent in our efforts to control our environment and entertain ourselves. [. . .] In it the styles and the techniques of the past are adjusted to the needs of the present, and in its integrative action the high styles of the past are democratized' (Ellison 2003c: 612). While Ellison's concept of the 'vernacular' is functionally equivalent to 'antagonistic cooperation', I focus on the latter because it dramatises the dialectical dynamism of the process it names.
16. While Ellison and Adorno share a striking number of similarities in biography and intellectual orientation (e.g., early training and ambitions in classical music; roots in a Marxist tradition, yet resistance to orthodox Marxism; an intensely dialectical imagination (Jay 1996); an aesthetic orientation towards politics, yet strong allergy to 'political' or 'protest' art; and a reputation for aesthetic elitism), they appear to split decisively on the artistic (and thus political) merits of jazz. Adorno famously objects to jazz as a commodity through which the masses take pleasure in their own alienation (Adorno 2002a, 2002b), whereas Ellison admires jazz as a means by which Black artists reveal and affirm their equality with whites. However, as James Harding points out, a closer look at their respective jazz writings reveals 'a surprising correlation' between the two thinkers (Harding 1995: 130; see also Okiji 2018). In particular, Ellison's distinction between 'jazz as experience' and 'jazz as entertainment' (Ellison 2003i: 269; 2003f: 277) suggests that he shares Adorno's concerns about the commercialisation of music.

17. We can read Ellison's concept of 'antagonistic cooperation' as a gloss on Marx's account of cooperation in Chapter 13 of *Capital* (Volume 1). Marx argues that the cooperation among labourers that fuels the emergence and accumulation of capital is simultaneously the product and source of labour's necessary antagonism with capital: 'The co-operation of wage-labourers is entirely brought about by the capital that employs them. [. . .] Hence the interconnection between their various labours confronts them [. . .] as the powerful will of a being outside them, who subjects their activity to his purpose' (Marx 1990: 449–50). Marx continues: 'As the number of the co-operating workers increases, so too does their resistance to the domination of capital, and, necessarily, the pressure put on by capital to overcome this resistance' (449). For Marx, as for Ellison, cooperation and antagonism are intricately and inexorably bound up with one another in modern society, and the possibility of an emancipatory politics hinges on mobilising their dialectical relationship.
18. We can also interpret Black laughter in this scene as antagonistically cooperating with the laughter of the white spectators. White laughter begins as 'antagonistic' chuckles of superiority directed at the 'irrationality' of the Black laughter emanating from the barrels. But in their co-presence, these two antagonistic forms of laughter begin to deconstruct each other: Black laughter appears more rational (or 'civilised'), while white laughter appears more irrational (or 'primitive'). Through their antagonism, Black and white laughter cooperate to democratise the racial order.

Chapter 4
The Best Medicine?
Repoliticising Laughter for Contemporary Feminist and Queer Politics

> There is nothing like the sound of women really laughing. The roaring laughter of women is like the roaring of the eternal sea. [. . .] [T]his laughter is the one true hope, for as long as it is audible there is evidence that someone is seeing through the Dirty Joke.
>
> Mary Daly, Gyn/ecology (1990: 17)

> Laughter's the best medicine, they say. I don't. I reckon penicillin might give it the nudge.
>
> Hannah Gadsby, Nanette (2018b)

On 27 September 2018, Dr Christine Blasey Ford testified to the US Senate Judiciary Committee that she had been the victim of sexual assault by Supreme Court nominee Brett Kavanaugh and his friend Mark Judge at a high school summer house party in 1982. Ford alleged that an intoxicated Kavanaugh and Judge trapped her in an upstairs bedroom, pinned her on a bed, covered her mouth, groped her and tried to remove her clothing. Ford recalled not being able to breathe and believing that the young men were about to rape her (*The Washington Post* 2018). Asked by Senator Patrick Leahy to identify the strongest memory she had of the assault, Ford delivered a startling response:

> *Ford*: Indelible in the hippocampus is the laughter, the laugh – the uproarious laughter between the two, and their having fun at my expense.
> *Leahy*: You've never forgotten that laughter. You've never forgotten them laughing at you.
> *Ford*: They were laughing with each other.
> *Leahy*: And you were the object of the laughter?
> *Ford*: I was, you know, underneath one of them while the two laughed, two friend – two friends having a really good time with one another.

Drawing on her training as a psychologist, Ford explained that the laughter of Kavanaugh and Judge – not the physical attack or her own feelings of fear or pain – etched itself into her memory most permanently. Without further prompting, Ford recalled this 'uproarious laughter' several more times over the course of the hearing, describing how Kavanaugh and Judge were 'drunkenly laughing during the attack' and how she 'could hear them talking as they went down the stairwell, they were laughing . . .'.

Notably, Ford resists Leahy's suggestion that Kavanaugh and Judge were laughing *at her*, insisting that the two young men were instead laughing *with one another*. Ford appears to believe that characterising Kavanaugh and Judge as laughing at her gives the men too much credit by implying that they acknowledged the presence of another human being in the room. According to Ford, she wasn't even really there in Kavanaugh and Judge's eyes: there was simply a body that they were enjoying together. The situation amounted to nothing more than 'two friends having a really good time with one another'. A celebration of their power, the laughter of Kavanaugh and Judge was premised on and worked to secure Ford's reduction to mere body; it signalled and created a situation where Ford did not count as fully human. 'Indelible in the hippocampus', this laughter and the trauma it inflicted impacted Ford for years to come in the form of anxiety, claustrophobia and PTSD-like symptoms. Ford is not alone in this experience. Victims and witnesses of sexual violence regularly recall attackers and onlookers laughing.[1] Ford's testimony highlights laughter as a key experience through which male power is achieved, enjoyed and entrenched.[2]

What resources does feminist and queer theory offer for understanding laughter's role in the (re)production of patriarchal and heteronormative behaviours and modes of social organisation? As it turns out, laughter has been at the centre of feminist and queer political visions for the past four decades. Beginning with Hélène Cixous's 1975 essay 'The Laugh of the Medusa' and continuing in the work of Luce Irigaray, Judith Butler and others, a rich discourse has emerged around the view that laughter is an experience that is uniquely capable of undermining the rigid and violent conceptions of gender identity and sexual desire at the root of patriarchy and heteronormativity. If in 2012 Jack Halberstam could propose a 'gaga feminism' featuring 'an unusual mix of whimsy and fierce purposefulness, ludic improvisation and staying power, passive resistance and loud refusals' (Halberstam 2012: 133) and Cynthia

Willett could advance an 'erotic politics of feminist laughter' that 'deconstructs the disciplinary matrix through a style of comportment that is egalitarian and even visionary' (Willett, Willett and Sherman 2012: 230), it was because in 1975 Cixous introduced a 'laughter that breaks out, overflows, a humor no one would expect to find in women – which is nonetheless surely their greatest strength because it's a humor that sees man much further away than he has ever been seen' (Cixous 1981: 55).

The present chapter questions whether this discourse equips contemporary feminist and queer politics with an adequate account of laughter. In particular, is theorising laughter as intrinsically opposed to patriarchy and heteronormativity – that is, as naturally aligned with feminist and queer political goals – sufficient for grasping how it operates with respect to sex and gender? Can this approach, for instance, illuminate the political origins and effects of the laughter haunting Ford and other victims of sexual violence? In light of the critical theory of laughter articulated and practised in the preceding chapters, my wager is that laughter participates in sex and gender politics in a multiplicity of ways that exceed and are often at odds with its ability to resist patriarchy and heteronormativity. Laughter, I propose, is a site of politics through which these structures of power are not only undermined and transformed but also built and sustained.

I advance three arguments along these lines. First, the prevailing feminist and queer discourse hinges on a curiously under-politicised conception of laughter. This discourse's abstract, philosophical view of laughter as naturally subversive unduly limits its own critical efficacy by obscuring laughter's concrete political polyvalence around sex and gender. Second, and consequently, a fully politicised feminist/queer[3] account of laughter requires an attention to laughter's political productivity. Laughter is not simply an experience that disrupts and undermines formations of gender identity and sexual desire; it is an experience/event that constructs and maintains them as well. Third, such an account of gelopolitics requires attending to the question of the social order as a whole. Because laughter today arises and exerts effects within a society that is patriarchal and heteronormative in its basic structure, even the most radical, emancipatory laughter remains parasitic on and reinscribes these oppressive logics. I conclude that rather than being, as Willett suggests, 'just the medicine for what ails us in our social norms' (Willett, Willett and Sherman 2012: 239), laughter is a privileged site of political contestation over sex and gender – a site distinguished not by its power to emancipate, but by its peculiar efficacy in creating, enforcing and resisting the formations of gender identity and sexual desire that compose the social order.

As was the case in the previous chapter on racial gelopolitics, this chapter does not simply apply the critical theory of laughter developed thus far to the issues of sex and gender. Because the terms governing our experiences and accounts of laughter are themselves already heavily gendered, the present chapter learns from and engages existing accounts of sex and gender gelopolitics in order to further articulate the critical theory of laughter itself. It proceeds in three sections. Section I offers a genealogy of the late twentieth- and early twenty-first-century feminist and queer discourse on laughter. I trace how a philosophical fascination with laughter as an emancipatory experience emerges in Cixous's 'The Laugh of the Medusa' and is taken up by Irigaray, Butler, D. Diane Davis, Willett and others. Drawing on dissident moments in this discourse, Section II begins the task of repoliticising laughter by returning to modernity's first systematic account of laughter and human sexuality: Freud's 1905 book *The Joke and Its Relation to the Unconscious*. Whereas the theorists in Section I interpret Freud as conceiving of laughter as intrinsically liberating – a view they seek to weaponise against patriarchy, heteronormativity and even Freud himself – I demonstrate that Freud also reveals laughter's ability to produce and sustain traditional formations of gender identity and sexual desire. Section III takes the next step in repoliticising laughter by turning to Linda Mizejewski's 2014 book *Pretty/Funny* and Hannah Gadsby's 2018 stand-up special *Nanette* to show that even the most ostensibly subversive laughter draws on and fuels the patriarchal and heteronormative logics governing the social order as a whole. Mizejewski and Gadsby highlight the dialectic of laughter within which feminist and queer politics labours today: laughter that resists the hetero-patriarchal social order does so only by reinscribing the terms of life of that order.

I. Feminist and Queer Gelopolitics: A Genealogy

Laughter first emerges as an object of feminist theoretical interest in Hélène Cixous's 1975 essay 'The Laugh of the Medusa' (Cixous 1976). While feminists had certainly discussed laughter prior to 1975 – mainly as a means by which men express their hostility to and dismissal of women's political demands (Friedan 1983: 80; Millett 1970: 45, 303–4; Wollstonecraft 1995: 5) – the urgency of proving that feminism was a serious political movement militated against making laughter an object of sustained theoretical attention (Barreca 1988: 4; Gray 1994: 19).[4] Regina Barreca traces the prevailing view of laughter to which Cixous responds. According to Barreca, patriarchy – the form of social and political organisation where men rule due to the belief that they alone possess *logos* – holds that only men know how to create laughter and laugh properly. Quoting the mid-twentieth-century English author Reginald Blyth, Barreca argues that patriarchy understands women as 'the unlaughing at which men laugh' (Barreca 1988: 4). Women are 'unlaughing' in two interlocking ways. First, they are seen as incapable of generating laughter in others. Blyth writes:

> The truth is [. . .] that women have not only no humour in themselves but are the cause of the extinction of it in others. This is almost too cruel to be true, but in every way women correspond to and are representative of nature. Is there any humour in nature? (Barreca 1988: 4; see also Congreve 1964)

Second, women are 'unlaughing' because they are held to be incapable of themselves laughing in appropriate or rational ways. Women's laughter is not *really* laughter – i.e., the politically generative interplay of *logos* and *phōnē* – but instead mere *phōnē* – i.e., mindless giggles (Barreca 1988: 4), hysterical howls (16) and inscrutable smiles (4–5). As 'unlaughing' creatures, women appear to be less than human, which in turn renders them laugh*able* by men – typically by way of sexist jokes. The 'unlaughing' nature of women is reconfirmed every time a woman refuses to laugh at these jokes (hence the trope of the 'humourless feminist') (7). The discourse inaugurated by Cixous aims to redeem this maligned 'unlaughing' and 'laughable' laughter of women as the source and centrepiece of a radical feminist politics.

Replete with allusions to Greek mythology, modern literature and psychoanalytic theory, Cixous's 'The Laugh of the Medusa' envisions a specifically 'feminine' form of writing, or *écriture féminine*. *Écriture féminine* differs from 'masculine' writing not because it is written by women or focuses on issues of particular concern to women, but because it obeys a distinctively 'feminine' discursive and libidinal economy.[5] Masculine writing, Cixous argues, is *logocentric*. Whether in the form of the essay, treatise or novel, masculine writing analyses, classifies and hierarchises, all with the goal of establishing rational mastery over an essentially irrational objective world (Cixous 1976: 879). According to Cixous, masculine writing obeys the same logic that has historically characterised male domination of women: the possession of *logos* requires and justifies rule over bodies held to be capable of only *phōnē*. 'Logocentrism subjects all thought – all concepts, codes and values – to a binary system, related to "the" couple, man/woman' (Cixous and Clément 1986: 64; see also Cixous 1981: 44). Masculine writing is consequently a key vector through which patriarchy establishes, exercises and secures its rule:

> I maintain unequivocally that there is such a thing as *marked* writing; that, until now, far more extensively and repressively than is ever suspected or admitted, writing has been run by a libidinal and cultural – hence political, typically masculine – economy; that this is a locus where the repression of women has been perpetuated, over and over, more or less consciously [. . .]. [T]his locus has grossly exaggerated all the signs of sexual opposition (and not sexual difference), where woman has never *her* turn to speak. (Cixous 1976: 879)

For Cixous, the history of the human *logos* is bound up with masculine, phallic power: *logo*-centrism is really *phallo-logocentrism*, or *phallogocentrism* (885; Cixous and Clément 1986: 65).

Rather than attempting to occupy the position of *logos* that has historically been denied to women (which would only reinscribe the patriarchal *logos/phōnē* dichotomy), *écriture féminine* establishes an alternative discursive and libidinal economy that gives voice to the bodies silenced by phallogocentrism. 'Write your self', Cixous encourages her readers; 'your body must be heard' (Cixous 1976: 880). Against the reason-giving, distinction-drawing and hierarchy-building of masculine writing, *écriture féminine* unleashes and articulates the energies and desires of oppressed bodies. Cixous demands that 'women must write through their bodies, they must invent the impregnable language that will wreck partitions, classes, and rhetorics, regulations and codes' (886). *Écriture féminine* does not look or sound anything like masculine writing; charged with *eros*, it is passionate, disorderly and excessive. Cixous explains that

> it is impossible to *define* a feminine practice of writing, and this is an impossibility that will remain, for this practice can never be theorized, enclosed, coded – which doesn't mean that it doesn't exist. But it will always surpass the discourse that regulates the phallocentric system [. . .]. It will be conceived of only by subjects who are breakers of automatisms, by peripheral figures that no authority can ever subjugate. (883)

The radical political potential of *écriture féminine* consists in how its inscription of *phōnē* into the form of *logos* (i.e., into writing) undermines the stability and self-sufficiency of *logos* itself.

> If woman has always functioned 'within' the discourse of man [. . .] it is time for her to dislocate this 'within', to explode it, turn it around, and seize it; to make it hers, containing it, taking it in her own mouth, biting that tongue with her very own teeth to invent for herself a language to get inside of. (887)

As a fugitive form of *logos* that receives its shape and substance from the *phōnē* of the body, *écriture féminine* ultimately dissolves the *logos/phōnē* distinction constitutive of patriarchal power. Cixous concludes that *écriture féminine* is revolutionary: it allows women to 'do more than modify power relations or toss the ball over to the other camp; she will bring about a mutation in human relations, in thought, in all praxis' (882).

Cixous associates *écriture féminine* with the experience of laughter: 'this open and bewildering prospect goes hand in hand with a certain kind of laughter' (Cixous 1981: 55). While masculine writing is serious, sombre and reserved, *écriture féminine* is light-hearted and joyous, boasting an excessive Nietzschean irreverence. The laughter of *écriture féminine* revolts against the silences imposed by patriarchy; it is the tone taken by a *logos* that emerges out of the *phōnē* of oppressed bodies. Cixous writes: 'Our glances, our smiles, are spent; laughs exude from all our mouths' (Cixous 1976: 878). Resisting classification, categorisation or calcification into a set formula, *écriture féminine* never takes itself too seriously. It eschews the menacing image of woman as Medusa – the Greek mythological creature who Freud links to the threat of castration (Freud 1968: 273–4; Parvulescu 2010: 105–6). As Cixous assures her male readers, 'you only have to look at the Medusa straight on to see her. And she's not deadly. She's beautiful and she's laughing' (Cixous 1976: 885). For Cixous, laughter is the key in which a truly transformative feminist politics – one that fully repudiates and escapes the logic of phallogocentrism – must proceed:

> A feminine text cannot fail to be more than subversive. It is volcanic; as it is written it brings about an upheaval of the old property crust, carrier of masculine investments; there's no other way. There's no room for her if she's not a he. If she's a her-she, it's in order to smash everything, to shatter the framework of institutions, to blow up the law; to break up the 'truth' with laughter. (888)

If the 'feminine' is the power that interrupts masculine discursive and libidinal economies (882, 889), then the characteristic experience of the feminine is laughter. Cixous sees women and laughter as co-extensive, not mutually exclusive. Women, not men, know how to truly laugh.

Luce Irigaray follows Cixous in placing laughter at the centre of feminist politics. In *This Sex Which Is Not One* Irigaray argues that Western history and philosophy have been dominated by a phallogocentrism that values the discovery of stable truths, the imposition of hierarchical orders and exercises of mastery (Irigaray 1985: 86, 161–2). This masculine libidinal and discursive economy presupposes its object to be a mute, irrational and mysteriously seductive 'lack' of *logos* known as 'the feminine': 'It is inasmuch as she does not exist that she sustains the desire of these "speaking beings" that are called men [. . .]. Man seeks her out, since he has inscribed her in discourse, but as lack, as fault or flaw' (89). While the 'feminine' has so far only been known in the terms provided by phallogocentrism, Irigaray believes that its position as 'other' means that it threatens that economy (89–90). Resisting patriarchy likewise entails allowing feminine desires and pleasures to speak on their own terms, 'to practice that difference' as an alternative libidinal and discursive economy (159). Laughter stands at the heart of such a project. 'Isn't laughter the first form of liberation from a secular oppression?' Irigaray asks. *'Isn't the phallic tantamount to the seriousness of meaning?* Perhaps woman, and the sexual relation, transcend it "first" in laughter?' (163). As an affirmative enjoyment of bodily pleasure, logical contradiction and openness to difference, laughter displaces the false choice of 'silence' or 'seriousness' imposed by phallogocentrism. 'Women among themselves begin by laughing', Irigaray explains. 'To escape from a pure and simple reversal of the masculine position means in any case not to forget to laugh' (163). Like Cixous, Irigaray associates feminine political power with the experience of laughter.

The turn to queer theory inaugurated by Judith Butler's *Gender Trouble* reimagines this relationship between laughter and the feminine. Butler objects to accounts like Cixous's and Irigaray's due to how their conception of two diametrically opposed 'masculine' and 'feminine' economies reinscribes the totalising and essentialising gestures of phallogocentrism (Butler 1990: 13).[6] Because even the most radical attempts to give voice to patriarchy's 'other' (i.e., the feminine) are informed by judgements about gender identity and sexual desire belonging to existing patriarchal society, they necessarily yield an impoverished sexual and gender imaginary. Against the view that 'the feminine as the repudiated/excluded within that system constitutes the possibility of a critique and disruption of that hegemonic conceptual scheme', Butler claims that such a 'feminine' is bound up with and bears the traces of that which it resists: 'the utopian notion of a sexuality freed from heterosexual constructs, a sexuality beyond "sex," failed to acknowledge the ways in which power relations continue to construct sexuality for women even within the terms of a "liberated" heterosexuality or lesbianism' (28–9). Butler believes an overhaul in theoretical approach is therefore required. Rather than offering an abstract philosophical account of the 'masculine' and the 'feminine', she advocates a genealogical analysis of the concrete practices of power that produce and regulate gender identity and sexual desire in a given social order (2).

Butler's departure from Cixous and Irigaray on the usefulness of the 'feminine' as a category for feminist politics does not, however, entail a corresponding abandonment of laughter. On the contrary, Butler insists that 'laughter in the face of serious categories is indispensable for feminism' (viii), and she articulates her alternative approach *through* a reimagination of the politics of laughter. Whereas Cixous and Irigaray conceive of laughter as the characteristic experience of an oppositional feminine economy, Butler theorises laughter as an experience that calls into question the very concepts of the 'masculine' and the 'feminine'. We see this most clearly in *Gender Trouble*'s account of parody. According to Butler, parodic practices like drag undermine the distinction between a subject's 'inner' and 'outer' identities, challenging the notion that subjects have an original or primary gender identity that they then express in their behaviour (137). Parody highlights how gender is the product of imitative performances within the context of society's various regulatory regimes: 'gender parody reveals that the original identity after which gender fashions itself is an imitation without an origin' (138). The laughter generated by such practices likewise *un-grounds* gender:

> The loss of the sense of 'the normal', however, can be its own occasion for laughter, especially when 'the normal', 'the original' is revealed to be a copy, and an inevitably failed one, an ideal that no one *can* embody. In this sense, laughter emerges in the realization that all along the original was derived. (138–9)

Butler holds that while Cixous and Irigaray have learnt to laugh at patriarchy and heteronormativity, their commitment to a feminine economy of laughter indicates that they continue to take laughter *itself* too seriously. Instead of embodying a philosophical alternative to phallogocentrism, laughter for Butler constitutes a historically specific experience that undermines, transforms and proliferates – that is, that *queers* – concrete formations of gender identity and sexual desire. This queer/ing laughter is 'a subversive laughter in the pastiche-effect of parodic practices in which the original, the authentic, and the real are themselves constituted as effects' (146). A feminist politics geared towards the subversion and multiplication of gender identities and forms of sexual desire is a politics of queer/ing laughter.

Despite the centrality of laughter to Butler's queer political vision, she cautions against theorising laughter in exclusively emancipatory terms. Butler advises that amid all the attention paid to the laughter of Bataille, Derrida, Foucault and Cixous (see Introduction), 'let us not forget Herculine's relation to the laugh' (103). Herculine Barbin, a nineteenth-century French hermaphrodite whose journals were edited and republished by Foucault, fears the 'incredulous laughter' of the officials at her school and laughs scornfully at her incompetent doctor (Foucault 2010: 23, 71; Butler 1990: 103–4). Butler argues that laughter in Herculine's case emerges within and thus helps reproduce the terms of the prevailing discursive regime: 'For Herculine, then, laughter appears to designate either humiliation or scorn, two positions unambiguously related to a damning law, subjected to it either as its instrument or object' (Butler 1990: 104). Departing from Nietzschean and feminist celebrations of laughter's capacity to exceed and displace discursive boundaries, Butler suggests that laughter always arises, operates and exerts effects *within* discourse. Not simply an experience that signals a breakdown of the law, laughter is also an experience through which the law exercises and reinforces its power. If Herculine's 'sexuality is not outside the law, but is the ambivalent production of the law' (105), we can say the same about her laughter: it stands in a necessarily fraught relation to the discourse from which it emerges and to which it responds. Butler's reflections on Herculine Barbin show that *Gender Trouble* offers a much more nuanced assessment of laughter's relation to patriarchy and heteronormativity than a cursory reading might suggest. As we will see below, these passages prove decisive to articulating a critical mode of theorising laughter for feminist and queer politics today.

Perhaps the most ambitious and sustained feminist account of gelopolitics is provided by D. Diane Davis in her 2000 book *Breaking Up [at] Totality*. Drawing on a wide range of deconstructionist and post-structuralist thought, Davis seeks to articulate a 'rhetoric of laughter' capable of 'breaking up' discursive regimes on behalf of identities and practices that remain unthinkable within their terms (Davis 2000: 17). According to Davis, there exists an ineliminable excess to *logos*: something always slips through, breaks out or resists human attempts to understand and master the world. She writes: 'The excess re/turns, perpetually, in the form, for instance, of an unruly twig of hair and/or an irrepressible burst of laughter, to keep "identity" shaken up, unfixable, uncontrollable' (39). The human *logos* is thus a laughing *logos*: there is a '*Laughing*-in-language that will not and cannot be suppressed' (94). This is not an 'angelic' laughter that delights in the discovery of meaning (33), nor a 'devilish' laughter that revels in meaninglessness (25). Rather, it is a 'co(s)mic' laughter that displaces the angelic–devilish dichotomy itself by affirming the historical plurality, contingency and open-endedness of systems of meaning (63). In the burst of laughter, 'the negative de(con)struction exceeds itself, bursting forth into an unchecked *affirmation* that is neither positive nor negative, but something totally other, something explosive, which up/sets binary logic from the inside' (56). Davis believes that those committed to emancipatory politics must attune themselves to and participate in this laughter-in-language. Laughter stands at the heart of an anti-fascistic sensibility that resists the calcification of the human *logos* and invites pluralisation by identities and practices that are currently disqualified or unintelligible in its terms. We must learn, Davis concludes, to 'laugh with the Laughter that is laughing language' (114).

Davis contends that this rhetoric of laughter has major implications for feminist politics. Because *logo*-centrism is always already *phallo*-centrism (137), by exceeding and disrupting *logos*, laughter exceeds and disrupts patriarchal power. Like Cixous and Irigaray, Davis associates this capacity of laughter with the 'feminine':

> [L]aughter *releases* the 'feminine', 'desire-in-language' from its binary bondage. [Feminists] are willing to laugh and to be laughed, to take the chance of losing consciousness and *forgetting*, if only for an instant, about the old battle [against patriarchy]. And it is here, in the space of this affirmative forgetting, that an/other politics and an/other feminism gets underway, a *feminist politics* that breaks up the Phallocratic Order by breaking up *at* it. (208; brackets added)

This 'feminine' laughter, Davis continues, is the same as that identified by Butler in her analysis of parody (205–8). Davis believes that despite Butler's objections to the discourse of phallogocentrism, her critique of 'gynocentric' and representational feminisms – that is, feminisms grounded in the category of 'woman' – constitutes the next logical step in the fight against phallogocentrism.[7] A queer/ing laughter, in other words, strikes at the very heart of the 'Phallocratic Order'. Davis writes: 'The logocentric linguistic structure that many American feminists uphold in their struggle is a phallocentric one that will continually misfire for "women" *because* it demands that one be either male or female, active or passive, subject or object' (151). For Davis, laughter characterises an affirmative, 'post-identity' feminist politics that overcomes the residual phallogocentrism of traditional feminisms by proliferating new gender identities and sexual practices (19–20, 136–40).

The work of Cixous, Irigaray, Butler and Davis has informed and been informed by a large, interdisciplinary body of scholarship that affords laughter a privileged role in feminist and queer politics.[8] This fascination with the emancipatory possibilities of laughter has carried over into the artistic realm as well (Isaak 1996). Perhaps most notable is Marleen Gorris's 1982 film *A Question of Silence* (Gorris 1982). This Dutch drama tells the story of three previously unacquainted women who suddenly and seemingly inexplicably murder the male clerk of a local boutique. A series of interviews with Janine, the court-appointed psychiatrist, reveals each woman's discontent with life under patriarchy. For the homemaker Christine, the problem is a distant husband who saddles her with the children; for the secretary Andrea, it is the disrespect of her male colleagues; and for the waitress Annie, it is abandonment by her husband and lack of career mobility. In the film's pivotal closing scene, the women are on trial and the male prosecutor questions Janine about why she refuses to diagnose them as insane. When Janine suggests that the clerk's identity as a man is germane to the investigation, the prosecutor insists that it would make no difference if the clerk were female. The three defendants burst into laughter at this comment, and before long all the women in the courtroom, including Janine, are laughing along with them, forcing a suspension of the trial. Gorris's film illustrates the feminist/queer discourse's claim that women's laughter interrupts and literally breaks male-dominated social institutions and can likewise form the basis of a revolutionary feminist politics.

'The Seriously Erotic Politics of Feminist Laughter', a 2012 essay by Cynthia Willett, Julie Willett and Yael Sherman (later expanded into the 2019 book *Uproarious*), exemplifies the political vision in which this feminist/queer discourse of gelopolitics culminates and thus serves as a convenient bookend to it. Willett et al. explain that due to the historical domination of the comedy genre by men (Willett, Willett and Sherman 2012: 217) and the prevalence of sexist jokes as a means of social control (219–20), feminists have traditionally distrusted laughter in favour of a more serious, 'schoolmarmish' tone (226). Against this brand of feminism, the authors point to the subversive humour of American female comics like Roseanne Barr (pre-Trump era, at least), Margaret Cho and Wanda Sykes as illustrating laughter's capacity to 'jolt' (229) audiences out of reactionary attitudes: 'the sting of ridicule or the contagion of joyous laughter prove to be [. . .] effective weapons for social change' (218). Willett et al. believe that laughter is uniquely well suited for achieving the social and political goals of feminism because in addition to allowing women to reclaim an experience that has been historically deployed against them ('to joyfully re-appropriate the energy and eros from systems of domination'; 240), its disruption of established hierarchies and identities serves egalitarian ends. They write: 'The techniques of inversion and leveling that can account for the pleasure of the joke are well suited for the central aim of a feminist ethical vision – one of social equality and inclusion' (228–9; see also Isaak 1996: 27). While Cixous, Irigaray, Butler and Davis would all likely take issue with Willett et al.'s instrumentalist description of laughter as a 'weapon' for feminism (Parvulescu 2010: 112), their essay reveals the logical endpoint of this discourse's theoretical vision: joyously irreverent and rebellious feminist comedy. As Frances Gray puts it:

> Cixous works out the image in vivid, powerful and erotic terms to adumbrate a new form of writing, a new use of language. A woman who both writes and performs, as so many woman comedians do, is making this image concrete, flesh and blood. (Gray 1994: 37)

Depoliticising Laughter

The above genealogy demonstrates how a particular conception of laughter has become central to feminist and queer theory over the last four decades. Cixous, Irigaray, Davis, Gorris, Willett et al. and to a certain extent Butler all discover in laughter an emancipatory experience that undermines patriarchy and heteronormativity. They are united by the view 'that women have always been on the laughing side, that women have a stake in laughter's indissoluble and essential relation to freedom' (Isaak 1996: 20). For Cixous and Irigaray, laughter is bound up with the necessarily oppositional and liberatory power of the 'feminine'; for Butler, laughter queers entrenched gender identities and forms of sexual desire; for Davis, laughter operates as the extra-discursive, co(s)mic force to which feminist politics must attune itself; for Gorris, laughter dismantles institutions that are deaf to the claims of women; and for Willett et al., laughter constitutes the ideal weapon for women to employ to achieve equality and inclusion.

Yet for all of this discourse's insights, its view of gelopolitics *itself* remains curiously one-dimensional. To its incisive accounts of laughter as a site of resistance there correspond no similarly rich accounts of (a) laughter as an exercise, celebration and entrenchment of male power, as it was in the case of Christine Blasey Ford and other victims of sexual violence; (b) how gender identities are constituted, governed and reproduced through the social regulation of laughter (e.g., the existence of different rules for women/girls and men/boys about when it is appropriate to laugh, the body's movements during laughter and the volume and duration of one's laughter; Barreca 1991; Douglas 2015); and (c) the role gender plays in the social determination of which bodies, lives and experiences count as laughable. In place of such a multifaceted study of the sex and gender politics of laughter, the feminist and queer discourse simply flips the traditional patriarchal discourse on its head such that *men* are the 'unlaughing' at which women or queer subjects laugh. Indeed, while the theorists reviewed above highlight laughter as a political experience that exerts important political effects, their insistence that laughter is *naturally* opposed to patriarchy and heteronormativity and is never *itself* affected or shaped by politics amounts to a depoliticising gesture at odds with the critical and radical ambitions of their own discourse.

One might object that the feminist and queer discourse never actually aims to provide an extensive political analysis of laughter along the lines I am describing. Laughter for Cixous, Irigaray and Davis instead operates merely as a *metaphor* for the political style or affective sensibility they believe is necessary for resisting patriarchy and heteronormativity. As Jo Anna Isaak notes, laughter

> is meant to be thought of as a metaphor for transformation, for thinking about cultural change. In providing libidinal gratification, laughter can also provide an analytic for understanding the relationships between

the social and the symbolic while allowing us to imagine these relationships differently. (Isaak 1996: 5; see also Gray 1994: 35)

While it is correct that many of the above theorists do understand laughter mainly as a metaphor – and therefore do not seek to explain how laughter operates more concretely within sex and gender politics – it does not follow that their accounts are without bearing on this question. A metaphorical treatment of laughter entails a conception of where laughter comes from, how it operates and the political effects it exerts. The feminist/queer discourse's view of laughter as intrinsically emancipatory – that is, as properly aligned with the 'feminine' – makes it difficult to see and account for occasions when laughter functions in very different ways. (For example, Isaak simply dismisses non-subversive laughter as not *really* laughter, writing that laughter rooted in 'contemporary parody [. . .] is in effect a strengthening of the law, [. . .] not laughter at all but rhetoric'; Isaak 1996: 20.) Grasping the full scope of sex and gender gelopolitics requires an alternative theoretical approach – one that does not find in laughter a metaphor for politics, but a site of politics itself.

Foucault argues that genealogy dramatises historical paths not taken, rescuing them from the obscurity imposed by the smooth, linear narratives of traditional history (Foucault 1977). The above genealogy of the feminist/queer discourse provides glimpses of such untaken paths in the more explicitly *political* conceptions of laughter it occasionally offers. Butler's discussion of the laughter of Herculine Barbin is the most notable example of this. As described earlier, Butler suggests that Herculine's relation to the laugh indicates how in addition to challenging the bounds of a discursive regime (e.g., patriarchy or heteronormativity), laughter is an experience through which such a regime exercises and reproduces its power. Davis, meanwhile, interrupts her celebration of laughter to agree with Butler that laughter's emancipatory effects always unfold within discourse: 'all subversive activities ("liberatory" practices) necessarily take place *within* the constraints of established citational boundaries' (Davis 2000: 40). Finally, while Willett et al. claim that humour may be just what the doctor ordered, a lengthy footnote warns that 'humor is not a cure-all for our social ills', and that laughter can serve a 'reactionary function or aim'; 'reinvoke insider/outsider and hierarchical social structures'; and 'sow the seeds of resentment and backlash rather than progressive social change' (Willett, Willett and Sherman 2012: 241–2n6). If the recent feminist/queer discourse hinges on an under-politicised conception of laughter's relation to sex and gender, its dissident moments provide the basis for a more fully politicised account that better satisfies its own critical and radical aims.

The next section begins the task of repoliticising laughter for contemporary feminist and queer politics by revisiting modernity's first systematic treatment of the relation between laughter and human sexuality. Freud's account of laughter as an inherently emancipatory experience constitutes the (at times unacknowledged) point of departure for the feminist/queer discourse. Cixous, Irigaray, Butler, Davis, Gorris and Willett et al. reappropriate Freud's theory of laughter as a means of resisting the patriarchy and heteronormativity that his account largely takes for granted. In what follows I argue that *The Joke and Its Relation to the Unconscious* actually offers a much more nuanced conception of gelopolitics than is generally appreciated by these thinkers. For Freud, laughter plays a decisive role not merely in the disruption of conventional sex and gender norms, but in their *production* and *preservation* as well. Moving beyond the depoliticising tendencies of the feminist/queer discourse requires first moving back in time to reconsider that discourse's intellectual wellspring and arch-nemesis: Freud.

II. Freud, Laughter and the Production of Sexual Character

According to Freud, laughter is the pleasure enjoyed by a subject upon the sudden lifting of a psychical inhibition: 'laughter arises when an amount of psychical energy previously used in charging certain psychical pathways has become unusable, so that it can be freely released' (Freud 2003: 142). Freud's book focuses specifically on the laughter produced by jokes.[9] He explains that a joke's technique and/or content brings to consciousness an impulse that was previously repressed by either the listener's rational faculty (121–7) or an external social authority (97–110). The saving of the psychical energy employed to maintain that inhibition yields the pleasure of laughter: 'the person listening to the joke is laughing with the amount of psychical energy that has become free through the lifting of the inhibitory energy-charge; he is laughing away this amount, as it were' (143).

Freud's use of the pronoun 'he' in the above quotation is not a mere historical artefact; it reflects the strictly gendered terms of

The Best Medicine? Laughter in Feminist and Queer Politics 139

his theory of laughter. Freud tells numerous jokes to illustrate the psychic patterns and tendencies of 'the joke' in general, and they are often deeply misogynistic. A sampling:

> A physician, leaving a wife's sickbed, shakes his head and says to her husband accompanying him: 'I don't *like the look* of your wife.' 'I haven't *liked the look of her* for a long time', the husband hastens to agree. (28)

> According to one view, the husband is supposed to have *earned a lot* and so put *a bit on one side*, according to another, the wife is supposed to have been *a bit on the side* and *so to have earned a lot*. (30)

> The *Schadchen* [Jewish marriage-broker] is defending the girl he has proposed in face of the young man's objections. 'I don't like the mother-in-law', the young man says. 'She is a malicious, stupid person.' – 'You're not marrying the mother-in-law, you're marrying the daughter.' – 'Yes, but she's no longer so young, and she's not exactly pretty either.' – 'That doesn't matter. If she's not young and pretty, she'll be all the more faithful to you.' – 'There's not much money going, either.' – 'Who's talking about money? Are you marrying the money? It's a wife you want.' – 'But she's got a hump-back as well.' – 'Now what *are* you after? *So she's not to have one single fault?*'. (50)

Freud leaves readers with the distinct impression that joking is an activity enjoyed by men at the expense of women. It is likewise not surprising when, about halfway through the text, Freud argues that the 'bawdy talk' at the root of joking is '*in origin* directed at women' (92; italics added). It is to this claim that I direct my attention.

Freud contends that tendentious jokes – the kind of jokes that provoke truly 'irresistible', 'sudden outbursts' of laughter due to their content (or 'tendency') – fall into two categories: hostile and obscene (92).[10] A hostile joke reflects an act of aggression against an enemy, and the laughter it generates stems from a momentary relaxation of social rules against attacking others (97–8). The motivation behind an obscene (or 'dirty') joke, meanwhile, is sexual. An obscene joke reflects an attempt to 'strip someone naked' (92), and the laughter it produces stems from a momentary relaxation of social rules against discussing sexual matters (96–7). Despite these differences, Freud explains that both hostile and obscene jokes reflect aggressive attempts by the psyche to '*open up sources of pleasure that have become inaccessible*' due to social restrictions (98). In fact, obscene jokes appear to be a type of hostile joke, as Freud describes them as 'hostile', 'cruel' and 'sadistic' (94). However, Freud's insistence on discussing the more limited category of obscene jokes first leads one to suspect that the aggression characterising all tendentious joking is ultimately sexual in nature. This suspicion receives support when Freud classifies jokes about marital sexual frustration as hostile (106) and when he suggests the importance of obscene jokes to unpacking the psychological mechanisms of joking in general, writing that the obscene joke is 'a borderline kind of joke which promises to throw light on more than one dark point' (92).

Freud argues that the origin of obscene joking is the practice of 'bawdry' or 'bawdy talk' – that is, raunchy, 'dirty' talk directed at one's object of desire (92, 95). The subject who engages in bawdry achieves a degree of sexual satisfaction by publicly imagining a person of the opposite sex stripped naked: 'Bawdry is like an act of unclothing the person of different sex at whom it is directed. [. . .] There is no doubt that the pleasure in gazing on what is sexual revealed in its nakedness is the original motive of bawdy talk' (93). While bawdry pleases the speaker, it also advances the sexual aim by forcing the person targeted to imagine themselves stripped naked (93). Even if the target reacts with shame or hostility, such reactions amount to a tacit admission of their own arousal. When it comes to bawdy talk, for Freud, 'no' really does mean 'yes'. Bawdry

> is meant to make [the target] aware of this arousal by listening to the bawdry and so becoming sexually aroused themselves. Instead of being aroused, the person might also be made to feel shame or embarrassment, which only implies a reaction against their arousal and, in this roundabout way, an admission of it.[11] (92)

Freud claims that the enjoyment of bawdry is limited to those belonging to lower socio-economic classes, as the increased levels of repression that mark higher social strata restrict such open discussion of sexual matters (95). The wittiness introduced by the joke form refines bawdry such that its pleasures become acceptable in polite society: 'Only when we rise into more cultivated society do we find the addition of the formal requirements for jokes. The bawdry becomes witty, and is tolerated only if it is witty' (95).[12]

Freud contends that bawdy talk and obscene joking obey a strictly gendered economy. Men make, share and laugh at bawdry, while women are its targets: 'Bawdy talk, then, is in origin directed at women and is to be regarded as the equivalent of an attempt at seduction' (92).

A man employs bawdry to overcome or compensate for a woman's resistance to his sexual advances: 'the woman's intransigence, then, is the most immediate prerequisite for bawdry to develop' (94). In a section that recalls the testimony of Christine Blasey Ford, Freud depicts bawdry and obscene joking as a kind of homosocial ritual wherein men build solidarity with one another at the expense of a woman (Bird 1996; Rubin 1975; Sedgwick 1985). The ritual features three parties: a joke-teller (the man whose sexual desire is blocked), a target (the woman who has rebuffed him) and an audience (another man or group of men) (Freud 2003: 95). The joke-teller derives pleasure from creating and telling the joke (144), while the audience takes pleasure in the sexual images provided by the joke; they are 'laughing like a spectator at an act of sexual aggression' (93). The joke-teller builds solidarity with his audience by offering them the gift, as it were, of sexually satisfying images of the woman:

> [A]s the first person finds his satisfaction inhibited by the woman, his libidinal impulse develops a hostile tendency towards this second person and calls on the third, originally the intruder, to be his ally. The first person's bawdy talk strips the woman naked before the third, who is now, as listener, bribed – by the effortless satisfaction of his own libido. (95)

Laughter, in short, unites the male joke-teller and his audience against the woman targeted by the joke. If, as Freud suggests, tendentious jokes are originally obscene in nature, then the laughter they yield is originally *masculine* in character – that is, it constitutes a pleasure taken in the release of inhibitions against sexual access to women.

But there is a hiccup in Freud's argument. Shortly after introducing the key claim that 'bawdy talk, then, is in origin directed at women' (92), Freud appears gripped by uncertainty. Why does the aggressiveness of bawdry mean that it originates in men and targets women? Can women engage in bawdy talk or obscene joking at the expense of men? And why is bawdry always directed at a person of the opposite sex? What, in brief, does Freud's argument presuppose about male and female sexuality? 'It can only help to clarify matters if at this point we go back to fundamentals', Freud advises (93). When we return to the fundamentals of human sexuality, we find that 'the libido for looking and touching is of two kinds in everyone, active and passive, masculine and feminine, and develops in the one or the other direction according to which sexual character is predominant' (93). For Freud, the human libido, or sexual instinct, is originally bisexual – it contains both masculine ('active') and feminine ('passive') characteristics.[13] This is consistent with his position in *Three Essays on the Theory of Sexuality*, the landmark text on human sexual development published the same year as *The Joke* (Freud 2000: 7–14, 85–6). When Freud contends that the libido's status as masculine or feminine develops 'in the one or the other direction according to which sexual character is predominant', what does he mean by 'sexual character [*Geschlechtscharakter*]'? And how does this sexual character govern the activity of the libido within an economy of joking and laughter?

If we turn to the *Three Essays* for help with these questions, we are initially led into a corner. With the concept of 'sexual character', Freud means simply the libido's status as 'masculine' or 'feminine' (i.e., its tendency as active or passive). In the first essay's discussion of hermaphroditism, Freud notes that sexual character is distinct from anatomical sex:

> It is popularly believed that a human being is either a man or a woman. Science, however, knows of cases in which the sexual characters [*Geschlechtscharaktere*] are obscured, and in which it is consequently difficult to determine the sex. This arises in the first instance in the field of anatomy. [. . .] In every normal male or female individual, traces are found of the apparatus of the opposite sex. (Freud 2000: 7)

In the third essay, Freud associates sexual character with the tendency of one's libido. Before tracing the adolescent differentiation of the libido into its mature 'masculine' (active) or 'feminine' (passive) forms, he explains: 'As we all know, it is not until puberty that the sharp distinction is established between the masculine and feminine characters [*Charakters*]. From that time on, this contrast has a more decisive influence than any other upon the shaping of human life' (85). A 1915 footnote makes this connection between 'sexual character' and the libido's status as masculine or feminine even clearer:

> In human beings pure masculinity or femininity is not to be found either in a psychological or a biological sense. Every individual on the contrary displays a mixture of the character-traits [*Geschlechtscharakters*] belonging to his own and to the opposite sex; and he shows a combination of activity and passivity whether or not these last character-traits tally with his biological ones. (85–6n1)

If a subject's sexual character is identical to the tendency of their libido, then Freud's central claim in *The Joke* that 'the libido [. . .] develops in one or the other direction according to which sexual character is predominant' is a tautology: the sexual character develops in one or the other direction according to which sexual character is predominant. In light of this circularity, how do we account for the origin of a gendered economy of bawdry and obscene joking?

Freud suggests a way out of the impasse by explaining that the development of one's sexual character is shaped by social forces of repression that enter the picture during puberty. Puberty, he writes, 'is marked in girls by a fresh wave of *repression*' against the active, 'masculine' libido they originally share with boys (86). By 'repression', Freud is referring to Victorian moral codes enforced by schools, the family and the Church that prohibit girls from taking an interest or engaging in sexual activity. The adolescent girl 'holds herself back and [. . .] denies her sexuality' (87), leading to the emergence of both the mature feminine and masculine sexual characters. The girl's denial of her libido prepares the way for a transfer of sexual excitability from the clitoris to the vagina and the corresponding transformation of her libido from an 'active' to a 'passive' character: 'the fact that women change their leading erotogenic zone in this way, together with the wave of repression at puberty, which, as it were, puts aside their childish masculinity [. . .] are intimately related to the essence of femininity' (87; see also 101). Meanwhile, the reluctance of adolescent girls to indulge their sexual desires stimulates the development of the boy's libido such that it assumes its distinctively 'masculine' aggressiveness: 'the intensification of the brake upon sexuality brought about by pubertal repression in women serves as a stimulus to the libido in men and causes an increase of its activity' (87). For Freud, the 'masculine' and 'feminine' sexual characters that orient the economy of bawdry and obscene joking are products of the repressive forces that society levies on adolescent girls.

However, a key assumption of Freud's argument remains unexplained. If the development of sexual character stems from the repression of an originally masculine libido in girls, what accounts for the masculine quality of this pre-pubescent desire? Foucault famously identifies the belief that society regulates sexuality by restricting subjects' natural drives as 'the repressive hypothesis' (Foucault 1990: 10). According to Foucault and his followers like Judith Butler (1990), Ian Hacking (2004) and Arnold Davidson (2001), it is impossible to identify a form of desire – such as Freud's primordially 'masculine' libido – that exists prior to society's attempts to block or censor it. As Butler writes,

> prohibitions are invariably and inadvertently productive in the sense that 'the subject' who is supposed to be founded and produced in and through those prohibitions does not have access to a sexuality that is in some sense 'outside', 'before', or 'after' power itself. (Butler 1990: 29)

A society's repressive mechanisms construct and sustain the desires they claim to merely police: 'Dispositions are not the primary sexual facts of the psyche, but produced effects of a law imposed by culture' (64). Repressive measures – like those brought to bear on adolescent girls in Freud – conceal their political efficacy by positing the desires they help constitute as pre-social, pre-cultural, 'natural' dispositions in need of regulation (65).

If all of this is the case, then the 'originally' masculine libido identified by Freud is itself a creation of social forces of repression. In treating sexual aggressiveness as inappropriate for subjects whose bodies are marked 'female', the repressive forces that enter the scene during puberty *produce* a masculine libido that is recognised as the developmental norm from which the mature feminine sexual character deviates. The social construction of the libido thus does not, as Freud suggests, begin at some point during adolescence; as a product of repressive forces that are continuously operating in society, it is ongoing from the very earliest stages of childhood sexual development. Crucially, therefore, experiences through which the libido transgresses repressive codes are not as liberatory as they might at first appear. They instead presuppose and (re)produce the shape of desire constituted by those codes. As Foucault explains, 'We must not think that by saying yes to sex, one says no to power; on the contrary, one tracks along the course laid out by the general deployment of sexuality' (Foucault 1990: 157). Consequently, when we encounter an ostensibly emancipatory experience like laughter, the critical task is not, as Freud suggests, to trace how it 'makes the satisfaction of a drive possible [. . .] in face of an obstacle in its way' (Freud 2003: 96) or 'represents a rebellion against [. . .] authority, a liberation from the oppression it opposes' (100). The task is rather to determine how such an experience (re)produces the desire constituted by the prohibition it violates.

We should likewise conceive of the laughter generated by bawdy talk and obscene joking not as the satisfaction of a repressed sexual desire, but as constitutive of that desire itself. The parties to bawdy talk and obscene joking do not simply follow a pre-written script that assigns each person to a role 'according to which sexual character is predominant' (e.g., the men laugh together at a woman) (93). Instead, the laughter produced by these activities helps construct the masculine and feminine sexual characters in the first place. We catch glimpses of this political productivity of laughter at key junctures in *The Joke*. Pay attention in the following quote to how Freud describes laughter's effects on the character of sexual desire. Men, he writes, turn to obscene joking

> [f]irst, to lay claim to the woman, and second, because by summoning up the idea the words spoken may kindle the corresponding state of arousal in the woman herself and waken her inclination to passive exhibitionism. [. . .] For in a situation where the woman soon becomes willing, the obscene speech is short-lived, it promptly gives way to sexual action. It is different if the woman's willingness cannot be counted on, and a defensive reaction on her part makes its appearance instead. Then the sexually arousing speech becomes – in the form of bawdry – an end in itself; as the sexual aggression is checked in its advance towards the act, it lingers on the evocation of arousal and derives pleasure from signs of it in the woman. In doing so, the aggression probably also changes character, in the same way as every movement in the libido does when it meets an obstacle; it becomes plain hostile, cruel, that is, it calls on the sadistic components of the sexual drive for help against the obstacle. (94)

The experience of being the target of shared male laughter from bawdy talk constructs the quintessentially 'feminine' sexual character that finds satisfaction in 'passive exhibitionism' and in the choice between submission ('a situation where the woman soon becomes willing') or intransigence ('a defensive reaction'). Meanwhile, engaging in bawdy talk constructs a masculine libido that finds satisfaction in sexual aggression. As Freud explains, in 'lingering' on the response of the woman, the male subject's libido 'changes character' and becomes 'plain hostile, cruel' and increasingly 'sadistic'. The social (re)production of this masculine sexual character is bolstered by the collective nature of bawdry and obscene joking. The laughter yielded by these practices *produces* – rather than merely expresses – the sexual dichotomy identified by Freud: a defensive, intransigent, 'passive' femininity on the one hand and an aggressive, sadistic, 'active' masculinity on the other.

The answer to the question that troubled Freud – namely, why are bawdy talk and obscene joking in origin directed at women? – is now clear: because the laughter generated by these practices constructs libidos that work that way. The masculine libido has been shaped into an 'active', aggressive form and the feminine libido has been shaped into a 'passive', submissive form by laughter itself. Laughter does not express something 'natural' about the subject; it constructs the very idea of the subject having a nature. The first step towards repoliticising laughter for feminist and queer politics is recognising this capacity of laughter to create and sustain formations of sexual desire and gender identity. While laughter may indeed exert the subversive and emancipatory effects attributed to it by the feminist and queer discourse, Freud demonstrates that this is never simply or necessarily the case. Even at its most liberatory, laughter helps produce and entrench conventional conceptions of masculinity and femininity.

Several recent studies provide instructive models for how feminist and queer theory might attend to laughter's role in the social construction of sex and gender. Emily Douglas shows how laughter operates as both a source and site of disciplinary power shaping female subjectivities. 'The contemporary state of laughter practices works to uphold docile femininity', Douglas contends (Douglas 2015: 142). Meanwhile, Anna Hickey-Moody and Timothy Laurie argue that the custom of men laughing at one another over perceived failures of masculinity (e.g., physical weakness, emotional vulnerability, same-sex desire) 'is a form of mediated intimacy and collective identity building' that fuels 'hegemonic masculinity' (Hickey-Moody and Laurie 2017: 226). Finally, Sharon Lockyer and Heather Savigny (2020) demonstrate that rape jokes and media coverage of them are powerful vectors for the normalisation and legitimation of male sexual violence. The above rereading of Freud suggests that an appreciation of laughter's political productivity is essential for a critical feminist/queer account of gelopolitics.

III. *Pretty/Funny* and *Nanette*: Gelopolitics in a Hetero-patriarchal Social Order

If the first step in repoliticising laughter for feminist and queer politics is attending to how it constructs and sustains formations of gender identity and sexual desire, the second step is grasping its political function in a *social order* organised around those formations.

The Best Medicine? Laughter in Feminist and Queer Politics   147

This section considers two recent efforts to expose the political limits and dangers of even the most emancipatory laughter within the contemporary heteronormative and patriarchal – or 'hetero-patriarchal' – social order: Linda Mizejewski's 2014 book *Pretty/Funny: Women Comedians and Body Politics* and (ex-)comedian Hannah Gadsby's 2018 Netflix special *Nanette*. By 'hetero-patriarchal social order', I am referring to the form of social organisation structured around the notion that desire is naturally heterosexual and that cisgender males – due to the reason and strength attributed to them by the logic of heterosexuality – are fit to rule in a variety of realms (e.g., politics, business, the household) (Arvin, Tuck and Morrill 2013: 13). I begin with Mizejewski.

Pretty Funny? The Dialectic of Feminist/Queer Laughter

Linda Mizejewski's *Pretty/Funny* investigates the relationship between American female comedians and feminist politics in the early twenty-first century. According to Mizejewski, professional comedy in the United States has historically been governed by a logic of 'pretty versus funny': female performers can be 'pretty' or 'funny', but not both. Those considered 'pretty' (i.e., who appear young, slim, white, heterosexual and/or sexually available; Mizejewski 2014: 10, 23) may read comic lines or star alongside funny men, but they are not themselves sources of laughter (18–20). For example, Lucille Ball, Meg Ryan and Mila Kunis 'weren't known for their own wit but for their performances of witty comic scripts. Most of all they had to be pretty' (1). A pretty performer is the 'handmaid of laughter, not its creator' (Gray 1994: 21). On the other hand, 'funny' women (i.e., those who write and perform their own comedy) are not considered pretty. As Christopher Hitchens emits in his (in)famous 2007 'Why Women Aren't Funny' essay, women comics are usually 'hefty or dykey or Jewish, or some combo of the three' (Hitchens 2007). On this view, funny women exhibit masculine, 'un-ladylike' qualities such as being of a larger size or telling aggressive, crude jokes. Hitchens cites Roseanne Barr as an example of a funny – that is, not pretty – female comic (Hitchens 2007). Mizejewski argues that the 'body politics of comedy' in the United States are presumptively masculine: in order for a performer to be 'funny', they cannot be 'pretty' (i.e., feminine), and in order to be 'pretty', they cannot be 'funny' (i.e., masculine) (Mizejewski 2014: 15, 17). As Danielle Russell puts it, 'in "doing" comedian the woman ceases to "do" female' (Russell 2002). The hetero-patriarchal social order's imperative that subjects embody either a masculine or feminine gender functions in comedy as the imperative to be either funny or pretty.

Mizejewski contends that the generation of American female comedians that achieved celebrity status in the 2000s – Tina Fey, Sarah Silverman, Margaret Cho, Kathy Griffin, Ellen DeGeneres, among others – is distinctive for how it challenged the pretty/funny logic. Simply put, many of these comedians are both funny *and* pretty. Alessandra Stanley's 2008 rebuttal essay to Hitchens ('Who Says Women Aren't Funny?') was accompanied by a parodically glamorous Annie Leibovitz photoshoot of Fey, Silverman, Kristin Wiig, Maya Rudolph and Amy Poehler that sought to demonstrate that their funniness in no way detracts from their prettiness, and vice versa (Stanley 2008; Mizejewski 2014: 3). Mizejewski points to how DeGeneres serves as a model and spokeswoman for CoverGirl makeup (Mizejewski 2014: 28) and how the conventional physical attractiveness of comedians like Chelsea Handler, Olivia Munn and Whitney Cummings now counts as a professional asset: their 'sex appeal is intrinsic to their commercial appeal as comics' (3). There is no longer a trade-off between prettiness and funniness: 'pretty' female comedians succeed in getting laughs – even from raunchy and aggressive joke-telling – just like their male counterparts.

In light of these developments, one might assume that the pretty/funny logic has been overcome and that a comedian's success now depends solely on the quality of their performance. However, Mizejewski argues that what ultimately distinguishes the recent generation of female comedians is not their attractiveness but how they make traditional conceptions of femininity or 'prettiness' into objects of laughter. For example, Kathy Griffin's *My Life on the D List* lampoons conventional notions of female celebrity (26); Tina Fey's *30 Rock* pokes fun at consumerist feminisms (9–10, 26–7); and Ellen DeGeneres's daytime comedy explores the place of the lesbian body in American society (28). Because these comedians all produce laughter at the expense of conventional notions of femininity and 'prettiness', the pretty/funny logic actually has *not* been overcome; it has merely been displaced. The female comedian occupies the position of 'funny' in order to generate laughs at what counts as 'pretty':

> [I]n the historic binary of 'pretty' versus 'funny', women comics, *no matter what they look like*, have been located in opposition to 'pretty',

enabling them to engage in a transgressive comedy grounded in the female body [. . .]. In this strand of comedy, 'pretty' is the topic and target, the ideal that is exposed as funny. (5; italics added)

Instead of governing the distribution of bodies in the space of professional comedy, the pretty/funny logic now governs the relationship between these bodies and their targets of laughter. It remains impossible to be fully pretty and fully funny (i.e., to be both feminine and funny) at the same time. Prettiness must still be sacrificed to get a laugh. Mizejewski concludes that even the most ostensibly transgressive female comedy – that which produces laughter at patriarchal notions of sex and gender – obeys and reinscribes this sexist logic: 'the dynamic of stand-up performances by women often entails the male gaze even if the point is its subversion or elision' (14).

Mizejewski's analysis reveals that in the hetero-patriarchal social order, dominant conceptions of gender identity and sexual desire do not simply collapse in response to a feminist or queer/ing laughter. There persists a broader structural logic – pretty versus funny – within which such a subversive experience remains ensnarled. Generating laughter that undermines conventional notions of femininity and 'prettiness' entails temporarily occupying a masculine position that presupposes and sustains precisely those notions. As Mizejewski explains: 'the status of the female body itself – its visibility, availability, and presumed heterosexuality – is intrinsic to women's comedy even at its most transgressive' (19). To be clear, Mizejewski does not mean that the laughter produced by such comedy lacks *any* emancipatory efficacy. She acknowledges that 'when female comics hijack male space and the authority to be funny, they are also hijacking the cultural organization of heterosexuality itself' and 'once appropriate femininity becomes the site of satire or outrageous flippancy, the most basic assumptions about sex and gender are hilariously imperiled' (16). Yet these effects always unfold within the discursive structure that such laughter ostensibly resists.[14] A critical feminist/queer account of gelopolitics must attend to this dialectic. While it is possible for laughter to disrupt the hetero-patriarchal social order, such disruptions are always partial, contaminated and reversible. Rather than providing an escape from heteronormativity and patriarchy, laughter offers a way out that only ever brings one right back in (and out, and in) again. For Mizejewski, one is never on stable political ground with laughter.

Nanette: *Laughter as a Mere Sweetener*

Comedian Hannah Gadsby grapples directly with these structural constraints on feminist and queer/ing laughter in her award-winning 2018 Netflix special *Nanette*. An Australian comic who acknowledges that 'I get mistaken for a man quite a lot', Gadsby's career, at least until *Nanette*, obeyed the pretty/funny logic to a 't' (Gadsby 2018b). Gadsby used her distance from 'prettiness' to produce laughter about conventional notions of masculinity and femininity, in particular her experience coming out in the deeply conservative state of Tasmania (Burford 2018). While following this formula admitted Gadsby into the sphere of 'funny' people, she explains that she has recently been receiving a 'bit of negative feedback' from 'my people, the lesbians' who are upset that there is 'not enough lesbian content' in her act. There exists a belief, Gadsby suggests, that laughter at stand-up shows constitutes a radical (or at least progressive) experience through which audiences collectively resist and overcome a form of oppression (e.g., homophobia), even if only temporarily and in the space of the theatre. By selling an hour of laughs, the comic sells an hour of freedom. On this view, Gadsby is a comedic representative of the lesbian community, and she has a special responsibility to tell jokes with which 'her people' identify. Looking back at her earlier work, Gadsby lampoons this conception of the relationship between laughter, comedy and politics: 'I told lots of cool jokes about homophobia. Really solved that problem. Tick!'

Indeed, Gadsby worries that her comedy may not have been as politically radical as she at first thought. She explains that the self-deprecation that characterises so much of the stand-up genre misfires badly when practised by comics from historically oppressed groups:

> I built a career out of self-deprecating humor. That's what I've built my career on. And . . . I don't want to do that anymore. Because, do you understand . . . do you understand what self-deprecation means when it comes from somebody who already exists in the margins? It's not humility. It's humiliation.

Because the laughter Gadsby generated stemmed from a presentation of her identity as something odd, unusual and even abnormal, rather than subverting dominant notions of sex and gender, it functioned to affirm their validity. According to Gadsby, a fundamental asymmetry marks how laughter produced by self-deprecation operates politically when it is directed at subjects from dominant versus marginalised groups. In the former case, laughter exposes foibles and prompts self-questioning; in the latter, it entrenches conditions of subordination. As Gadsby puts it in a post-*Nanette* interview, 'The difference between Louis C.K. and I [sic] is that we can both say we're losers, and when I say it, the world goes, "Yeah, you are a bit," and when Louis does it, they go, "You're a genius!". And that was what pissed me off' (Gadsby 2018a). Gadsby fears that her comedy career hinges on sustaining a latent homophobia that marginalises herself and the lesbian 'community' she has been enlisted to represent.

Gadsby believes this problem can be traced back to the form of stand-up comedy itself. Joke-telling, she explains, is a technique of artificially creating and diffusing tension in an audience: 'Tension. I do that, that's my job. I make you all feel tense, and then I make you laugh, and you're like, "Thanks for that. I was feeling a bit tense"' (Gadsby 2018b). The imperative to generate laughs – that is, to relieve tension – requires that comics from marginalised groups distort the experiences that provide the content for their jokes. Gadsby illustrates these dynamics by telling a joke about a man who threatened her for flirting with his girlfriend:

> [O]ut of nowhere, he just comes up and starts shoving me, going, 'Fuck off, you fucking faggot!' And he goes, 'Keep away from my girlfriend, you fucking freak!' And she's just stepped in, going, 'Whoa, stop it! It's a girl!' And he's gone, 'Oh, sorry.' He said, 'Oh, I'm so sorry. I don't hit women', he said. What a guy! 'I don't hit women.' How about you don't hit anyone? Good rule of thumb.

Gadsby creates tension in the audience by suggesting she was in physical danger; she then relieves that tension by explaining how the misunderstanding was resolved. However, Gadsby soon reveals that this is not actually how the incident unfolded. After realising that Gadsby was a woman, the man assaulted her, saying 'You're a lady faggot. I'm allowed to beat the shit out of you'. Gadsby argues that it is these life experiences – being sexually assaulted as a child, beaten up as a teenager, and raped by two men as a young adult – that the joke form does not allow her to communicate: 'In order to balance the tension in the room with that story, I couldn't tell that story as it actually happened.' Tensions that are created and sustained by the very structure of society cannot be easily laughed away. Gadsby finds that the imperative to produce laughter prevents her and her audiences from confronting and coming to terms with the trauma inflicted by the hetero-patriarchal social order.

In this way, stand-up comedy fails to deliver the freedom that the genre's defenders insist is its distinctive feature. 'Comedy has suspended me in a perpetual state of adolescence', Gadsby confesses. 'What I had done, with that comedy show about coming out, was I froze an incredibly formative experience at its trauma point and I sealed it off into jokes.' Gadsby argues that what is socially and politically necessary today is not relieving tension but sharing and forcing a public reckoning with the stories responsible for those tensions in the first place:

> My story has value. [. . .] I will not allow my story . . . to be destroyed. What I would have done to have heard a story like mine. Not for blame. Not for reputation, not for money, not for power. But to feel less alone. To feel connected.

Gadsby's call for public storytelling resonates with Lynn Sanders's concept of 'testimony', or the practice of 'telling one's own story' that functions to 'open the possibility of reasonable, collective consideration of novel, if disquieting perspectives' (Sanders 1997: 372). Unlike the much-heralded democratic ideal of deliberation, testimony is unapologetically 'impassioned', 'extreme' and particularistic (370). As a form of testimony, Gadsby's performance forces her audience to listen to and acknowledge her story, and in doing so, it makes possible future deliberation that can actually hear her claims. From Gadsby's perspective, we need the difficult conversations prompted by truthful storytelling, not the easy laughs provided by stand-up comedy.

If we translate Gadsby's account of the politics of stand-up into the framework articulated by Mizejewski, we find that Gadsby occupies the position of 'funny' by telling self-deprecating jokes that obey and entrench the heteronormative and patriarchal logics governing the social order as a whole. What is 'other' about herself – her experience growing up as a lesbian in Tasmania – is not allowed to speak on its own terms. This part of her life remains a mute object of comic amusement – just like the 'pretty' female performers who are denied a comic voice of their own. While Mizejewski believes that the most recent generation of American female comedians reveals the possibility of chipping away at the pretty/funny logic from within, Gadsby is not as sanguine. She maintains that stand-up comedy that obeys the pretty/funny logic – which is more or less *all* stand-up comedy – necessarily entails a masculine perspective. In a November 2017

The Best Medicine? Laughter in Feminist and Queer Politics   153

tweet, Gadsby declares, 'I'LL SETTLE THIS: my show is NOT stand up comedy because i got jack of an art form designed by men for men' (Gadsby 2017). No matter how innovative, edgy or subversive a stand-up performance appears to be, in a hetero-patriarchal social order the laughter it creates feeds on and sustains the everyday traumas inflicted on women and gender 'not-normals' (Gadsby's term) (Gadsby 2018b). Gadsby refuses to participate in this politically toxic cycle any longer: 'I put myself down in order to speak, in order to seek permission . . . to speak. And I simply will not do that anymore. Not to myself or anybody who identifies with me.' 'I have to quit comedy', she resolves.

Gadsby pairs her structural critique of stand-up comedy with a historical one as well. She argues that the genre's reputation as subversive is entirely unearned when it comes to sexual politics. Woody Allen, Bill Cosby and Louis C.K. demonstrate that sexual violence is in the very DNA of stand-up:

> These men are not exceptions, they are the rule. And they are not individuals, they are our stories. And the moral of our story is, 'We don't give a shit. We don't give a fuck . . . about women or children. We only care about a man's reputation.'

The structural and historical entanglement of stand-up comedy with heteronormativity and patriarchy means that when what is needed is a reckoning with these forms of social organisation, we instead get 'throwaway jokes about priests being paedophiles and Trump grabbing the pussy'. By reducing accumulated tension and temporarily making audiences feel better, the laughter produced by such jokes forecloses any genuine confrontation with the hetero-patriarchal social structure at the root of that tension. As Gadsby reminds her audience, 'nobody here is leaving this room a better person. We're just rolling around in our own shit here'. In Gadsby's eyes, the conventional wisdom that laughter generated by stand-up – especially when it is performed by women or queer subjects – challenges entrenched formations of gender identity and sexual desire is merely an ideological rendering of this laughter's success at securing the hetero-patriarchal social order at its most vulnerable points.

The irony of Gadsby's attack on stand-up and announcement that she is leaving the genre is, of course, that both unfold within what is billed as and initially appears to be a stand-up comedy show. This raises an obvious and, for us, crucial question: does Gadsby believe that laughter is irredeemably bound up with heteronormativity and patriarchy? Can laughter serve *any* role in resisting these structures of domination? While Gadsby refuses to celebrate laughter for its supposed emancipatory power, she does not jettison it altogether. Gadsby instead *downgrades* laughter, characterising it as a mere technique subjects can employ when sharing their stories in public: 'Laughter is not our medicine. Stories hold our cure. Laughter is just the honey that sweetens the bitter medicine.' The last few minutes of *Nanette* suggest what this approach looks like. Gadsby delivers a searing monologue that situates the homophobia and misogyny she has experienced in her life and career within the context of the histories of art and stand-up comedy. Gadsby punctuates the story with a few brief laugh lines that ease – but do not relieve – the considerable tension that accumulates in the theatre. She concludes by declaring that the show will not end, as is customary, with a big cathartic punchline. Gadsby is done using laughter to diffuse the tension that the hetero-patriarchal social order has created and shouldered her with: 'This tension, it's yours. I am not helping you anymore. You need to learn what this feels like.' The medicine of honest, public storytelling is bitter, and laughter does nothing more – or less – than help get it down.[15]

Gadsby's conception of laughter as a mere sweetener – and not, as Willett et al. claim, 'just the medicine for what ails us in our social norms' (Willett, Willett and Sherman 2012: 239) – suggests a strategy for repoliticising laughter beyond the terms of the dialectic identified by herself and Mizejewski. Unlike laughter produced by so-called feminist or queer comedy that creates the illusion of an escape from heteronormativity and patriarchy, laughter that plays a merely supporting role in practices of public testimony facilitates a reckoning with the terms of life in the hetero-patriarchal social order. By deflating laughter's liberatory power and reinserting it into the field of politics itself, Gadsby's approach paradoxically unlocks new emancipatory potentialities for it. Gadsby introduces yet another dialectic to the feminist/queer study of gelopolitics: laughter's capacity to resist the hetero-patriarchal social order hinges on the extent to which it eschews a central role in this struggle. On the margins, laughter can assist in a confrontation with prevailing formations of gender identity and sexual desire, but at the heart of such a project, laughter risks becoming depoliticised and inadvertently bolstering these same formations. For Gadsby, an attention to laughter's structural and historical entanglement with heteronormativity and patriarchy motivates a measured and strategic – and for that reason,

The Best Medicine? Laughter in Feminist and Queer Politics   155

more productive – grappling with the perils and possibilities it presents for feminist and queer politics.

IV. A Critical Feminist/Queer Account of Gelopolitics

The previous chapter explored how race constitutes an essential concept in a critical theory of laughter and, conversely, how such a critical theory can illuminate laughter's role in contemporary racial politics. This chapter has performed a similar analysis by demonstrating how it is impossible to theorise laughter critically without an attention to sex and gender and how a critical theory of laughter reveals the dangers and opportunities laughter poses for feminist and queer politics today. My central claim has been that the feminist and queer discourse of laughter that began with Hélène Cixous's 'The Laugh of the Medusa' is unable to fully account for how laughter operates politically in the hetero-patriarchal social order. In particular, this discourse's conception of laughter as an intrinsically emancipatory experience obscures how laughter also functions to produce and entrench conventional notions of gender identity and sexual desire. Laughter's liminal position with respect to *logos* does not make it a political cure for patriarchy and heteronormativity; it makes it a crucial site of political contestation over sex and gender itself. Freud's *The Joke*, Mizejewski's *Pretty/Funny* and Gadsby's *Nanette* all illustrate how laughter is a key experience/event in and through which the hetero-patriarchal social order produces, sustains and transforms itself politically. As the joyfully irreverent laughter celebrated by Cixous; the drunken laughter of sexual violation haunting Christine Blasey Ford; and the tentative, uncomfortable laughter of Hannah Gadsby's audience all evince, laughter exercises a perhaps unparalleled capacity to shape and reshape sex and gender politics in contemporary society. It is the task of a critical feminist/queer account of gelopolitics to grasp and grapple with these opportunities and dangers of laughter in all of their contradictory complexity.

Notes

1. See, for instance, cases where onlookers laughed as a group of men raped and beat a California teenager at school (Greene 2009); Ohio teenagers were filmed joking and laughing about an alleged rape of a 16-year-old girl (Dahl 2013); cellphone video showed three Canadian teenagers laughing while they raped a young woman (Grant 2018);

members of a Maryland high school football team laughed as younger players were sodomised by brooms in a hazing ritual (Lewis 2018); and three Swedish men laughed during a gang rape that was live-streamed on Facebook (*The Local* 2017).
2. Indeed, a recent anthology of #MeToo essays, fiction and poetry titled itself *Indelible in the Hippocampus* after Ford's testimony (Oria 2019).
3. My linking of 'feminist' and 'queer' with a slash or 'and' may ruffle a few feathers. Indeed, queer theory is typically understood as marking a break with the traditional feminist commitment to 'women' as the subject of anti-patriarchal politics. However, as I show below, the queer appropriation of laughter in the 1990s by Judith Butler and others represents an extension of, rather than break with, the mode of theorising laughter initiated by feminist scholars (Hélène Cixous, Luce Irigaray and Julia Kristeva) in the 1970s and 1980s. While the latter group privileges the concept of the 'feminine', they use this notion to challenge and deconstruct (i.e., to *queer*) conventional conceptions of masculinity and femininity. The term 'feminist' in this chapter likewise refers to thinkers who, by way of their accounts of laughter, largely anticipate the theoretical innovations made by queer theorists. So while there certainly are crucial differences between feminist and queer theory writ large, when it comes to the thinkers considered here, the two traditions are actually not that far apart. The repoliticised feminist/queer account of laughter I articulate in Sections II and III follows Butler in conceiving of feminism as a project oriented towards queering conventional sex and gender norms and subject positions.
4. Two pre-Cixous feminist accounts of laughter deserve mention. First, Simone de Beauvoir makes the giggling of adolescent girls a minor theme in *The Second Sex*: 'High school girls and shopgirls burst into laughter while recounting love or risqué stories, while talking about their flirtations, meeting men, or seeing lovers kiss' (Beauvoir 2011: 365). What makes Beauvoir's account of laughter different from the discourse inaugurated by Cixous, however, is that she understands this 'silly' and occasionally 'hysterical' laughter as the expression of an immature political consciousness rather than the wellspring of a viable radical feminism. Beauvoir laments that the laughing girl 'does not accept the destiny nature and society assign to her; and yet she does not actively repudiate it: she is too internally divided to enter into combat with the world' (365). Second, French philosopher Annie Leclerc's untranslated (except for excerpts) 1974 book *Parole de Femme* (2007) discusses laughter in terms that resonate strongly with those employed a year later by Cixous. For example: 'Laughter, an immense and delicious sensual pleasure, wholly sensuous pleasure . . . I said to my sister, or she said to me, come over, shall we play laughter? [. . .] Laughable laughter. Laughter so laughable it made us laugh. Then it came,

real laughter, total laughter, taking us into its immense tide. Bursts of repeated, rushing, unleashed laughter, magnificent laughter, sumptuous and mad.... And we laugh our laughter to the infinity of laughter.... O laughter! Laughter of sensual pleasure, sensual pleasure of laughter; to laugh is to live profoundly' (Kundera 1999: 79). Or: 'Therefore I say (nothing will stop me): man's value has no value. My best proof: the laughter that takes hold of me when I observe him in those very areas where he wishes to be distinguished. And that is also my best weapon' (Gill 1980: 79). Leclerc may rightfully claim to be the 'first' to theorise laughter as the source of a radical feminist politics, but it was Cixous's essay that thematised the issue explicitly and inspired and informed several generations of feminist and queer theory. I consequently take her work to be this discourse's point of departure.

5. Cixous's concept of 'economy' can be traced to two main sources: Jacques Derrida's 1967 essay 'From Restricted to General Economy' (Derrida 1978) and Jean-François Lyotard's 1974 book *Libidinal Economy* (Lyotard 1993). The former is especially important for our purposes. For Cixous, Derrida's Hegel- and Bataille-inspired distinction between a 'restricted economy', or system that extracts value or meaning from the elements that compose it (e.g., capitalism, philosophy, psychoanalysis), and a 'general economy', or the non-significative, playful proliferation of differences within which all restricted economies operate, *is* the difference between masculinity and femininity. Restricted economies obey the 'masculine' logic of order, hierarchy and mastery, while a general economy embodies the inexhaustible power of the 'feminine' that disrupts this logic. As we will see, Cixous's *écriture féminine* deconstructs the two poles of the masculine economy – 'man' and 'woman' – in the same way imagined by Derrida's concept of 'sovereign writing' (Derrida 1978: 265).

6. Cixous and Irigaray would almost certainly object to this line of criticism. For them, the feminine is precisely that which resists all totalising and essentialising (i.e., all phallogocentrism). Cixous writes: '*defining* a feminine practice of writing is impossible with an impossibility that will continue; for this practice will never be able to be *theorised*, enclosed, coded, which does not mean it does not exist' (Cixous and Clément 1986: 92). Irigaray, meanwhile, claims that 'the feminine cannot signify itself in any proper meaning, proper name, or concept, not even that of woman. [. . .] [S]peaking of (a) woman underlines both the external position of the feminine with respect to the laws of discursivity' (Irigaray 1985: 156).

7. Davis does not take Butler's objections to Irigaray seriously enough here. Butler questions whether it is possible, as Irigaray proposes, 'to identify a monolithic as well as a monologic masculinist economy [i.e., phallogocentrism] that traverses the array of cultural and historical

contexts in which sexual difference takes place' (Butler 1990: 13; brackets added). Davis appears to interpret Butler's critique of Irigaray – and *Gender Trouble*'s broader deconstruction of the female subject – as an attempt to root out any remaining traces of phallogocentrism in feminist theory and to, as it were, complete the critique of phallogocentrism. But this interpretation overlooks the novelty of Butler's approach. Butler eschews abstract philosophising about sex and gender (no matter how radical and open-ended) in favour of a genealogical analysis of the concrete, regulatory practices – the 'surface politics of the body' – that produce certain types of subjectivities, identities and desires (135). Thus even while Butler's 'theory', as Davis shows, is broadly comprehensible in the terms of the critique of phallogocentrism begun by Cixous and Irigaray, Butler refuses to theorise in those terms. Butler finds that such an approach obscures more than it illuminates about the polyvalent construction of and resistance to sex and gender and, for the reasons described earlier, ultimately entrenches phallogocentrism. In other words, Butler believes that defeating phallogocentrism requires leaving behind the feminist philosophical discourse of phallogocentrism.
8. See, for instance, work by Regina Barreca (1988, 1991), Jacques Derrida (1979: 54–63), Frances Gray (1994), Jack Halberstam (2012), Jo Anna Isaak (1996), Julia Kristeva (1980, 1984), Jean-Luc Nancy (1993: 368–92), Anca Parvulescu (2010), Lisa Perfetti (2003), Kathleen Rowe (1995) and Cynthia Willett and Julie Willett (2019).
9. At first glance, *The Joke* appears to be primarily about jokes (their psychological origin, formal structure and social effects) and only secondarily about laughter. But as Samuel Weber remarks about Freud, 'to comprehend the joke theoretically, therefore, is to address the problem of laughter' (Weber 1987: 695). Because the 'jokiness' of a joke – what makes it *really* a joke – is its ability to generate the pleasure of laughter ('Joking [. . .] is an activity whose aim it is to obtain pleasure from psychical processes'; Freud 2003: 91) and 'explosive laughter [. . .] is the sign of a good joke'; 69), Freud's study of jokes is, in the final analysis, a study of laughter.
10. At the end of the book's third chapter, Freud introduces two additional types of tendentious jokes: cynical and sceptical jokes (Freud 2003: 110–11).
11. Freud's account of bawdry captures the logic of contemporary catcalling. Blocked from achieving the sexual aim, the catcaller seeks the substitute satisfaction of forcing his object of desire to listen to his sexual intentions. Catcalling is a win–win for the catcaller: either the woman accedes to his announced desires, or her hostility or indifference provides the substitute satisfaction of revealing that she 'secretly likes (or wants) it' (see also Bartky 1990: 27).

12. Freud here identifies *class* as yet another social hierarchy (in addition to race and sex/gender) that shapes and is in turn shaped by laughter. Just as a patriarchal society constructs and maintains itself by distinguishing between the mere *phōnē* of women's laughter and the complex interplay of *phōnē* and *logos* in men's laughter, a classed society constructs and maintains itself by distinguishing between the unsophisticated laughter yielded by the bawdy talk of the poor and the refined, polite laughter generated by the witty jokes of the wealthy.
13. For Freud, 'masculine' and 'feminine' describe tendencies of the libido, not anatomical, physiological or hormonal features (Freud 2000: 80n2, 82n1, 85–6n1).
14. Mizejewski thus recalls Butler's point about laughter's ambivalent relation to the 'damning law' (Butler 1990: 104) and Davis's reminder about laughter's 'place *within* the constraints of established citational boundaries' (Davis 2000: 40).
15. Gadsby has since backed down from her vow to leave comedy, and in 2020 she released a new Netflix special, *Douglas*. Gadsby explains in a *New York Times* interview, 'Quitting was always a theatrical device, and I'm delighted everyone took it so seriously. But that theatrical device, as I relived trauma night after night, felt really good to say it and mean it. I think I meant it and still mean it in the sense of the strictest definition of what comedy is – yeah, I've quit that' (Arditi 2019). Gadsby 'quits' stand-up again in *Douglas* by deconstructing the genre in new ways. For instance, she opens the show by offering a detailed preview of the jokes she will tell, thus undermining the standard set-up/punchline structure; she repeatedly breaks the fourth wall with facetious tips to the audience on how to react to her jokes (e.g., 'feel, but don't invest'); and she experiments by giving a 'lecture' that showcases the differences between her comedic style and 'lecturing' (a criticism levelled against *Nanette*) as well as the comedic possibilities of lecturing as a genre (Gadsby 2020). The challenge faced by Gadsby after *Nanette* – one that *Douglas* indicates she takes quite seriously – is to produce enough laughter to qualify as stand-up, but not so much laughter that her shows become *merely* stand-up.

The End of Laughter?
Gelopolitics and the New Agelasty

> We laugh at such simplicity as does not yet know how to dissemble, and yet we also rejoice in the natural simplicity here thwarting that art of dissimulation. We were expecting the usual custom, the artificial utterance carefully aimed at creating a beautiful illusion – and lo! there is uncorrupted, innocent nature, which we did not at all expect to find [. . .]. Here the beautiful, but false illusion, which usually has great significance in our judgment, is suddenly transformed into nothing, so that, as it were, the rogue within ourselves is exposed; and this is what agitates the mind alternately in two opposite directions, and is what also gives the body a wholesome shaking.
>
> Immanuel Kant, *Critique of Judgment* (1987: 206)

Immanuel Kant offers a surprisingly Nietzschean account of laughter in §54 of the *Critique of Judgment*. The discovery of innocence and simplicity where one expected to find a 'beautiful, but false illusion' ignites a pleasurable discordance within and between the mind's faculties and the body's organs through which 'the rogue within ourselves is exposed'. Laughter lays bare a previously hidden side of the subject – a roguish side refreshingly naive of the Kantian distinctions between the imagination, reason and the understanding; judgement and affect; duty and inclination. While Kant worries about the threat this rogue poses to the subject's rational and moral vocation (202–3), he also illuminates laughter as an experience that 'makes reason think more' (183; Giamario 2017) or that prompts reason to freely revise its ideas in response to the contingencies of empirical existence. In the playful, roguish self-transcendence sparked by laughter, the Kantian subject becomes, for a moment at least, a kind of Nietzschean free spirit.

Recent developments in gelopolitics suggest we ought to consider a darker and more troubling interpretation of Kant's account, however.

The End of Laughter? Gelopolitics and the New Agelasty

The rise in reactionary deployments of laughter – for example, the emergence of insult comedy as presidential speech (Webber 2019b; Wolcott 2015); Internet trolling as political discourse (Forestal 2017; Greene 2019; Lieback 2019); 'owning the libs' as a policymaking principle (Perticone 2018; Scocca 2019); 'parodic' celebrations of violence against journalists (Harwell and Romm 2019); and the pretence of 'just joking' to excuse these activities – indicate that the 'rogue within ourselves' exposed by laughter may not be a Nietzschean free spirit but rather a Trumpian neofascist. As Gilles Deleuze explains, only a minuscule distance separates these opposed political potentialities: 'fascism is constructed on an intense line of flight, which it transforms into a line of pure destruction and abolition' (Deleuze and Guattari 2011: 230). The question of whether the momentary suspension of sense in laughter facilitates an overcoming of *logos* – i.e., a making reason think more, as Kant and Nietzsche suggest – or a ruthless reinscription of *logos* – i.e., a doubling down on the terms of existing reason, as achieved by neofascist humour – is freshly urgent today.

Popular and scholarly discourse has taken a decidedly agelastic turn in response to this renewed uncertainty around gelopolitics. The decades-long celebration of laughter by liberal and Nietzschean thinkers has given way to widespread anxiety about laughter's role in the *polis*. (Hannah Gadsby's *Nanette* was one example of this anxiety.) Animating the discourse I am calling the 'new agelasty' is a sense that we have reached *the end of laughter* – that we have arrived at a point where arguments about laughter's centrality to a liberal polity geared towards the discovery of truth or a Nietzschean politics aimed at transforming what counts as true are no longer compelling. Does laughter still have a future in politics? Or has laughter, to invoke Bruno Latour's question about critique, 'run out of steam'? (Latour 2004).

This book closes by considering how the critical theory of laughter developed and deployed in the preceding chapters illuminates and responds to this latest question of laughter. I explore the new agelasty of Emily Nussbaum, Ken Jennings and Nidesh Lawtoo – three thinkers who are nostalgic for an (imagined) past when laughter's limited role in the *polis* ensured that it exerted emancipatory rather than oppressive effects. By longing for the re-establishment of these limits on laughter, the new agelasty – like all a/gelastic political theory – fails to grasp how the *polis* it aims to secure is itself constituted and sustained by laughter. I conclude that those seeking to resist reactionary deployments of laughter should abandon the illusory and ultimately counterproductive goal of erecting boundaries between laughter and the *polis* and should instead engage laughter as a site of political contestation replete with democratic opportunity and fascistic danger.

Laughter and Liberal Nostalgia

Emily Nussbaum's January 2017 *New Yorker* essay 'How Jokes Won the Election' grapples with the implications of Donald Trump's 2016 presidential campaign for the liberal discourse of gelopolitics. Writing in the period between Trump's election and inauguration, Nussbaum reassesses her long-held belief that laughter exposes and defeats reactionary political figures: 'I had the impression that jokes, like Woody Guthrie's guitar, were a machine that killed fascists' (Nussbaum 2017: 1). Just like Shaftesbury and his followers, Nussbaum viewed laughter, truth and freedom as naturally promoting and reinforcing each other. 'Jokes', she writes, 'were a superior way to tell the truth – that meant freedom for everyone' (1). However, Nussbaum's faith in laughter was tested when Trump made humour a centrepiece of his campaign (1). Trump's jokes about Hillary Clinton, other Republicans, disabled people, immigrants and others granted his supporters the thrill of violating the rules of 'political correctness' without any of the social costs associated with doing so in a non-comedic register. Trump weaponised laughter's suspension of *logos* to obscure and excuse the reactionary displacement of *logos* it enacted. 'On TV and on Twitter', Nussbaum writes, 'his jokes let him say the unspeakable and get away with it' (2). (This only became more the case over the course of the Trump presidency, as he used the joke form to excuse incitements of police violence, accusations of treason against Democrats and orders to slow COVID-19 testing.) The 2016 election revealed to Nussbaum that laughter can just as easily contribute to neofascist politics as defend against it.

Nussbaum argues that this reactionary appropriation of laughter puts liberals in a bind: 'How do you fight an enemy who's just kidding?' (1). On the one hand, continuing to laugh at right-wing politicians as if nothing has changed is irresponsible because it sustains a light-hearted atmosphere that provides cover for reactionary humour. Such an approach is inattentive to 'how quickly a liberating joke could corkscrew into a weapon' (5). As Adorno showed us, there is nothing safe about laughing at fascists. But on the other hand, failing to laugh at these figures legitimises them as 'serious' political actors and surrenders a powerful weapon to them. It also confirms right-wing claims about liberal humourlessness (which, as we saw in Chapter 4, often do double duty as claims about women's humourlessness). For Nussbaum, once laughter has lost its necessary connection to truth and freedom, 'every path [. . .] leads to humiliation' (7).

The end of laughter does not pose a mere tactical dilemma for liberals, however. If laughter – supposedly the truth-producing experience par excellence – cannot be trusted to enlighten and liberate, how can a liberal political order that identifies truthful speech as the source of human freedom survive at all? When fascists begin to laugh just as much as liberals, it becomes impossible to distinguish true from false discourse; serious discussion from 'just joking'; *logos* from *phōnē*. As Nussbaum explains, Trump and his troll army's 'quasi-comical memeing and name-calling was so destabilising, flipping between serious and silly, that it warped the boundaries of discourse' (6). Under these conditions, the 'overlapping consensus' that ensures the stability of a liberal polity (Rawls 1996: 133–72) gives way to a discursive free-for-all where unreasonable – i.e., racist, sexist and xenophobic – speech is not only tolerated but solicited and savoured as such. In 2016, the effect was that 'the distinction between a Nazi and someone pretending to be a Nazi for "lulz" had become a blur' (Nussbaum 2017: 1). Nussbaum fears that by undermining the foundational distinction between *logos* and *phōnē*, the end of laughter portends the end of liberalism as a viable governing philosophy.

Nussbaum does not have any easy answers for the crisis in liberal gelopolitics. 'Knowing what's wrong doesn't mean you know how to escape it', she confesses (8). A polity unmoored from *logos* has lost the means to rescue itself. Nussbaum's new agelasty thus amounts to nostalgia for a time when politics was not yet gelopolitics – that is, for when laughter's distance and difference from serious political discourse allowed it to effectively regulate that discourse. In Nussbaum's idyll, laughter is like a benevolent nightwatchman, securing the freedom of the *polis* by keeping out treacherous falsehoods. Today, however, laughter more closely resembles a band of rogue cops, fomenting unrest by legitimating untruths.

Planet Laughter

The new agelasty of Ken Jennings – yes, he of *Jeopardy!* fame – takes a broader view than Nussbaum. Jennings's 2018 book *Planet Funny: How Comedy Took Over Our Culture* explores how laughter has colonised nearly every aspect of early twenty-first-century social, cultural and political life. '*Everything* is getting funnier', Jennings argues. 'Today [. . .] our god is not strength or efficiency or even innovation, but funny' (Jennings 2018: 3–4). Jennings traces, for example, how comedians have supplanted academics as public intellectuals (7); advertising has traded earnestness for irony and absurdism (89–99); wittiness has replaced anger as the genre of protest signs (231); airlines have revamped staid safety presentations into self-mocking videos (107–8); and yoga has become 'laughter yoga' (21). All the while, streaming stand-up shows and comedy podcasts explode in popularity (117–27); companies contrive 'fun' office environments to increase productivity (135); and Twitter operates as a 'real time joke factory of pitiless efficiency' for ordinary citizens to hone their comedic skills (100). The imperative on Planet Funny, Jennings contends, is to extract the maximum amount of laughter from everything: 'The world that has been delivered to us now seems to have the goal of packing in as many laughs into every second of the day as possible' (21).

Jennings believes that while this laughter 'arms race' (262) has made comedy 'faster, weirder, more complex, more self-aware than ever before' (26), such gains have come at a steep moral and political cost. The endless pursuit of laughs heightens one's sensitivity to even the slightest flaws in others and erodes one's moral shame in exploiting them for humour. '[B]eing funny is not making me a better person', Jennings confesses (270). Meanwhile, when politics becomes the object of incessant laughter – as *The Daily Show*, *Saturday Night Live* and Twitter memes have made it – and is itself practised through laughter – for example, Obama's appearance on *Between Two Ferns* and Trump's insult comedy – citizens find it difficult to believe that any political issue or cause is actually worth taking seriously. Jennings writes that 'we're learning to laugh at problems instead of solving them, or self-medicating with jokes so we don't have to face ominous facts' (268). The end result of this refusal to take a non-ironic stance on anything is the rise of dangerously vacuous and cynical political leaders like Trump, Johnson and Bolsonaro. 'When we finally voted in the showman whose candidacy had seemed the funniest, no one felt much like laughing at all', he laments (229).

Jennings responds to these moral and political crises on Planet Funny by calling for the *polis*'s partial insulation from laughter. '[L]et's keep some part of the public sphere laughter-optional, so that serious engagement and earnest emotion don't become completely taboo', he advises (274). From Jennings's perspective, both *gelōs* and the *polis* are best served when their interactions are strictly regulated. Establishing a 'laughter-optional' sector of the public sphere preserves the possibility of (a) virtuous attitudes and behaviour uninfected by the imperative to make jokes; (b) non-ironic political discourse and action; (c) meaningful and effective political satire and humour (i.e., '*principled* irony'; 182); and (d) the enjoyment of non-political laughter without fear of it enabling reactionary humour. Restoring laughter to its proper place in the *polis* ensures that it exerts only positive moral and political effects. Jennings likewise insists that he does not oppose laughter, only its misuse: 'I come to praise comedy, not to bury it' (273). For Jennings, preventing the end of laughter requires refusing to treat laughter as our only end.

Whereas Nussbaum mourns the loss of limits on laughter, Jennings calls for reinstating them. It is on this point that Nussbaum's account, though narrower and more tentative than Jennings's, is ultimately more perceptive. Nussbaum understands that appeals to insulate a part of the *polis* from laughter misapprehend the magnitude of the contemporary crisis. If laughter has colonised as much of social, cultural and political life as Jennings claims, how can we determine where to draw the line between the *polis* and laughter? Once laughter has discredited everything, there no longer exists a 'serious', 'earnest', 'principled' sphere to which one can simply retreat. While Nussbaum's prescription of nostalgia may be a mere palliative, unlike Jennings's proposed remedy, it at least grasps the nature of the disease at hand.

The Pathology of Laughing Too Much

Scholarship on laughter, comedy and humour has also grown markedly more agelastic in the last several years. For example, political theorist Julie Webber's 2019 edited volume *The Joke is On Us* (2019a) studies the laughter produced by Trump-era political satire as a means by which neoliberal governmentality exercises and secures its rule. Meanwhile, the essays comprising Krista Giappone, Fred Francis and Iain MacKenzie's 2018 volume *Comedy and Critical Thought: Laughter as Resistance* are, despite the book's title, actually quite sceptical about laughter's critical power. As the editors ask about contemporary political comedians, 'are these comic voices genuinely effective in their critique, or does, perhaps, humour act as a mask for a platform deliberately antithetical to the philosophical project of critique?' (Giappone, Francis and MacKenzie 2018: 10). And although two recent texts I have already cited – Nicholas Holm's *Humour as*

Politics (2017) and Alfie Bown's *In the Event of Laughter* (2019) – depart from the new agelasty in key ways, they share this discourse's suspicions about laughter's salutary political effects.

I would like to examine one particularly sophisticated scholarly example of the new agelasty. Nidesh Lawtoo's 2019 essay 'The Powers of Mimesis: Simulation, Encounters, Comic Fascism' explores the 'genealogical link' (Lawtoo 2019: 722) between the critical study of mimesis and William Connolly's pluralist and anti-fascist political theory. Mimesis, Lawtoo explains, refers to the immanent powers of imitation flowing beneath the level of consciousness that generate affective bonds between human and non-human bodies (723–5). Lawtoo considers whether contemporary satirical news programmes like *The Daily Show* mobilise powers of mimesis to combat neofascism (a topic of shared interest to himself and Connolly; Connolly and Lawtoo 2017). Lawtoo argues that, on the one hand, these shows expose the lies of right-wing politicians in such a way that helps build anti-fascist affective communities. He writes:

> [P]rofessional mimes like comedians who host satirical television news programs [. . .] play an increasingly important role not only in unmasking lies and in identifying new symptoms of fascist behavior at the level of content, but also in re-enacting the powers of mimesis within a formal genre that triggers positive forms of mimetic communication that culminate in healthy and liberating laughter. (Lawtoo 2019: 736)

Although satirists 'provide a daily antidote to a sick(ening) politics' (736), Lawtoo worries that, on the other hand, the pleasures of laughter risk generating a perverse affective attachment to this very same politics. Because 'pleasure generates an attraction, a desire, and thus a demand, perhaps even an *addiction* for what triggers pleasure in the first place', these programmes 'might also unwittingly contribute to creating an infectious spiral of human, all-too-human dependency on the kinds of political pathologies they denounce at the level of the message' (739–40). Such a pathological laughter, while not immediately reactionary like that generated by Trumpian humour, is nevertheless complicit with the latter by fostering affective communities devoted to the mere ridicule – rather than defeat – of neofascism. Lawtoo finds that although Trump-era satirists oppose reactionary politics on the level of *message*, on the level of *medium*, they inadvertently fuel a 'comic fascism' (735).

Lawtoo believes that the danger of comic fascism stems from how satirical news programmes blur the distinction between news and entertainment (737). When the serious and the comedic become discursively indistinguishable from one another – as it does, for instance, for someone whose primary news source is Stephen Colbert (Martin, Kaye and Harmon 2018) – what begins as a 'healthy and liberating laughter' that exposes lies and builds affective solidarity devolves into a 'pathological' laughter that takes pleasure in the reactionary politics it ostensibly opposes (Lawtoo 2019: 736). Lawtoo contends that the political-ethical imperative under such conditions is to restrict one's laughter to the 'right moments' and 'right dosages' (740). Laughter that is enjoyed prudently preserves the critical distance between its subject and object, while unregulated laughter collapses this distance such that the subject becomes complicit with their object. Lawtoo explains that

> it is only in homeopathic doses that the powers of mimesis have positive and noble [. . .] effects; in massive doses they might easily contribute to the problem they appear to simply represent by re-*producing* a chain of hyper-mimetic contagion that generates pathological mirroring effects. (740)

For Lawtoo, laughter's mimetic powers must be wielded wisely: whereas the deliberate, tactical deployment of laughter can undermine neofascist political assemblages, the unrestrained enjoyment of laughter risks empowering them even further. 'The diagnostic value of comedy has everything to do with time – and timing', he concludes (737).

Although the discourse of mimesis – with its emphasis on affective flows, contagion and simulacra – would seem to preclude the possibility of securing the *polis* from a mimetically charged experience like laughter, this is precisely what Lawtoo presents as an ethical-political imperative. Laughter that arises at the 'right moments' and in the 'right dosages and genres' (740) is 'healthy' and 'noble' (741) and has a place in the *polis*, while laughter that overflows these limits is 'sick' and 'base' (741) such that it 'infect[s] the body politic' (735). Lawtoo's agelastic political theory is more theoretically advanced and explicitly political than Jennings's, but its prescription is ultimately the same: police *gelōs* in order to secure the *polis* from the dangers of gelopolitics.[1] Lawtoo and Jennings imagine a *polis* where citizens laugh less, and for that reason, laugh better.

The theorists of the new agelasty are all reluctant, even embarrassed agelasts. Theirs is a discourse that is surprised and discomfited by its own existence. Nussbaum had always counted on laughter as liberalism's secret weapon against fascism; Jennings had always enjoyed laughter as an incentive for deeper, quicker and more critical engagement with the world; and Lawtoo had discovered in laughter a Dionysian affect that activates the powers of mimesis like few others. Yet for all these past and would-be gelasts, laughter has gone too far. The saturation of social, cultural and political life by laughter has blurred the basic distinctions between true and false, news and comedy, fascist and anti-fascist that are necessary for it to exert emancipatory rather than reactionary effects. The new agelasts do not seek to eliminate laughter from the *polis*; they merely seek to restore its proper role. In their view, only laughter that arises in the right places and at the right times can effectively check oppressive political power. The solution to the end of laughter as they knew and loved it is to bring gelopolitics – or the contemporary Age of Hilarity where politics proceeds in and through laughter – to an end.

Laughter as Politics has sought to demonstrate the impossibility of this task. *Politics has always been gelopolitics*. If humans are political animals due to their possession of *logos*, then laughter – as an experience/event that arises at the intersection of *logos* and *phōnē* – does not merely affect the *polis*; it constitutes the *polis*. All a/gelastic political theory – even the reluctant, minimalist new agelasty of Nussbaum, Jennings and Lawtoo – hinges on the illusion that it is possible to separate laughter from the political life within which it arises and whose bounds and contours it shapes. There is not, never was and never will be a sphere of 'serious', non-ironic, 'real news' discourse within which laughter makes only an occasional, salutary intervention because laughter helps determine what counts as 'serious' discourse in the first place. No *polis* exists apart from the *gelōs* that constitutes it; all there is is gelopolitics. The task today is neither to mourn the loss of a non-gelopolitical life that never existed nor to chase after one that necessarily remains out of reach. Instead of asking 'what role should laughter play in politics?' we must ask 'how does laughter itself operate politically, and what are the political dangers and opportunities it presents?'

The book's first two chapters on Hobbes and Adorno developed a theoretical framework for answering this question. Hobbes's conception of laughter as a groundless feeling of superiority that is nevertheless taken seriously by others means that it obeys a political logic of counter/sovereignty. Laughter undermines sovereign authority only by reinscribing it anew, and it bolsters sovereign authority only by dramatising the latter's vulnerability to challenge. A source of neither anarchy nor peace in the *polis*, laughter is an experience/event through which the *polis*'s very sovereign structure (i.e., a particular distribution of *logos* and *phōnē*) is made, undone and made again. Meanwhile, Adorno demonstrates how laughter always arises and exerts effects within a broader social order. Adorno uncovers the social logic of gelopolitics: laughter entrenches structures of social power only by prompting the imagination of alternative forms of social organisation, and it resists structures of social power only when it bears their violence within itself. Adorno understands laughter as neither a straightforward tool of nor threat to a broken social order, but as a site of social non-identity replete with fascistic danger and emancipatory opportunity. Taken together, Hobbes and Adorno articulate a discourse of gelopolitics that is irreducible to a/gelasty – a critical theory that grasps laughter as a privileged site of politics wherein the contemporary social order produces, sustains and transforms itself.

The book's next two chapters further articulated this critical theory of laughter by investigating laughter's relation to two of the social order's most important and entrenched political structures: race and sex/gender. The laughing barrel joke recounted by Ellison illustrates how the American racial order produces and sustains itself by policing the laughter of Black subjects. Ellison theorises Black laughter as an intensely dialectical site of politics: neither the 'irrational', 'primitive' force imagined by white supremacy nor the intrinsically liberatory force envisioned by many Black thinkers, the sounds, styles and tonalities of Black laughter bear the marks of a history of oppression and democratise the white supremacist social order by 'antagonistically cooperating' with it. Recent feminist and queer theory features a similar conflict between essentialising and dialectical approaches to gelopolitics. Despite the success of Cixous, Irigaray, Gorris, Willett and others in challenging men's historical monopoly on laughter, their view that laughter is a naturally anti-patriarchal and anti-heteronormative experience obscures its role in the production, enforcement and transformation of a wide range of gender identities and modes of sexual desire. The work of Butler, Freud, Mizejewski and Gadsby reveals that laughter is neither the nemesis nor ally of feminist and queer politics but rather a uniquely efficacious site of political contestation over sex and gender in the contemporary social order.

By refusing to conceive of laughter as naturally aligned with either sovereignty or counter-sovereignty (Hobbes); social power or resistance (Adorno); white supremacy or democracy (Ellison); heteropatriarchy or feminist/queer politics (Butler, Mizejewski, Gadsby), the critical theory of laughter articulated and practised over the course of this book has challenged the depoliticisations of laughter at the heart of a/gelastic political theory. Laughter is depoliticised when its valence as either emancipatory or reactionary is imagined to be a *natural* characteristic that merits either allowing or prohibiting it in the *polis*. For instance, the new agelasty holds that it is in the nature of laughter to be helpful to the *polis* in limited doses but detrimental when left unregulated. Depoliticised accounts of laughter identify the nature of laughter as exogenous to the *polis* in which it arises, circulates and exerts effects. *Laughter as Politics* rejects this move. Laughter does not have a 'nature'; it is an experience/event through which what counts as 'nature' emerges and entrenches itself. Laughter is a product of the *polis* that it in turn helps shape, sustain and transform. From the perspective of this relentlessly politicised account of laughter, the traditional a/gelastic question about laughter's proper role in the *polis* quite simply makes no sense.

The core problem with the new agelasty is not only that the depoliticisation of laughter it pursues is impossible to achieve (because politics has always been gelopolitics); it is that even trying to do so undermines its stated goal of resisting neofascism. Attempts to insulate the *polis* from laughter would have the effect of blocking the politicisations of both laughter and the *polis* that are necessary to combat neofascist politics. For example, when Lawtoo advocates protecting 'a serious and informed political context' (Lawtoo 2019: 738) from the 'pathological mirroring effects' of laughter (740), he neglects the possibility that what counts as a 'serious' and 'informed' political context is precisely what is pathological today. Instead of approaching the contemporary imbrications of politics and laughter as an opportunity for revisiting and revising the prevailing terms of seriousness (i.e., what counts as *logos* versus *phōnē*), Lawtoo works to shore up these terms. Conversely, his prescription of 'homeopathic doses' of laughter overlooks the anti-fascist possibilities incipient in so-called 'pathological' laughter (740). If the problem with the latter form of laughter is that it reproduces 'a chain of hypermimetic contagion' (740), then there is no guarantee that its effects will *always* or *only* be reactionary. As he writes, 'Dionysian contagion is fundamentally Janus-faced for it can be put to both fascist and anti-fascist uses' (735). We have seen throughout this book that even the most reactionary laughter is never *simply* reactionary; as a site of social non-identity, it often gives rise to surprisingly emancipatory effects. Such anti-fascist redeployments of laughter are foreclosed by

Lawtoo's reduction of gelopolitics to a matter of 'right moments' and 'right dosages' (740). The new agelasty, in sum, overlooks the irreducible entanglement of politics and laughter, and in promoting their disentanglement, shields both from much-needed examination and challenge. It likewise fails as both an analysis of and response to neofascist deployments of laughter today.

By dramatising the political dangers and opportunities of the current moment, the dizzying intensification of gelopolitics in recent years indicates a *polis* that is freshly uncertain about how to govern itself.[2] The neoliberal consensus that ruled in hegemonic fashion from the mid-1970s to the mid-2010s is collapsing under the enormous strain of its own failures and crises, and new right- and left-wing political projects are springing up out of the wreckage (Brown 2019; Fraser 2019). When confronted with the enormous quantity and variety of laughter generated in and around this conjuncture, the task for theory is not to prop up teetering institutions and ideologies, but to *dwell in* and *engage* this laughter as an experience/event through which new political institutions and ideologies can be thought and fought either for or against. This book has found in laughter not a *source* of social transformation and emancipation, but an unusually fecund *site* of political struggle and contestation that makes such transformation and emancipation possible. Despite the new agelasty's fear that we have reached the end of the road with laughter – that it has nothing left to offer us besides a *jouissance* that is mindless at best and fascistic at worst – this is true only if we follow this discourse's advice and aim to bring gelopolitics to an end. That the 'rogue within ourselves' exposed by laughter might be a fascist is not an argument for limiting laughter; it is an argument for harnessing laughter's inexhaustible political energy on behalf of projects that are resolutely democratic and anti-fascist in ambition.

Notes

1. The new agelasty reveals just how porous the liberal and Nietzschean discourses of gelopolitics have become to one another in recent years. For instance, Emily Nussbaum's liberal critique of Trumpian laughter highlights how the latter reshapes the prevailing discursive terrain (a classic Nietzschean insight), while Lawtoo's Nietzschean critique of satirical television programmes calls for securing the *polis* so that laughter can exert its proper truth-producing function (a traditional liberal goal). Confronted with the challenges posed by neofascist

laughter, the liberal and Nietzschean discourses turn to one another to remedy their respective blind spots. Their failures dramatise the need for the approach articulated over the course of this book – a critical theory of laughter that does not view laughter as merely affecting or affected by the *polis* but as a site of politics in its own right.

2. In a sense, the prediction made by Dominic Boyer and Alexei Yurchak in their influential 2010 article 'American Stiob' – namely that the prevalence of satire that parodically over-identifies with hegemonic modes of discourse (*stiob*, in Russian) signals and contributes to a dangerous breakdown in political order – appears to be coming to fruition (Boyer and Yurchak 2010).

References

Adorno, Theodor W. 1969. 'Society'. Translated by Fredric Jameson. *Salmagundi* 10/11: 144–53.
Adorno, Theodor W. 1973. *Negative Dialectics*. Translated by E. B. Ashton. New York: Continuum.
Adorno, Theodor W. 1974. 'Commitment'. *New Left Review* 87–8: 75–89.
Adorno, Theodor W. 1976. 'On the Logic of the Social Sciences', in Glyn Adley and David Frisby (trans.), *The Positivist Dispute in German Sociology*. London: Heinemann Educational Books, 105–22.
Adorno, Theodor W. 1977. 'The Actuality of Philosophy'. *Telos* 31: 120–33.
Adorno, Theodor W. 1991a. 'The Essay as Form', in Rolf Tiedemann (ed.), *Notes to Literature, Volume 1*. New York: Columbia University Press, 3–23.
Adorno, Theodor W. 1991b. 'Trying to Understand *Endgame*', in Rolf Tiedemann (ed.), *Notes to Literature, Volume 1*. New York: Columbia University Press, 241–75.
Adorno, Theodor W. 1992. 'Is Art Lighthearted?', in Rolf Tiedemann (ed.), *Notes to Literature, Volume 2*. New York: Columbia University Press, 247–53.
Adorno, Theodor W. 1996. 'Chaplin Times Two'. Translated by John MacKay. *The Yale Journal of Criticism* 9.1: 57–61.
Adorno, Theodor W. 1997. *Aesthetic Theory*. Translated by Robert Hullot-Kentor. Minneapolis: University of Minnesota Press.
Adorno, Theodor W. 1999. '47: Wiesengrund-Adorno to Benjamin, London 1936', in Henri Lonitz (ed.) and Nicholas Walter (trans.), *Theodor W. Adorno and Walter Benjamin: The Complete Correspondence 1928–1940*. Cambridge, MA: Harvard University Press, 127–34.
Adorno, Theodor W. 2000. *Introduction to Sociology*. Translated by Edmund Jephcott. Oxford: Polity Press.
Adorno, Theodor W. 2002a. 'On Jazz', in Richard Leppert (ed.), *Essays on Music*. Berkeley: University of California Press, 470–95.

Adorno, Theodor W. 2002b. 'On the Fetish-Character in Music and the Regression of Listening', in Richard Leppert (ed.), *Essays on Music*. Berkeley: University of California Press, 288–317.

Adorno, Theodor W. 2005a. 'Critique', in Henry Pickford (trans.), *Critical Models: Interventions and Catchwords*. New York: Columbia University Press, 281–8.

Adorno, Theodor W. 2005b. 'Marginalia to Theory and Praxis', in Henry Pickford (trans.), *Critical Models: Interventions and Catchwords*. New York: Columbia University Press, 259–78.

Adorno, Theodor W. 2005c. *Minima Moralia: Reflections from Damaged Life*. Translated by E. F. N. Jephcott. London: Verso.

Adorno, Theodor W. 2005d. 'Notes on Philosophical Thinking', in Henry Pickford (trans.), *Critical Models: Interventions and Catchwords*. New York: Columbia University Press, 127–34.

Adorno, Theodor W. 2005e. 'On Subject and Object', in Henry Pickford (trans.), *Critical Models: Interventions and Catchwords*. New York: Columbia University Press, 245–58.

Adorno, Theodor W. 2005f. 'The Meaning of Working Through the Past', in Henry Pickford (trans.), *Critical Models: Interventions and Catchwords*. New York: Columbia University Press, 89–104.

Ahmed, Sara. 2004a. 'Affective Economies'. *Social Text* 22.2: 117–39.

Ahmed, Sara. 2004b. *The Cultural Politics of Emotion*. New York: Routledge.

Allen, Danielle. 2004a. 'Ralph Ellison on the Tragi-Comedy of Citizenship', in Lucas E. Morel (ed.), *Ralph Ellison and the Raft of Hope: A Political Companion to* Invisible Man. Lexington: The University Press of Kentucky, 37–57.

Allen, Danielle. 2004b. *Talking to Strangers: Anxieties of Citizenship since Brown v. Board of Education*. Chicago: University of Chicago Press.

Almond, Steve. 2019. 'Stephen Colbert and *Saturday Night Live*'s Mockery only Makes Trump Stronger'. *Los Angeles Times*, 10 February. https://www.latimes.com/opinion/op-ed/la-oe-almond-how-comics-support-trump-20190210-story.html (accessed 20 July 2021).

Althusser, Louis. 2005. *For Marx*. Translated by Ben Brewster. London: Verso.

Alvarez, Lizette. 2010. 'Stretch: Laughter Yoga, Serious Benefits'. *The New York Times*, 21 August. http://goo.gl/catQR (accessed 20 July 2021).

Anderson, Luvell. 2015. 'Racist Humor'. *Philosophy Compass* 10.8: 501–9.

Anderson, Luvell. 2020. 'Why so Serious? An Inquiry on Racist Jokes'. *Journal of Social Philosophy*. doi: 10.1111/josp.12384.

AP. 2019. 'NY School Denies That Girls Were Strip Searched'. *FOX5 DC*, 25 January. https://www.fox5dc.com/news/ny-school-denies-that-girls-were-strip-searched (accessed 20 July 2021).

Appelbaum, David. 1990. *Voice*. Albany: State University of New York Press.
Arditi, Sara. 2019. 'Hannah Gadsby to Return to New York With "Douglas"'. *The New York Times*, 8 April. https://www.nytimes.com/2019/04/08/arts/television/hannah-gadsby-douglas-american-tour.html (accessed 20 July 2021).
Aristotle. 1996. *The Politics and The Constitution of Athens*. Edited by Stephen Everson. Cambridge: Cambridge University Press.
Aristotle. 2001. *On the Parts of Animals*. Translated by James Lennox. Oxford: Clarendon Press.
Arnold, Jeremy. 2009. 'Laughter, Judgment, and Democratic Politics'. *Culture, Theory and Critique* 50.1: 7–21.
Arvin, Maile, Eve Tuck and Angie Morrill. 2013. 'Decolonizing Feminism: Challenging Connections between Settler Colonialism and Heteropatriarchy'. *Feminist Formations* 25.1: 8–34.
Attardo, Salvatore, ed. 2014. *Encyclopedia of Humor Studies*. Los Angeles: SAGE.
Badiou, Alain. 2005. *Being and Event*. Translated by Oliver Feltham. London: Continuum.
Badiou, Alain. 2007. 'The Event in Deleuze'. Translated by Jon Roffe. *Parrhesia* 2: 37–44.
Bakhtin, Mikhail. 1984. *Rabelais and His World*. Translated by Helene Iswolsky. Bloomington: Indiana University Press.
Balapurwala, Tasneem. 2015. 'Five Global Versions of *The Daily Show*'. *The Economic Times*, 14 August. https://economictimes.indiatimes.com/magazines/panache/five-global-versions-of-the-daily-show/articleshow/48478153.cms (accessed 20 July 2021).
Barker, Colin. 2001. 'Fear, Laughter, and Collective Power: The Making of Solidarity at the Lenin Shipyard in Gdansk, Poland, August 1980', in Jeff Goodwin, James M. Jasper and Francesca Polletta (eds), *Passionate Politics: Emotions and Social Movements*. Chicago: University of Chicago Press, 175–94.
Barreca, Regina, ed. 1988. *Last Laughs: Perspectives on Women and Comedy*. New York: Gordan and Breach.
Barreca, Regina. 1991. *They Used to Call Me Snow White . . . But I Drifted*. New York: Viking.
Bartky, Sandra Lee. 1990. *Femininity and Domination: Studies in the Phenomenology of Oppression*. New York: Routledge.
Basu, Sammy. 1999. 'Dialogic Ethics and the Virtue of Humor'. *Journal of Political Philosophy* 7.4: 378–403.
Bataille, Georges. 2001a. 'Aphorism for the "System"', in Stuart Kendall (ed.), *The Unfinished System of Nonknowledge*. Translated by Michelle Kendall and Stuart Kendall. Minneapolis: University of Minnesota Press, 153–82.

Bataille, Georges. 2001b. 'Nonknowledge, Laughter, and Tears', in Stuart Kendall (ed.), *The Unfinished System of Nonknowledge*. Translated by Michelle Kendall and Stuart Kendall. Minneapolis: University of Minnesota Press, 133–50.

Baumgartner, Jody C. and Amy Becker, eds. 2018. *Political Humor in a Changing Media Landscape*. London: Lexington Books.

Baumgartner, Jody C. and Jonathan S. Morris. 2006. 'The Daily Show Effect: Candidate Evaluations, Efficacy, and American Youth'. *American Politics Research* 34.3: 341–67.

Baumgartner, Jody C. and Jonathan S. Morris. 2008. *Laughing Matters: Humor and Politics in the Media Age*. New York: Routledge.

Baumgartner, Jody C. and Jonathan S. Morris. 2011. 'The 2008 Presidential Primaries and Differential Effects of "The Daily Show" and "The Colbert Report" on Young Adults'. *Midsouth Political Science Review* 12: 87–102.

Baumgartner, Jody, Jonathan S. Morris and Natasha L. Walth. 2012. 'The Fey Effect: Young Adults, Political Humor, and Perceptions of Sarah Palin in the 2008 Presidential Election Campaign'. *Public Opinion Quarterly* 76.1: 95–104.

Beard, Mary. 2014. *Laughter in Ancient Rome*. Oakland: University of California Press.

Beauvoir, Simone de. 2011. *The Second Sex*. Translated by Constance Borde and Sheila Malovany-Chevallier. New York: Vintage.

Becker, Amy B. and Leticia Bode. 2018. 'Satire as a Source for Learning? The Differential Impact of News Versus Satire Exposure on Net Neutrality Knowledge Gain'. *Information, Communication & Society* 21.4: 612–25.

Beckett, Samuel. 1978. *Endgame: A Play in One Act*. New York: Grove Press.

Bell, Jamel Santa Cruze and Ronald L. Jackson II. 2014. *Interpreting Tyler Perry*. New York: Routledge.

Benhabib, Seyla. 1986. *Critique, Norm, and Utopia*. New York: Columbia University Press.

Benjamin, Rich. 2017. '*Get Out* and the Death of White Racial Innocence'. *The New Yorker*, 27 March. https://www.newyorker.com/culture/culture-desk/get-out-and-the-death-of-white-racial-innocence (accessed 20 July 2021).

Benjamin, Walter. 2002. 'The Work of Art in the Age of Its Technological Reproducibility (Second Version)', in Michael W. Jennings (ed.), *Selected Writings*. Vol. 3, *1935–1938*. Cambridge, MA: Belknap, 101–33.

Benjamin, Walter. 2007. 'The Author as Producer', in Peter Demetz (ed.), *Reflections: Essays, Aphorisms, Autobiographical Writings*. Translated by Edmund Jephcott. New York: Schocken Books, 220–38.

Bennington, Geoffrey. 2009. 'Political Animals'. *Diacritics* 39.2: 21–35.

Bercaw, Nancy and Ayla M. Amon. 2016. Personal communication with scholars at National Museum of African American History and Culture, 6 July.

Bergson, Henri. 1999. *Laughter: An Essay on the Meaning of the Comic*. Translated by Cloudesley Shovell and Henry Brereton. København: Green Integer.

Berlant, Lauren and Sianne Ngai. 2017. 'Comedy Has Issues'. *Critical Inquiry* 43.2: 233–49.

Berlatsky, Noah. 2020. 'Fascists Know How to Turn Mockery into Power'. *Foreign Policy*, 20 August. https://foreignpolicy.com/2020/08/20/fascists-know-how-to-turn-mockery-into-power/ (accessed 20 July 2021).

Biard, Gérard. 2015. 'Charlie Hebdo Editorial: Will There Continue to be "yes, but?"'. *CNN*, 15 January. https://goo.gl/qZqTas (accessed 20 July 2021).

Billig, Michael. 2005. *Laughter and Ridicule: Towards a Social Critique of Humour*. London: SAGE.

Bird, Sharon R. 1996. 'Welcome to the Men's Club: Homosociality and the Maintenance of Hegemonic Masculinity'. *Gender & Society* 10.2: 120–32.

Black, Zachariah. 2020. 'Laughing with Leviathan: Hobbesian Laughter in Theory and Practice'. *Political Theory*. doi: 10.1177/0090591720952056.

Boonin-Vail, David. 1994. *Thomas Hobbes and the Science of Moral Virtue*. Cambridge: Cambridge University Press.

Boskin, Joseph. 1986. *Sambo: The Rise & Demise of an American Jester*. New York: Oxford University Press.

Bown, Alfie. 2019. *In the Event of Laughter: Psychoanalysis, Literature and Comedy*. New York: Bloomsbury.

Boyer, Dominic and Alexei Yurchak. 2010. 'American Stiob: Or, What Late-Socialist Aesthetics of Parody Reveal about Contemporary Political Culture in the West'. *Cultural Anthropology* 25.2: 179–221.

Brand, Russell and Jeremy Paxman. 2013. 'Paxman vs Russell Brand: Full Interview'. BBC. YouTube. https://www.youtube.com/watch?v=3YR4CseY9pk (accessed 20 July 2021).

Brown, Sterling A. 2000. *The Collected Poems of Sterling A. Brown*. Edited by Michael S. Harper. Evanston, IL: TriQuarterly Books.

Brown, Wendy. 2019. *In the Ruins of Neoliberalism: The Rise of Antidemocratic Politics in the West*. New York: Columbia University Press.

Bruner, M. Lane. 2005. 'Carnivalesque Protest and the Humorless State'. *Text and Performance Quarterly* 25.2: 136–55.

Buck-Morss, Susan. 1977. *The Origin of Negative Dialectics*. New York: Free Press.

Bunch, Sonny. 2017. 'I promise: It's Okay to Laugh at Trump – and Ourselves.' *The Washington Post*, 8 November. https://www.washingtonpost.

com/news/act-four/wp/2017/11/08/i-promise-its-okay-to-laugh-at-trump-and-ourselves/ (accessed 20 July 2021).

Burford, Corinna. 2018. 'A Guide to Hannah Gadsby's Pre-*Nanette* Work'. *Vulture*, 28 June. https://www.vulture.com/2018/06/a-guide-to-hannah-gadsbys-pre-nanette-work.html (accessed 20 July 2021).

Burrell, Jalylah. 2020. '"We Always Somebody Else": Inherited Roles and Innovative Strategies in Black Women's Stand-Up Comedy'. *WSQ: Women's Studies Quarterly* 48.1–2: 182–98.

Bussie, Jacqueline. 2007. *The Laughter of the Oppressed: Ethical and Theological Resistance in Wiesal, Morrison, and Endo*. New York: T&T Clark.

Butler, Judith. 1990. *Gender Trouble: Feminism and the Subversion of Identity*. New York: Routledge.

Cao, Xiaoxia. 2010. 'Hearing It from Jon Stewart: The Impact of *The Daily Show* on Public Attentiveness to Politics'. *International Journal of Public Opinion Research* 22.1: 26–46.

Cardoso, Joana Amaral. 2009. 'Gato Fedorento em versão Daily Show entram na campanha eleitoral'. *Público*, 9 September. http://www.publico.pt/temas/jornal/gato-fedorento-em-versao-daily-show--entram-na-campanha-eleitoral-17754273 (accessed 20 July 2021).

Carpio, Glenda. 2008. *Laughing Fit to Kill: Black Humor in the Fictions of Slavery*. New York: Oxford University Press.

Chait, Jonathan. 2015. '*Charlie Hebdo* and the Right to Commit Blasphemy'. *New York*, 7 January. http://nymag.com/daily/intelligencer/2015/01/charlie-hebdo-and-the-right-to-commit-blasphemy.html (accessed 20 July 2021).

Chakrabortty, Aditya. 2019. 'This Milkshake Spring Isn't Political Violence – It's Political Theatre'. *The Guardian*, 21 May. https://www.theguardian.com/commentisfree/2019/may/21/far-right-milkshake-nigel-farage-tommy-robinson (accessed 20 July 2021).

Chambers, Samuel A. 2003. *Untimely Politics*. New York: New York University Press.

Chambers, Samuel A. 2014. *Bearing Society in Mind: Theories and Politics of the Social Formation*. Lanham, MD: Rowman & Littlefield.

Chambers, Samuel A. 2018. 'Undoing Neoliberalism: Homo Œconomicus, Homo Politicus, and the Zōon Politikon'. *Critical Inquiry* 44.4: 706–32.

Chappell, Bill. 2019. 'Ukraine's Comedian President Takes Office, Says He's Dissolving Parliament'. *NPR*, 20 May. https://www.npr.org/2019/05/20/724961911/ukraines-comedian-president-takes-office-says-he-s-dissolving-parliament (accessed 20 July 2021).

Chappelle, Dave. 2006. 'Chappelle's Story'. *The Oprah Winfrey Show*, 3 February. http://www.oprah.com/oprahshow/chappelles-story/all (accessed 20 July 2021).

Chasar, Mike. 2008. 'The Sounds of Black Laughter and the Harlem Renaissance: Claude McKay, Sterling Brown, Langston Hughes'. *American Literature* 80.1: 57–81.

Chokshi, Niraj. 2016. 'The 100-plus Times Donald Trump Assured Us that America is a Laughingstock'. *The Washington Post*, 27 January. http://goo.gl/x1Kpdv (accessed 20 July 2021).

Christofaro, Beatrice. 2019. 'The President of Brazil Slams Carnival and Tweets an Explicit Video after South America's Biggest Street Party Made Him a Laughing Stock'. *Insider*, 6 March. https://www.insider.com/brazil-jair-bolsonaro-war-on-carnaval-after-protests-2019-3 (accessed 20 July 2021).

Churchwell, Sarah. 2020. 'American Fascism: It Has Happened Here'. *The New York Review of Books*, 22 June. https://www.nybooks.com/daily/2020/06/22/american-fascism-it-has-happened-here/ (accessed 20 July 2021).

Cixous, Hélène. 1976. 'The Laugh of the Medusa'. Translated by Keith Cohen and Paula Cohen. *Signs* 1.4: 875–93.

Cixous, Hélène. 1981. 'Castration or Decapitation?' Translated by Annette Kuhn. *Signs* 7.1: 41–55.

Cixous, Hélène and Catherine Clément. 1986. 'Sorties: Out and Out: Attacks/Ways Out/Forays', in *The Newly Born Woman*. Translated by Betsy Wing. Minneapolis: University of Minnesota Press. 63–132.

Classen, Albrecht, ed. 2010. *Laughter in the Middle Ages and Early Modern Times*. Berlin: Walter de Gruyter.

Coates, Ta-Nehisi. 2015. *Between the World and Me*. New York: Spiegel & Grau.

Cohen, Joshua. 2003. 'Deliberation and Democratic Legitimacy', in Derek Matravers and Jon Pike (eds), *Debates in Contemporary Political Philosophy: An Anthology*. London: Routledge, 342–60.

Congreve, William. 1964. 'Concerning Humour in Comedy', in Paul Lauter (ed.), *Theories of Comedy*. Garden City, NY: Doubleday.

Connolly, William E. 1993. *Political Theory and Modernity*. Ithaca, NY: Cornell University Press.

Connolly, William E. 2002. *Identity\Difference: Democratic Negotiations of Political Paradox*. Ithaca, NY: Cornell University Press.

Connolly, William E. 2017. *Aspirational Fascism: The Struggle for Multifaceted Democracy under Trumpism*. Minneapolis: University of Minnesota Press.

Connolly, William E. and Nidesh Lawtoo. 2017. 'Rhetoric, Fascism and the Planetary: A Conversation between William Connolly and Nidesh Lawtoo'. *The Contemporary Condition*. http://contemporarycondition.blogspot.com/2017/07/rhetoric-fascism-and-planetary.html (accessed 20 July 2021).

Conway, Daniel W. and John Seery. 1992. *The Politics of Irony: Essays in Self-Betrayal*. New York: St. Martin's Press.

Cosgrove-Mather, Bootie. 2004. 'Young Get News from Comedy Central'. *CBS*, 1 March. http://www.cbsnews.com/news/young-get-news-from-comedy-central/ (accessed 20 July 2021).

Coulson, Shea. 2007. 'Funnier Than Unhappiness: Adorno and the Art of Laughter'. *New German Critique* 100: 141–63.

Cousins, Norman. 1976. 'Anatomy of an Illness (As Perceived by the Patient)'. *The New England Journal of Medicine* 295.26: 1458–63.

Critchley, Simon. 2002. *On Humour*. London: Routledge.

Dahl, Julie. 2013. 'Video Depicts Teens Laughing About Alleged Sexual Assault Victim: "She is so raped right now"'. *CBS*, 8 January. https://www.cbsnews.com/news/video-depicts-teens-laughing-about-alleged-sexual-assault-victim-she-is-so-raped-right-now/ (accessed 20 July 2021).

Daly, Mary. 1990. *Gyn/ecology: The Metaethics of Radical Feminism*. Boston, MA: Beacon Press.

Davidson, Arnold I. 2001. *The Emergence of Sexuality: Historical Epistemology and the Formation of Concepts*. Cambridge, MA: Harvard University Press.

Davis, D. Diane. 2000. *Breaking Up [at] Totality: A Rhetoric of Laughter*. Carbondale, IL: Southern Illinois University Press.

Davis, Jessica Milner, ed. 2017. *Satire and Politics: The Interplay of Heritage and Practice*. Sydney: Palgrave Macmillan.

Deleuze, Gilles. 1987. 'Leibniz and the Baroque'. *The Deleuze Seminars*. https://deleuze.cla.purdue.edu/seminars/leibniz-and-baroque/lecture-12 (accessed 20 July 2021).

Deleuze, Gilles. 1990. *The Logic of Sense*. Translated by Mark Lester. Edited by Constantin V. Boundas. New York: Columbia University Press.

Deleuze, Gilles and Félix Guattari. 1986. *Kafka: Toward a Minor Literature*. Translated by Dana Polan. Minneapolis: University of Minnesota Press.

Deleuze, Gilles and Félix Guattari. 2011. *A Thousand Plateaus: Capitalism and Schizophrenia*. Translated by Brian Massumi. Minneapolis: University of Minnesota Press.

Deloria, Jr, Vine. 1988. *Custer Died for Your Sins: An Indian Manifesto*. Norman, OK: University of Oklahoma Press.

Derrida, Jacques. 1978. 'From Restricted to General Economy: A Hegelianism Without Reserve', in *Writing and Difference*. Translated by Alan Bass. Chicago: University of Chicago Press, 251–77.

Derrida, Jacques. 1979. *Spurs / Éperons*. Chicago: University of Chicago Press.

Descartes, René. 1989. *The Passions of the Soul*. Translated by Stephen Voss. Indianapolis: Hackett.

Desta, Yohana. 2017. 'Is *Get Out* Really a Comedy? Don't Ask Jordan Peele'. *Vanity Fair*, 16 November. https://www.vanityfair.com/hollywood/2017/11/jordan-peele-get-out-golden-globes-comedy (accessed 20 July 2021).

Dolar, Mladen. 1986. 'Strel sredi koncerta', in *Uvod v socialogijo glasbe* by Thedoro Adorno. Ljubljana: DZS.

Douglas, Emily R. 2015. 'Foucault, Laughter, and Gendered Normalization'. *Foucault Studies* 20: 142–54.

Doxtader, Erik. 2003. 'Reconciliation – a Rhetorical Concept/ion'. *Quarterly Journal of Speech* 89.4: 267–92.

Du Bois, W. E. B. 1968. *Dusk of Dawn: An Essay Toward an Autobiography of a Race Concept*. New York: Schocken Books.

Du Bois, W. E. B. 2003. *The Souls of Black Folk*. New York: The Modern Library.

Dundes, Alan. 1973. *Mother Wit from the Laughing Barrel: Readings in the Interpretation of Afro-American Folklore*. Englewood Cliffs, NJ: Prentice Hall.

Eagleton, Terry. 2019. *Humour*. New Haven, CT: Yale University Press.

Egan, Timothy. 2019. 'We Need to Keep Laughing'. *The New York Times*, 4 January. https://www.nytimes.com/2019/01/04/opinion/trump-humor-political-satire.html (accessed 20 July 2021).

Ellison, Ralph. 1986. 'An Extravagance of Laughter', in *Going to the Territory*. New York: Random House, 145–97.

Ellison, Ralph. 1995. *Invisible Man*. New York: Vintage International.

Ellison, Ralph. 2002. *Living with Music: Ralph Ellison's Jazz Writings*. Edited by Robert G. O'Meally. New York: The Modern Library.

Ellison, Ralph. 2003a. 'Blues People', in John F. Callahan (ed.), *The Collected Essays of Ralph Ellison*. New York: The Modern Library, 278–87.

Ellison, Ralph. 2003b. 'Foreword to *The Beer Can by the Highway*', in John F. Callahan (ed.), *The Collected Essays of Ralph Ellison*. New York: The Modern Library, 847–52.

Ellison, Ralph. 2003c. 'Going to the Territory', in John F. Callahan (ed.), *The Collected Essays of Ralph Ellison*. New York: The Modern Library, 595–616.

Ellison, Ralph. 2003d. 'Haverford Statement', in John F. Callahan (ed.), *The Collected Essays of Ralph Ellison*. New York: The Modern Library, 431–6.

Ellison, Ralph. 2003e. 'Living with Music', in John F. Callahan (ed.), *The Collected Essays of Ralph Ellison*. New York: The Modern Library, 227–36.

Ellison, Ralph. 2003f. 'Remembering Jimmy', in John F. Callahan (ed.), *The Collected Essays of Ralph Ellison*. New York: The Modern Library, 273–7.

Ellison, Ralph. 2003g. 'Society, Morality, and the Novel', in John F. Callahan (ed.), *The Collected Essays of Ralph Ellison*. New York: The Modern Library, 698–729.

Ellison, Ralph. 2003h. 'That Same Pain, That Same Pleasure', in John F. Callahan (ed.), *The Collected Essays of Ralph Ellison*. New York: The Modern Library, 63–80.

Ellison, Ralph. 2003i. 'The Charlie Christian Story', in John F. Callahan (ed.), *The Collected Essays of Ralph Ellison*. New York: The Modern Library, 266–72.

Ellison, Ralph. 2003j. 'The Golden Age, Time Past', in John F. Callahan (ed.), *The Collected Essays of Ralph Ellison*. New York: The Modern Library, 237–49.

Ellison, Ralph. 2003k. 'The Little Man at Chehaw Station', in John F. Callahan (ed.), *The Collected Essays of Ralph Ellison*. New York: The Modern Library, 493–523.

Ellison, Ralph. 2003l. 'The Novel as a Function of American Democracy', in John F. Callahan (ed.), *The Collected Essays of Ralph Ellison*. New York: The Modern Library, 759–69.

Ellison, Ralph. 2003m. 'What America Would Be Like Without Blacks', in John F. Callahan (ed.), *The Collected Essays of Ralph Ellison*. New York: The Modern Library, 581–8.

Epstein, Jennifer. 2014. 'W.H.: "Ferns" Boosting ACA Traffic'. *Politico*, 4 April. https://www.politico.com/story/2014/03/barack-obama-between-two-ferns-healthcare-gov-104532 (accessed 20 July 2021).

Euben, J. Peter. 2003. *Platonic Noise*. Princeton, NJ: Princeton University Press.

Ewin, R. E. 2001. 'Hobbes on Laughter'. *The Philosophical Quarterly* 51.202: 29–40.

Fassin, Didier. 2015. 'In the Name of the Republic: Untimely Meditations on the Aftermath of the *Charlie Hebdo* Attack'. *Anthropology Today* 31.2: 3–7.

Fauset, Jessie. 1994. 'The Gift of Laughter', in Angelyn Mitchell (ed.), *Within the Circle: An Anthology of African American Literary Criticism from the Harlem Renaissance to the Present*. Durham, NC: Duke University Press, 45–50.

Feldman, Lauren and Dannagal G. Young. 2008. 'Late-Night Comedy as a Gateway to Traditional News: An Analysis of Time Trends in News Attention Among Late-Night Comedy Viewers During the 2004 Presidential Primaries'. *Political Communication* 25.4: 401–22.

Feola, Michael. 2014. 'Difference without Fear: Adorno contra Liberalism'. *European Journal of Political Theory* 13.1: 41–60.

Finley, Jessyka. 2020. 'Exposing "chocolate-covered bullshit": The Political Power of Black Women's Satire'. *Contemporary Political Theory*. doi: 10.1057/s41296-020-00451-z.

Fisher, Jonah. 2019. 'Zelensky Win: What Does a Comic President Mean for Ukraine?' *BBC*, 22 April. https://www.bbc.com/news/world-europe-47769118 (accessed 20 July 2021).

Flanagan, Caitlin. 2017. 'How Late-Night Comedy Fueled the Rise of Trump'. *The Atlantic*. https://www.theatlantic.com/magazine/archive/2017/05/how-late-night-comedy-alienated-conservatives-made-

liberals-smug-and-fueled-the-rise-of-trump/521472/ (accessed 20 July 2021).
Flathman, Richard. 2002. *Thomas Hobbes: Skepticism, Individuality, and Chastened Politics*. Lanham, MD: Rowman & Littlefield.
Flegenheimer, Matt and Ashley Parker. 2016. 'Donald Trump Heckled by New York Elite at Charity Dinner'. *The New York Times*, 20 October. https://goo.gl/EeNuOR (accessed 20 July 2021).
Fletcher, Angus. 2016. *Comic Democracies: From Ancient Athens to the American Republic*. Baltimore, MD: Johns Hopkins University Press.
Foley, Barbara. 2010. *Wrestling with the Left: The Making of Ralph Ellison's* Invisible Man. Durham, NC: Duke University Press.
Forestal, Jennifer. 2017. 'The Architecture of Political Spaces: Trolls, Digital Media, and Deweyan Democracy'. *American Political Science Review* 111.1: 149–61.
Foucault, Michel. 1977. 'Nietzsche, Genealogy, History', in Donald Bouchard (ed.), *Language, Counter-memory, Practice*. Ithaca, NY: Cornell University Press, 139–64.
Foucault, Michel. 1984. 'Truth and Power', in Paul Rabinow (ed.), *The Foucault Reader*. New York: Penguin.
Foucault, Michel. 1990. *The History of Sexuality*. Vol. 1, *An Introduction*. Translated by Robert Hurley. New York: Vintage.
Foucault, Michel. 1994. *The Order of Things: An Archaeology of the Human Sciences*. New York: Vintage.
Foucault, Michel, ed. 2010. *Herculine Barbin: Being the Recently Discovered Memoirs of a Nineteenth Century Hermaphrodite*. Translated by Richard McDougall. New York: Vintage.
Framke, Caroline. 2017. 'Watch: Trevor Noah Explains Why It's so Important to Laugh at Donald Trump'. *Vox*, 7 September. https://www.vox.com/culture/2017/9/7/16267334/trevor-noah-trump-comedian-seth-meyers (accessed 20 July 2021).
Frank, Jason. 2015. 'The Living Image of the People'. *Theory & Event* 18.1.
Fraser, Mariam. 2006. 'Event'. *Theory, Culture & Society* 23.2–3: 129–32.
Fraser, Nancy. 2019. *The Old is Dying and the New Cannot Be Born: From Progressive Neoliberalism to Trump and Beyond*. London: Verso.
Freedland, Jonathan. 2019. 'Donald Trump Wants to Be a Dictator. It's Not Enough Just to Laugh at Him'. *The Guardian*, 5 July. https://www.theguardian.com/commentisfree/2019/jul/05/donald-trump-dictator-not-enough-laugh (accessed 20 July 2021).
Freud, Sigmund. 1968. 'Medusa's Head', in *The Standard Edition of the Complete Psychological Works of Sigmund Freud, Vol. XVIII (1920–1922): Beyond the Pleasure Principle, Group Psychology and Other Works*. Translated and edited by James Strachey. London: The Hogarth Press and the Institute of Psychoanalysis.

Freud, Sigmund. 2000. *Three Essays on the Theory of Sexuality*. Translated and edited by James Strachey. Basic Books.

Freud, Sigmund. 2003. *The Joke and Its Relation to the Unconscious*. Translated by Joyce Crick. New York: Penguin.

Friedan, Betty. 1983. *The Feminine Mystique*. New York: W. W. Norton.

Funny or Die. 2010. 'The 53 Funniest Signs from the Rally to Restore Sanity and/or Fear'. 1 November. http://goo.gl/ThW82 (accessed 20 July 2021).

Gadsby, Hannah. 2017. Twitter post. 2 November, 12:41pm. https://twitter.com/Hannahgadsby/status/926127034526560258 (accessed 20 July 2021).

Gadsby, Hannah. 2018a. 'Hannah Gadsby Chats About Her Netflix Special, "Hannah Gadsby: Nanette"'. BUILD Series. YouTube. https://www.youtube.com/watch?v=dwcIon2flLU (accessed 20 July 2021).

Gadsby, Hannah. 2018b. *Nanette*. Netflix. https://www.netflix.com/title/80233611 (accessed 20 July 2021).

Gadsby, Hannah. 2020. *Douglas*. Netflix. https://www.netflix.com/title/81054700 (accessed 20 July 2021).

Garcia, Patricia. 2015. 'Late-Night TV Is an Official Stop on the Campaign Trail'. *Vogue*, 23 September. https://www.vogue.com/article/late-night-presidential-candidates-2016 (accessed 20 July 2021).

Gates, Jr, Henry Louis. 1988. *The Signifying Monkey: A Theory of Afro-American Literary Criticism*. New York: Oxford University Press.

Genot, Louis. 2020. 'Duvivier a Satirical Troublemaker in Bolsonaro's Brazil'. *Yahoo!*, 30 January. https://sg.style.yahoo.com/duvivier-satirical-troublemaker-bolsonaros-brazil-014316454.html (accessed 20 July 2021).

Giamario, Patrick T. 2016. 'The Laughing Body Politic: The Countersovereign Politics of Hobbes's Theory of Laughter'. *Political Research Quarterly* 69.2: 309–19.

Giamario, Patrick T. 2017. '"Making Reason Think More": Laughter in Kant's Aesthetic Philosophy'. *Angelaki: Journal of the Theoretical Humanities* 22.4: 161–76.

Giamario, Patrick T. 2020. 'Laughter as Dissensus: Kant and the Limits of Normative Theorizing Around Laughter'. *Contemporary Political Theory*. doi: 10.1057/s41296-020-00447-9.

Giappone, Krista, Fred Francis and Iain MacKenzie, eds. 2018. *Comedy and Critical Thought: Laughter as Resistance*. London: Rowman & Littlefield.

Gilhus, Ingvild Sælid. 2004. *Laughing Gods, Weeping Virgins: Laughter in the History of Religion*. New York: Routledge.

Gill, Gillian C., trans. 1980. 'Woman's Word', by Annie Leclerc, in Elaine Marks and Isabelle de Courtivron (eds), *New French Feminisms: An Anthology*. Amherst: University of Massachusetts Press, 79–86.

Goldstein, Donna. 2013. *Laughter Out of Place: Race, Class, Violence, and Sexuality in a Rio Shantytown*. Berkeley: University of California Press.
Gorris, Marleen, dir. 1982. *A Question of Silence*. Quartet Films.
Grant, Meghan. 2018. 'Victim Says She Was Gang Raped as Teens Laughed, Egged Each Other On'. *CBC*, 22 November. https://www.cbc.ca/news/canada/calgary/gang-rape-trial-adham-el-sakaan-timothy-fanning-sexual-assault-1.4916816 (accessed 20 July 2021).
Gray, Frances. 1994. *Women and Laughter*. Charlottesville, VA: University Press of Virginia.
Greene, Jessica. 2009. 'Gang Rape 911 Caller Speaks Out'. *NBC Bay Area*, 29 October. https://www.nbcbayarea.com/news/local/Gang-Rape-911-Caller-Speak-Out-67244402.html (accessed 20 July 2021).
Greene, Viveca. 2019. 'All They Need is Lulz: Racist Trolls, Unlaughter, and Leslie Jones', in Julie Webber (ed.), *The Joke is On Us: Political Comedy in (Late) Neoliberal Times*. Lanham, MD: Lexington Books, 37–64.
Gutmann, Amy and Dennis Thompson. 2004. *Why Deliberative Democracy?* Princeton, NJ: Princeton University Press.
Haberman, Maggie and Alex Burns. 2016. 'Donald Trump's Presidential Run Began in an Effort to Gain Stature'. *The New York Times*, 12 March. https://goo.gl/yDG0rB (accessed 20 July 2021).
Habermas, Jürgen. 1983. *Philosophical-Political Profiles*. Translated by Frederick G. Lawrence. Cambridge, MA: MIT Press.
Habermas, Jürgen. 1984. *The Theory of Communicative Action*. Vol. 1, *Reason and the Rationalization of Society*. Translated by Thomas McCarthy. Boston, MA: Beacon Press.
Habermas, Jürgen. 1990. *The Philosophical Discourse of Modernity*. Translated by Frederick Lawrence. Cambridge, MA: MIT Press.
Hacking, Ian. 2004. 'Making Up People', in *Historical Ontology*. Cambridge, MA: Harvard University Press, 99–114.
Halberstam, J. Jack. 2012. *Gaga Feminism: Sex, Gender, and the End of Normal*. Boston, MA: Beacon Press.
Halliwell, Stephen. 2008. *Greek Laughter: A Study of Cultural Psychology from Homer to Early Christianity*. Cambridge: Cambridge University Press.
Hamburger, Jacob. 2017. 'What Charlie Hebdo Taught Me About Freedom of Speech'. *Los Angeles Review of Books*, 7 January. https://lareviewofbooks.org/article/what-charlie-hebdo-taught-me-about-freedom-of-speech/ (accessed 20 July 2021).
Hansen, Miriam. 2012. *Cinema and Experience: Siegfried Kracauer, Walter Benjamin, and Theodor W. Adorno*. Berkeley: University of California Press.
Harding, James M. 1995. 'Adorno, Ellison, and the Critique of Jazz'. *Cultural Critique* 31: 129–58.

Harwell, Drew and Tony Romm. 2019. 'Violent Spoof Video of Trump Killing His Critics Shows How Memes Have Reshaped Politics'. *The Washington Post*, 14 October. https://www.washingtonpost.com/technology/2019/10/14/violent-spoof-video-trump-killing-his-critics-shows-how-memes-have-reshaped-politics/ (accessed 20 July 2021).

Heyd, David. 1982. 'The Place of Laughter in Hobbes's Theory of Emotions'. *Journal of the History of Ideas* 43.2: 285–95.

Hickey-Moody, Anna and Timothy Laurie. 2017. 'Masculinity and Ridicule', in Bettina Papenburg (ed.), *Gender: Laughter*. Macmillan Reference USA, 215–28.

Hietalahti, Jarno. 2020. 'Smash and Laugh: A Philosophical Analysis on the Relationship between Humour and Violence'. *Comedy Studies* 11.1: 36–46.

Hirschkop, Ken. 2001. *Mikhail Bakhtin: An Aesthetic for Democracy*. Oxford: Oxford University Press.

Hitchens, Christopher. 2007. 'Why Women Aren't Funny'. *Vanity Fair*, 1 January. https://www.vanityfair.com/culture/2007/01/hitchens200701 (accessed 20 July 2021).

Hobbes, Thomas. 1983. 'Letter 28: Hobbes to the Hon. Charles Cavendish, from Chatsworth', in Noel Malcolm (ed.), *Thomas Hobbes: The Correspondence*. Vol. 1. Oxford: Clarendon Press, 52–4.

Hobbes, Thomas. 1985. *Leviathan*. Edited by C. B. Macpherson. London: Penguin.

Hobbes, Thomas. 1991. *Man and Citizen (*De Homine *and* De Cive*)*. Edited by Bernard Gert. Indianapolis: Hackett.

Hobbes, Thomas. 1994a. *De Corpore*, in Sir William Molesworth (ed.), *The Collected Works of Thomas Hobbes*, Vol. I. London: Routledge/Thoemmes Press.

Hobbes, Thomas. 1994b. 'The Answer to Sir William Davenant's Preface before Gondibert', in Sir William Molesworth (ed.), *The Collected Works of Thomas Hobbes*, Vol. IV. London: Routledge/Thoemmes Press, 441–58.

Hobbes, Thomas. 2008. *The Elements of Law Natural and Politic*. New York: Oxford.

Hobbes, Thomas. 2012. *Leviathan*. Edited by Noel Malcolm. Oxford: Clarendon Press.

Hollander, Barry A. 2005. 'Late-Night Learning: Do Entertainment Programs Increase Political Campaign Knowledge for Young Viewers?' *Journal of Broadcasting & Electronic Media* 49.4: 402–15.

Holm, Nicholas. 2017. *Humour as Politics: The Political Aesthetics of Contemporary Comedy*. Basingstoke: Palgrave Macmillan.

Hong, Caroline Kyungah. 2019. 'Comedy, Humor, and Asian American Representation', in Josephine Lee (ed.), *The Oxford Encyclopedia of Asian American Literature and Culture*. New York: Oxford University Press.

Honneth, Axel. 2009. *Pathologies of Reason: On the Legacy of Critical Theory*. Translated by James Ingram. New York: Columbia University Press.

Horkheimer, Max. 1999. *Critical Theory: Selected Essays*. New York: Continuum.

Horkheimer, Max and Theodor W. Adorno. 2002. *Dialectic of Enlightenment: Philosophical Fragments*. Translated by Edmund Jephcott. Stanford, CA: Stanford University Press.

Hughes, Langston. 1995. *Not Without Laughter*. New York: Scribner.

Hughes, Sarah. 2017. 'The Mash Report Hopes to Put a UK Spin on US Topical Satire'. *The Guardian*, 16 July. https://www.theguardian.com/tv-and-radio/2017/jul/15/mash-report-bbc2-satirical-news-show-nish-kumar (accessed 20 July 2021).

Hulatt, Owen. 2016. *Adorno's Theory of Philosophical and Aesthetic Truth*. New York: Columbia University Press.

Iqbal, Nosheen. 2011. 'Missing Jon Stewart? Meet His Daily Show Equivalents Worldwide'. *The Guardian*, 25 June. https://www.theguardian.com/tv-and-radio/2011/jun/25/daily-show-jon-stewart-world (accessed 20 July 2021).

Irigaray, Luce. 1985. *This Sex Which Is Not One*. Translated by Catherine Porter and Carolyn Burke. Ithaca, NY: Cornell University Press.

Isaak, Jo Anna. 1996. *Feminism and Contemporary Art: The Revolutionary Power of Women's Laughter*. London: Routledge.

Itzkoff, Dave. 2017. 'Jimmy Fallon Was on Top of the World. Then Came Trump'. *The New York Times*, 17 May. https://www.nytimes.com/2017/05/17/arts/television/jimmy-fallon-tonight-show-interview-trump.html (accessed 20 July 2021).

Jackson, Lawrence. 2002. *Ralph Ellison: Emergence of Genius*. New York: Wiley.

Jackson, Patrick. 2015. 'Paris Attacks: I am Not Charlie'. *BBC*, 13 January. http://www.bbc.com/news/world-europe-30790412 (accessed 20 July 2021).

Jameson, Fredric. 1990. *Late Marxism: Adorno, or, The Persistence of the Dialectic*. London: Verso.

Jay, Martin. 1984. *Adorno*. Cambridge, MA: Harvard University Press.

Jay, Martin. 1996. *The Dialectical Imagination: A History of the Frankfurt School and the Institute of Social Research, 1923–1950*. Berkeley: University of California Press.

Jennings, Ken. 2018. *Planet Funny: How Comedy Took Over Our Culture*. New York: Scribner.

Kahn, Victoria. 1985. *Rhetoric, Prudence, and Skepticism in the Renaissance*. Ithaca, NY: Cornell University Press.

Kant, Immanuel. 1987. *Critique of Judgment*. Translated by Werner S. Pluhar. Indianapolis: Hackett.

Kay, Jeanne. 2016. 'Suis-Je Charlie? A Postcolonial Genealogy of the French Response to the *Charlie Hebdo* Attack', in Šarūnas Paunksnis (ed.), *Dislocating Globality: Deterritorialization, Difference and Resistance*. Leiden, Netherlands: Brill.

Kein, Katie. 2017. 'Let's All Laugh at Donald Trump: A Comedy Scholar's Call to Arms'. *The Huffington Post*, 17 January. https://www.huffpost.com/entry/lets-all-laugh-at-donald_b_14226788 (accessed 20 July 2021).

Kopano, Baruti N. and Jared A. Ball. 2014. 'Tyler Perry and the Mantan Manifesto', in Bell and Jackson (eds), *Interpreting Tyler Perry*. New York: Routledge, 32–46.

Kristeva, Julia. 1980. *Desire in Language: A Semiotic Approach to Literature and Art*. Translated by Thomas Gora, Alice Jardine and Leon S. Roudiez. New York: Columbia University Press.

Kristeva, Julia. 1984. *Revolution in Poetic Language*. Translated by Margaret Waller. New York: Columbia University Press.

Kristof, Nicholas. 2020. 'To Beat Trump, Mock Him'. *The New York Times*, 26 September. https://www.nytimes.com/2020/09/26/opinion/sunday/trump-politics-humor.html (accessed 20 July 2021).

Kuipers, Giselinde. 2011. 'The Politics of Humour in the Public Sphere: Cartoons, Power and Modernity in the First Transnational Humour Scandal'. *European Journal of Cultural Studies* 14.1: 63–80.

Kundera, Milan. 1999. *The Book of Laughter and Forgetting*. Translated by Aaron Asher. New York: HarperCollins.

Latour, Bruno. 2004. 'Why Has Critique Run out of Steam? From Matters of Fact to Matters of Concern'. *Critical Inquiry* 30: 225–48.

Lawtoo, Nidesh. 2019. 'The Powers of Mimesis: Simulation, Encounters, Comic Fascism'. *Theory & Event* 22.3: 722–41.

Leclerc, Annie. 2007. *Parole de Femme*. Arles, France: Actes Sud.

Leng, Kirsten. 2019. 'Pleasure and Pedagogy: The Role of Humor in Florynce Kennedy's Political Praxis'. *Feminist Formations* 31.2: 205–28.

Lewis, Kevin. 2018. '4 Damascus JV Football Players Accused in Locker Room Broomstick Rapes Released on Bond'. *WJLA*, 26 November. https://wjla.com/news/local/students-accused-of-md-high-school-hazing-assault-to-appear-in-court (accessed 20 July 2021).

Lichter, S. Robert, Jody C. Baumgartner and Jonathan S. Morris. 2018. *Politics is a Joke! How TV Comedians Are Remaking Political Life*. New York: Routledge.

Liebeck, Hedwig. 2019. 'Truth-Telling and Trolls: Trolling, Political Rhetoric in the Twenty-First Century, and the Objectivity Norm'. *Aspeers* 12: 9–36.

Lincoln, Kenneth. 1993. *Indi'n Humor: Bicultural Play in Native America*. New York: Oxford University Press.

Lockyer, Sharon. 2016. 'Comedy Matters: On the Impact of Comedy'. *Humor* 29.2: 153–5.

Lockyer, Sharon and Heather Savigny. 2020. 'Rape Jokes Aren't Funny: The Mainstreaming of Rape Jokes in Contemporary Newspaper Discourse'. *Feminist Media Studies* 20.3: 434–9.
Lombardini, John. 2013. 'Civic Laughter: Aristotle and the Political Virtue of Humor'. *Political Theory* 41.2: 203–30.
Lombardini, John. 2018. *The Politics of Socratic Humor*. Oakland: University of California Press.
Lyotard, Jean-François. 1988. *The Differend*. Translated by Georges Van Den Abbeele. Minneapolis: University of Minnesota Press.
Lyotard, Jean-François. 1993. *Libidinal Economy*. Translated by Iain Hamilton Grant. Bloomington: Indiana University Press.
Marasco, Robyn. 2015. *The Highway of Despair: Critical Theory after Hegel*. New York: Columbia University Press.
Martel, James. 2007. *Subverting the Leviathan*. New York: Columbia University Press.
Martin, Amanda, Barbara K. Kaye and Mark D. Harmon. 2018. 'Silly Meets Serious: Discursive Integration and the Stewart/Colbert Era'. *Comedy Studies* 9.2: 120–37.
Martinich, A. P. 2005. *Hobbes*. New York: Routledge.
Marx, Karl. 1990. *Capital, Vol. I*. Translated by Ben Fowkes. London: Penguin.
Marx, Nick and Matt Sienkiewicz, eds. 2018. *The Comedy Studies Reader*. Austin: University of Texas Press.
Marx, Wilhelm. 2012. 'Bassem Youssef: Egypt's Jon Stewart'. *Bloomberg*, 29 March. https://www.bloomberg.com/news/articles/2012-03-29/bassem-youssef-egypts-jon-stewart (accessed 20 July 2021).
Mbembe, Achille. 2017. *Critique of Black Reason*. Translated by Laurent Dubois. Durham, NC: Duke University Press.
McGowan, Todd. 2017. *Only a Joke Can Save Us: A Theory of Comedy*. Evanston, IL: Northwestern University Press.
McGrogan, Manus. 2017. 'Charlie Hebdo: The Poverty of Satire'. *Jacobin*, 7 January. https://www.jacobinmag.com/2017/01/charlie-hebdo-satire-islamophobia-laicite-terrorism-free-speech/ (accessed 20 July 2021).
McWilliams, Wilson Carey. 1995. 'Poetry, Politics, and the Comic Spirit'. *PS: Political Science and Politics* 28.2: 197–200.
Meyers, Seth. 2011. 'Seth Meyers at the 2011 White House Correspondents' Dinner – Full Transcript'. https://scrapsfromtheloft.com/2017/04/09/seth-meyers-2011-white-house-correspondents-dinner-transcript/ (accessed 20 July 2021).
Mill, John Stuart. 2002. *The Basic Writings of John Stuart Mill: On Liberty, The Subjection of Women, & Utilitarianism*. New York: The Modern Library.
Millett, Kate. 1970. *Sexual Politics*. Garden City, NY: Doubleday.
Mills, Charles W. 1997. *The Racial Contract*. Ithaca, NY: Cornell University Press.

Mizejewski, Linda. 2014. *Pretty/Funny: Women Comedians and Body Politics*. Austin: University of Texas Press.

Momen, Mehnaaz. 2020. 'Has Political Satire Turned Rational in Our Post-rational World?' *Contemporary Political Theory*. doi: 10.1057/s41296-020-00451-z.

Montopoli, Brian. 2010. 'Jon Stewart Rally Attracts Estimated 215,000'. *CBS*, 31 October. goo.gl/GK1fXD (accessed 20 July 2021).

Mora-Ripoll, Ramon. 2010. 'The Therapeutic Value of Laughter in Medicine'. *Alternative Therapies in Health and Medicine* 16.6: 56–64.

Morel, Lucas E. 2004. 'Ralph Ellison's American Democratic Individualism', in Lucas E. Morel (ed.), *Ralph Ellison and the Raft of Hope: A Political Companion to* Invisible Man. Lexington: The University Press of Kentucky, 58–90.

Morreall, John. 1983. *Taking Laughter Seriously*. Albany: State University of New York Press.

Morris, Jonathan S. 2009. 'The Daily Show with Jon Stewart and Audience Attitude Change during the 2004 Party Conventions'. *Political Behavior* 31.1: 79–102.

Mudde, Cas. 2019. *The Far Right Today*. Cambridge: Polity Press.

Nancy, Jean-Luc. 1993. *The Birth to Presence*. Translated by Brian Holmes et al. Stanford, CA: Stanford University Press.

Ngangura, Tari. 2017. 'White Liberals Are Taking the Wrong Lessons Away from "Get Out"'. *Vice*, 11 March. https://www.vice.com/en_us/article/mg4333/white-liberals-are-taking-the-wrong-lessons-away-from-get-out (accessed 20 July 2021).

Nietzsche, Friedrich. 1982. *Thus Spoke Zarathustra*, in Walter Kaufmann (ed.), *The Portable Nietzsche*. New York: Penguin, 103–439.

Nietzsche, Friedrich. 1989. *Beyond Good and Evil*. Translated by Walter Kaufmann. New York: Vintage.

Nietzsche, Friedrich. 1996. *Human, All Too Human: A Book for Free Spirits*. Translated by R. J. Hollingdale. Cambridge: Cambridge University Press.

Noerr, Gunzelin Schmid. 2002. 'Editor's Afterword: The Position of "Dialectic of Enlightenment" in the Development of Critical Theory', in Max Horkheimer and Theodor W. Adorno, *Dialectic of Enlightenment: Philosophical Fragments*. Stanford, CA: Stanford University Press, 217–47.

Nozick, Robert. 1974. *Anarchy, State, and Utopia*. New York: Basic Books.

NPR. 2010. 'Signs We Saw at the Sanity/Fear Rally'. 31 October. https://www.npr.org/templates/story/story.php?storyId=130953793 (accessed 20 July 2021).

Nussbaum, Emily. 2017. 'How Jokes Won the Election'. *The New Yorker*, 15 January. https://www.newyorker.com/magazine/2017/01/23/how-jokes-won-the-election (accessed 20 July 2021).

Nussbaum, Martha C. 2006. *Frontiers of Justice: Disability, Nationality, Species Membership*. Cambridge, MA: Belknap Press.

Nussbaum, Martha C. 2009. 'Stoic Laughter: A Reading of Seneca's *Apocolocyntosis*', in Shadi Bartsch and David Wray (eds), *Seneca and the Self*. Cambridge: Cambridge University Press, 84–112.

Nussbaum, Martha C. 2013. *Political Emotions: Why Love Matters for Justice*. Cambridge, MA: Belknap Press.

Oakeshott, Michael. 1965. Introduction to *Leviathan*, by Thomas Hobbes, vii–lxvi. Edited by Michael Oakeshott. Oxford: Basil Blackwell.

Oakeshott, Michael. 1991. *Rationalism in Politics and Other Essays*. Indianapolis: Liberty Press.

Okiji, Fumi. 2018. *Jazz as Critique: Adorno and Black Expression Revisited*. Stanford, CA: Stanford University Press.

Olen, Helaine. 2019. 'Ivanka Trump Wants Power, and Laughing at her Expense Won't Stop Her'. *The Washington Post*, 1 July. https://www.washingtonpost.com/opinions/2019/07/01/ivanka-trump-wants-power-laughing-her-expense-wont-stop-her/ (accessed 20 July 2021).

Oliver, John. 2014. 'FIFA and the World Cup: Last Week Tonight with John Oliver (HBO)'. HBO. YouTube. https://www.youtube.com/watch?v=DlJEt2KU33I (accessed 20 July 2021).

Olson, Joel. 2004. *The Abolition of White Democracy*. Minneapolis: University of Minnesota Press.

Oria, Shelly, ed. 2019. *Indelible in the Hippocampus: Writings from the Me Too Movement*. San Francisco, CA: McSweeney's.

Oxford English Dictionary. 2019. Oxford University Press. https://www.oed.com/.

Parikh, Tej. 2019. 'Comedians Will Soon Rule the World'. *Foreign Policy*, 13 February. https://foreignpolicy.com/2019/02/13/the-age-of-comedy-populism/ (accessed 20 July 2021).

Parrish, Timothy L. 1995. 'Ralph Ellison, Kenneth Burke, and the Form of Democracy'. *Arizona Quarterly* 51.3: 117–48.

Parvulescu, Anca. 2010. *Laughter: Notes on a Passion*. Cambridge, MA: MIT Press.

PBS. 2016. 'Inside the Night President Obama Took on Donald Trump'. 22 September. https://goo.gl/q23oL1 (accessed 20 July 2021).

Peele, Jordan, dir. 2017. *Get Out*. United States: Universal Pictures. DVD. https://scriptslug.com/assets/uploads/scripts/get-out-2017.pdf (accessed 20 July 2021).

Perez, Maria. 2018. '"Laughing while Black": Man Awarded $80K After He Was Arrested, Beaten, for Allegedly Laughing at Police'. *Newsweek*, 20 December. https://www.newsweek.com/laughing-black-man-settlement-arrested-beaten-police-1267278 (accessed 20 July 2021).

Perfetti, Lisa. 2003. *Women and Laughter in Medieval Comic Literature*. Ann Arbor: University of Michigan Press.

Perticone, Joe. 2018. 'How "owning the libs" Became the Ethos of the Right'. *Business Insider*, 28 July. https://www.businessinsider.com/how-owning-the-libs-became-the-ethos-of-the-right-2018-7 (accessed 20 July 2021).

Plato. 1991. *The Republic of Plato*. Translated by Allan Bloom. Basic Books.

Plato. 2016. *The Laws*. Edited by Malcolm Schofield. Translated by Tom Griffith. Cambridge: Cambridge University Press.

Provine, Robert. 2000. *Laughter: A Scientific Investigation*. New York: Penguin.

Rampersad, Arnold. 2007. *Ralph Ellison: A Biography*. New York: Knopf.

Rancière, Jacques. 1999. *Disagreement*. Translated by Julie Rose. Minneapolis: University of Minnesota Press.

Rancière, Jacques. 2001. 'Ten Theses on Politics'. Translated by Davide Panagia. *Theory & Event* 5.3.

Rasmussen Reports. 2009. 'Nearly One-Third of Younger Americans See Colbert, Stewart as Alternatives to Traditional News Outlets'. goo.gl/r6ejmN (accessed 20 July 2021).

Rawls, John. 1971. *A Theory of Justice*. Cambridge, MA: Belknap Press.

Rawls, John. 1996. *Political Liberalism*. New York: Columbia University Press.

Rea, Christopher. 2015. *The Age of Irreverence: A New History of Laughter in China*. Oakland: University of California Press.

Rifkind, Hugo. 2019. 'Milkshake Throwing Isn't as Funny as it Looks'. *The Times*, 20 May. https://www.thetimes.co.uk/article/throwing-milkshakes-may-be-funny-but-it-s-not-smart-zdlp5s2s7 (accessed 20 July 2021).

Rocha, Veronica. 2015. 'Group of Black Women Kicked off Napa Wine Train after Laughing too Loud'. *The Los Angeles Times*, 24 August. http://www.latimes.com/local/lanow/la-me-ln-black-women-kicked-off-napa-wine-train-20150824-htmlstory.html (accessed 20 July 2021).

Rogers, Will. 1932. 'Weekly Column'. *The New York Times*, 23 November.

Rolling Stone. 2020. 'Marcelo Adnet sobre imitações e críticas à Bolsonaro: "Ele sempre foi perigoso"'. 18 August. https://rollingstone.uol.com.br/noticia/marcelo-adnet-sobre-imitacoes-e-criticas-bolsonaro-ele-sempre-foi-perigoso/ (accessed 20 July 2021).

Rorty, Richard. 1989. *Contingency, Irony, and Solidarity*. New York: Cambridge University Press.

Rose, Gillian. 2014. *The Melancholy Science: An Introduction to the Thought of Theodor W. Adorno*. London: Verso.

Rowe, Kathleen. 1995. *The Unruly Woman: Gender and the Genres of Laughter*. Austin: University of Texas Press.

Rowson, Martin. 2015. 'Charlie Hebdo: We Must Not Stop Laughing at These Murderous Clowns'. *The Guardian*, 8 January. https://goo.gl/mq7HU1 (accessed 20 July 2021).

Rubin, Gayle. 1975. 'The Traffic in Women: Notes on the "Political Economy" of Sex', in Rayna R. Reiter (ed.), *Toward an Anthropology of Women*. New York: Monthly Review Press, 157–210.

Russell, Danielle. 2002. 'Self-deprecatory Humour and the Female Comic: Self-destruction or Comedic Construction?' *thirdspace: a journal of feminist theory & culture* 2.1.

Sanders, Barry. 1995. *Sudden Glory: Laughter as Subversive History*. Boston, MA: Beacon Press.

Sanders, Lynn M. 1997. 'Against Deliberation'. *Political Theory* 25.3: 347–76.

Schmitt, Carl. 2005. *Political Theology: Four Chapters on the Concept of Sovereignty*. Chicago: University of Chicago Press.

Schoolman, Morton. 2020. *A Democratic Enlightenment: The Reconciliation Image, Aesthetic Education, Possible Politics*. Durham, NC: Duke University Press.

Schulman, Kori. 2011. '"The President's Speech" at the White House Correspondents' Dinner'. https://obamawhitehouse.archives.gov/blog/2011/05/01/president-s-speech-white-house-correspondents-dinner (accessed 20 July 2021).

Schwartz, Matthew S. 2019. 'Comedian Wins Ukrainian Presidency in Landslide'. *NPR*, 22 April. https://www.npr.org/2019/04/22/715858365/comedian-wins-ukrainian-presidency-in-landslide (accessed 20 July 2021).

Schwarz, Jon. 2017. 'Here's Why We Shouldn't Laugh at Donald Trump's 100-Day Faceplant'. *The Intercept*, 29 April. https://theintercept.com/2017/04/29/heres-why-we-shouldnt-laugh-at-donald-trumps-100-day-faceplant/ (accessed 20 July 2021).

Schwirtz, Michael and Andrew E. Kramer. 2019. 'Ukraine's President: "I Wanted to Be World Famous," but Not This Way"'. *The New York Times*, 24 October. https://www.nytimes.com/2019/10/10/world/europe/ukraine-trump-zelensky-burisma-blackmail.html (accessed 20 July 2021).

Scocca, Tom. 2019. 'Governing by Owning the Libs'. *Slate*, 3 September. https://slate.com/news-and-politics/2019/09/donald-trumps-innovation-governing-by-owning-the-libs.html (accessed 20 July 2021).

Scott, Sophie. 2015. 'Why We Laugh'. TED video, 17:05. https://www.ted.com/talks/sophie_scott_why_we_laugh#t-1011291 (accessed 20 July 2021).

Screech, Michael A. 2015. *Laughter at the Foot of the Cross*. Chicago: University of Chicago Press.

Sedgwick, Eve Kosofsky. 1985. *Between Men: English Literature and Male Homosocial Desire*. New York: Columbia University Press.

Seery, John. 1990. *Political Returns: Irony in Politics and Theory from Plato to the Antinuclear Movement*. Boulder, CO: Westview Press.

Shaftesbury, Anthony Ashley-Cooper. 1999. 'Sensus Communis, an Essay on the Freedom of Wit and Humour in a Letter to a Friend', in Lawrence E. Klein (ed.), *Characteristics of Men, Manners, Opinions, Times*. Cambridge: Cambridge University Press, 29–69.

Shrimsley, Robert. 2019. 'We Should Be Stirred by Nigel Farage's Milkshake'. *Financial Times*, 22 May. https://www.ft.com/content/31b6c7b0-7be8-11e9-81d2-f785092ab560 (accessed 20 July 2021).

Skinner, Quentin. 1996. *Reason and Rhetoric in the Philosophy of Hobbes*. Cambridge: Cambridge University Press.

Skinner, Quentin. 2002a. 'Hobbes and the Purely Artificial Person of the State', in *Visions of Politics III: Hobbes and Civil Science*. Cambridge: Cambridge University Press, 177–208.

Skinner, Quentin. 2002b. 'Hobbes on Rhetoric and the Construction of Morality', in *Visions of Politics III: Hobbes and Civil Science*. Cambridge: Cambridge University Press, 87–141.

Skinner, Quentin. 2002c. 'The Classical Theory of Laughter', in *Visions of Politics III: Hobbes and Civil Science*. Cambridge: Cambridge University Press, 142–76.

Sorell, Tom. 1996. 'Hobbes's Scheme of the Sciences', in Tom Sorell (ed.), *The Cambridge Companion to Hobbes*. Cambridge: Cambridge University Press, 45–61.

Sorell, Tom. 2007. 'Hobbes's Moral Philosophy', in Patricia Springborg (ed.), *The Cambridge Companion to Hobbes's* Leviathan. Cambridge: Cambridge University Press, 128–53.

Stanley, Alessandra. 2008. 'Who Says Women Aren't Funny?' *Vanity Fair*, 3 March. https://www.vanityfair.com/news/2008/04/funnygirls200804 (accessed 20 July 2021).

Stanley, Jason. 2020. *How Fascism Works: The Politics of Us and Them*. New York: Random House.

Steele, Meili. 1996. 'Metatheory and the Subject of Democracy in the Work of Ralph Ellison'. *New Literary History* 27.3: 473–502.

Stelter, Brian. 2019. 'Welcome to the Stephen Colbert Primary'. *CNN*, 14 January. https://www.cnn.com/2019/01/14/media/stephen-colbert-primary/index.html (accessed 20 July 2021).

Stevens, Kyle. 2021. 'The Politics of Humor, From Dry to Wet'. *Cultural Critique* 112: 1–23.

Stewart, Jon. 2010. 'Jon Stewart's Closing Speech at the Rally to Restore Sanity'. http://faculty.washington.edu/jwhelan/Documents/Speeches/Stewart%20Sanity%20Rally.pdf (accessed 20 July 2021).

Stone, Alison. 2014. 'Adorno and Logic', in Deborah Cook (ed.), *Adorno: Key Concepts*. New York: Routledge, 47–62.

Strauss, Leo. 1984. *The Political Philosophy of Hobbes*. Translated by Elsa Sinclair. Chicago: University of Chicago Press.

Strong, Tracy. 1993. 'How to Write Scripture: Words, Authority, and Politics in Thomas Hobbes'. *Critical Inquiry* 20: 128–59.

Taylor, A. E. 1938. 'The Ethical Doctrine of Hobbes'. *Philosophy* 13.52: 406–24.

The Economist. 2019. 'The Boundaries between Politics and Stand-Up Comedy Are Crumbling'. 18 May. https://www.economist.com/international/2019/05/18/the-boundaries-between-politics-and-stand-up-comedy-are-crumbling (accessed 20 July 2021).

The Local. 2017. 'Man in Sweden "live-streamed gang rape on Facebook"'. 22 January. https://www.thelocal.se/20170122/three-in-sweden-live-streamed-gang-rape-on-facebook (accessed 20 July 2021).

The Washington Post. 2018. 'Senate Judiciary Committee Hearing on the Nomination of Brett M. Kavanaugh to be an Associate Justice of the Supreme Court, Day 5, Focusing on Allegations of Sexual Assault'. 27 September. https://www.washingtonpost.com/news/national/wp/2018/09/27/kavanaugh-hearing-transcript/ (accessed 20 July 2021).

Thompson, Catherine. 2014. 'Bill O'Reilly Attacks "Deceiver" Stephen Colbert for Income Inequality "Lie"'. *Talking Points Memo*, 9 April. http://talkingpointsmemo.com/livewire/bill-oreilly-attacks-stephen-colbert-deceiver (accessed 20 July 2021).

Time. 2015. 'Donald Trump's Presidential Announcement Speech'. 16 June. http://time.com/3923128/donald-trump-announcement-speech/ (accessed 20 July 2021).

Tønder, Lars. 2014. 'Comic Power: Another Road Not Taken?' *Theory & Event* 17.4.

Toscano, Alberto. 2020. 'The Long Shadow of Racial Fascism'. *Boston Review*, 28 October. http://bostonreview.net/race-politics/alberto-toscano-long-shadow-racial-fascism (accessed 20 July 2021).

Traverso, Enzo. 2019. *The New Faces of Fascism: Populism and the Far Right*. London: Verso.

Trudeau, Garry. 2015. 'The Abuse of Satire'. *The Atlantic*, 11 April. https://www.theatlantic.com/international/archive/2015/04/the-abuse-of-satire/390312/ (accessed 20 July 2021).

Trump, Donald. 2016a. Twitter post. 20 November, 8:26am. https://twitter.com/realdonaldtrump/status/800329364986626048 (accessed 20 July 2021).

Trump, Donald. 2016b. Twitter post. 4 December, 12:13am. https://twitter.com/realdonaldtrump/status/805278955150471168 (accessed 20 July 2021).

Trump, Donald. 2017. Twitter post. 17 January, 5:46pm. https://twitter.com/realdonaldtrump/status/820764134857969666 (accessed 20 July 2021).

Trump, Donald. 2019. Twitter post. 19 March, 6:59am. https://twitter.com/realdonaldtrump/status/1107250037854212096 (accessed 20 July 2021).

Tuck, Richard. 1989. *Hobbes*. Oxford: Oxford University Press.

Tuck, Richard. 1996. 'Hobbes's Moral Philosophy', in Tom Sorell (ed.), *The Cambridge Companion to Hobbes*. Cambridge: Cambridge University Press, 175–207.

Turner, Jack. 2008. 'Awakening to Race: Ralph Ellison and Democratic Individuality'. *Political Theory* 36.5: 655–82.

Twain, Mark. 1922. *The Mysterious Stranger and Other Stories*. New York: Harper & Brothers.

Warren, Robert Penn. 1965. *Who Speaks for the Negro?* New York: Random House.
Warrender, Howard. 1961. *The Political Philosophy of Hobbes.* Oxford: Clarendon Press.
Watts, Jerry Gafio. 1994. *Heroism and the Black Intellectual: Ralph Ellison, Politics, and Afro-American Intellectual Life.* Chapel Hill: University of North Carolina Press.
Webber, Julie, ed. 2019a. *The Joke Is on Us: Political Comedy in (Late) Neoliberal Times.* Lanham, MD: Lexington Books.
Webber, Julie. 2019b. '"You're Fired!" Neoliberalism, (Insult) Comedy, and Post-network Politics', in Julie Webber (ed.), *The Joke Is on Us: Political Comedy in (Late) Neoliberal Times.* Lanham, MD: Lexington Books, 293–314.
Weber, Samuel. 1987. 'Laughing in the Meanwhile'. *MLN* 102.4: 691–706.
Weeks, Mark. 2004. 'Beyond a Joke: Nietzsche and the Birth of "Super-Laughter"'. *Journal of Nietzsche Studies* 27: 1–17.
Whitman, James Q. 2017. *Hitler's American Model: The United States and the Making of Nazi Race Law.* Princeton, NJ: Princeton University Press.
Wilkie, Ian, ed. 2020. *The Routledge Comedy Studies Reader.* Abingdon: Routledge.
Willett, Cynthia. 2008. *Irony in the Age of Empire.* Bloomington: Indiana University Press.
Willett, Cynthia and Julie Willett. 2019. *Uproarious: How Feminists and Other Subversive Comics Speak Truth.* Minneapolis: University of Minnesota Press.
Willett, Cynthia, Julie Willett and Yael D. Sherman. 2012. 'The Seriously Erotic Politics of Feminist Laughter'. *Social Research* 79.1: 217–46.
Wolcott, James. 2015. 'How Donald Trump Became America's Insult Comic in Chief'. *Vanity Fair*, 6 November. https://www.vanityfair.com/culture/2015/11/wolcott-trump-insult-comic (accessed 20 July 2021).
Wolin, Sheldon. 2004. *Politics and Vision.* Princeton, NJ: Princeton University Press.
Wollstonecraft, Mary. 1995. *A Vindication of the Rights of Men* and *A Vindication of the Rights of Women.* Edited by Sylvana Tomaselli. Cambridge: Cambridge University Press.
Wood, Katelyn Hale. 2018. 'Standing Up: Black Feminist Comedy in the Twentieth and Twenty-first Centuries', in Kathy A. Perkins, Sandra L. Richards, Renée Alexander Craft and Thomas F. DeFrantz (eds), *The Routledge Companion to African American Theatre and Performance.* London: Routledge, 323–9.
Xenos, Michael A. and Amy B. Becker. 2009. 'Moments of Zen: Effects of *The Daily Show* on Information Seeking and Political Learning'. *Political Communication* 26.3: 317–32.

Young, Dannagal G. and Lindsay Hoffman. 2012. 'Acquisition of Current-Events Knowledge from Political Satire Programming: An Experimental Approach'. *Atlantic Journal of Communication* 20: 290–304.

Yu, Roger. 2015. '"Charlies Hebdo" Satirical Journalism Drew Fans, Critics'. *USA Today*, 7 January. https://www.usatoday.com/story/money/business/2015/01/07/charlie-hebdo-profile/21386729/ (accessed 20 July 2021).

Yuan, Jada and Hunter Harris (2018). 'The First Great Movie of the Trump Era'. *Vulture*. 22 February. http://www.vulture.com/2018/02/making-get-out-jordan-peele.html (accessed 20 July 2021).

Zuidervaart, Lambert. 1991. *Adorno's Aesthetic Theory*. Cambridge, MA: MIT Press.

Zumbrunnen, John. 2012. *Aristophanic Comedy and the Challenge of Democratic Citizenship*. Rochester, NY: University of Rochester Press.

Zupančič, Alenka. 2008. *The Odd One In: On Comedy*. Cambridge, MA: MIT Press.

Index

a/gelasty dispute, 1–5, 7, 12, 33, 34
   Adorno and, 30–1, 65, 67, 85–6, 91–2, 169
   critical theory of laughter and, 27, 34, 65, 67, 169–71, 172n1
   fascism and, 2, 5, 33, 161–4, 166–7, 168, 170–1
   feminist theory and, 32–3
   vs gelopolitics, 6–7, 16–17, 24–5, 27–8, 34, 91, 167, 168–71
   Hobbes and, 4, 31, 61, 169
   liberal discourse of gelopolitics and, 19–20, 24–5, 33, 161, 162–3, 167
   Lyotard and, 3–5, 24
   new agelasty, 33, 161–8, 170–1, 171n1
   Nietzschean discourse of gelopolitics and, 4, 24–5, 33, 161, 171n1
   participants in, 4
   philosophical underpinnings of, 17–25
   Plato and, 3–5, 24
   political theory and, 4, 7, 17, 29, 161, 167, 168, 170–1
   queer theory and, 32–3
   Trump and, 1–2, 33, 161–5, 171n1
A Question of Silence, 134
Adorno, Theodor, 72–3, 97, 118
   a/gelasty dispute and, 30–1, 65, 67, 85–6, 91–2, 168–9
   aesthetic experience, 65, 68, 79–82
   aesthetic philosophy, 76, 79–82
   Aesthetic Theory, 68, 79–82, 85, 91
   Beckett and, 31, 67, 68, 74, 76, 81–3
   Benjamin and, 71–3, 78–9, 94n10
   Chaplin and, 31, 67, 68, 75, 76, 81, 83–5, 90, 94n11
   clowning, 83–5
   critical theory of laughter, 31, 61, 65–8, 70–92, 86, 169
   critical theory of society, 25–6, 36n17, 66–70, 91, 96
   critique of laughter, 70–6, 78–9, 82, 162, 169
   culture industry, 31, 65–8, 70–3, 75, 76, 77, 81, 88, 90
   Dialectic of Enlightenment, 65, 68–70, 71, 78, 94n9, 119n3
   dialectics and, 37n19, 65, 91, 120n11
   Ellison and, 121n16
   enlightenment, 68–70, 77, 83, 84, 93n3
   fascism, 68–70, 72–3, 75–6, 162
   gelopolitics, 65–68, 91
   Get Out and, 90–1
   humour, 75, 82, 84
   identity, logic of, 68–70, 73, 75–6, 77, 83
   'In Malibu', 83–4
   irony, 74
   'Is Art Lighthearted?', 75–6, 81–2
   jazz, 121n16
   light-hearted art, 31, 67, 68, 76, 81–2
   mimesis, 83–4

Minima Moralia, 70, 72, 73–4, 78, 91
Negative Dialectics, 69, 77, 91
non-identical, the, 25, 26, 31, 37n19, 57, 69, 77–81, 83, 89, 91–2, 120n11, 169
parody, 83–5
polemical laughter, 68, 70–1, 73–6, 81, 82, 84, 88
power *see* social power
race, 119n3
reconciled laughter, 68, 76–9, 81–6, 88–92
reconciliation, 77–8, 80–1, 83, 85, 91–2, 94n8
satire, 74–5
social order, 25–7, 36n17, 61, 66–70, 73, 92n1, 93n2, 169
theory and practice, 91
theory of critical laughter, 85–6, 90–2
'Trying to Understand *Endgame*', 74–5, 82–3
wrong laughter, 77–8, 85–6, 87–91
aesthetic experience (Adorno), 65, 68, 79–82
reconciled laughter as, 81–5
see also non-identical, the (Adorno)
Aesthetic Theory, 68, 79–82, 85, 91
affect, 160, 166–7, 168
laughter as affective economy, 14–16, 20
Age of Hilarity, 7–17, 28, 33, 34, 66, 168
Allen, Danielle, 111–12, 117
Allen, Woody, 154
Althusser, Louis, 36n17, 93n2
'An Extravagance of Laughter', 31–2, 96, 98–101, 103–11, 115, 116, 118
antagonistic cooperation (Ellison), 111–19
Black laughter and, 112, 115–16, 118–19, 122n18, 169
democracy as, 32, 98, 111–12, 114, 115–19, 122n18, 169
as dialectical relationship, 113–18, 122n17

equality and, 117, 119
jazz and, 112–16
in Marx, 122n17
social order and, 115–19, 122n17, 169
as vernacular style, 121n15
Appelbaum, David, 6
Aristophanes, 4
Aristotle, 19, 22
Hobbes and, 39–40, 47
logos/phōnē dialectic, 5–7, 39–40
art, 79–81
autonomy of, 79–82
double character of, 80–2
light-hearted, 31, 67, 68, 76, 81–2
see also aesthetic experience (Adorno)
authoritarianism, 3
comedy and, 2, 75–6, 94n11
enlightenment and, 69, 93n3
satire and, 2
autonomy
Adorno and, 79–82
liberal conception of, 80–1
Nietzschean conception of, 80–1
of theory, 91

Badiou, Alain, 36n18
Bakhtin, Mikhail, 4, 23, 24, 36n16
Barbin, Herculine, 132, 137
Barker, Colin, 57–8
Barr, Roseanne, 135, 147
Barreca, Regina, 127
Bataille, Georges, 21, 22, 62n1, 132, 157n5
a/gelasty dispute and, 4
bawdry (Freud), 139–41, 143–6, 158n11
class dimensions of, 159n12
as homosocial ritual, 141, 145
see also obscene joking
bawdy talk *see* bawdry (Freud)
Beard, Mary, 93n2, 120n8
Beauvoir, Simone de, 156n4
Beckett, Samuel, 31, 67, 68, 74, 76, 81–3, 88
Benjamin, Rich, 87
Benjamin, Walter, 25, 28, 66, 71–3, 78–9, 94n10

Bergson, Henri, 28
Berlant, Lauren, 10
The Big Bang Theory, 66
Billig, Michael, 29, 93n2
Black, Zachariah, 64n11
Black laughter, 31–2, 87–91, 95–112, 115–16, 118–19, 169
  antagonistic cooperation and, 112, 115–16, 118–19, 122n18, 169
  democratic politics and, 31–2, 96–8, 105–12, 115–16, 118–19, 120n10, 122n18, 169
  dialectics of, 32, 96–8, 103–7, 169
  dissensus and, 32, 98, 105
  Du Bois and, 95, 119n5
  emancipatory nature of, 32, 98, 105, 169
  equality and, 101, 105, 107, 111, 116, 120n10
  at *Get Out*, 87–91
  'irrationality' of, 98, 100–5, 118, 122n18, 169
  political polyvalence of, 105, 107, 116
  regulation of, 95–6, 98, 100–8, 110, 116, 118–19, 119n6, 120n9, 121n12, 169
  self-regulation of, 106
  shaped by white supremacy, 32, 96–100, 102, 169
  as survival strategy, 100, 109–10
  vs white laughter, 98, 99–100, 102–7, 118, 122n18
  see also white supremacist regime of laughter
Black nationalism, 117
Blackness, 120n11
Blyth, Reginald, 127
body, 6, 19, 45, 160, 166
body politic (Hobbes), 30, 53–7
  as laughing body politic, 56
  sovereignty and, 53–61
  temporality of, 55
  see also laughing body politic
Bolsonaro, Jair, 2, 164
Borges, Jorge Luis, 22
Bown, Alfie, 36n18, 93n2, 166
Boyer, Dominic, 172n2

Brand, Russell, 10–12, 13, 17, 23, 35n12
Brecht, Bertolt, 75
Brexit, 2
Brown, Sterling, 101–2
Butler, Judith, 5, 143–4, 157n7
  Gender Trouble, 33, 130–2, 158n7
  laughter and, 4, 17, 33, 124, 126, 130–2, 133–4, 135, 137, 138, 156n3, 159n14, 169
  parody and, 131–2, 133
  queer/ing laughter, 131–2, 134, 136

Caldwell, Erskine, 98, 107, 111
Capital, Volume 1, 65, 122n17
capitalism, 122n17
  Adorno's critique of, 68–70
  critical theory and, 25–6, 81, 93n4
  Ellison and, 119n3
  enlightenment and, 69–70
  fascism and, 71–3, 76
  laughing at, 73, 75
  laughter and, 29, 31, 79, 86, 92, 97
  logic of identity and, 69–70, 73, 75–6
  violence of, 85
  see also culture industry
Carlson, Tucker, 4
carnival, 7, 23
cartoons, 9–10, 71–2, 90
catcalling, 158n11
Chait, Jonathan, 9
Chambers, Samuel, 93n2
Chaplin, Charlie, 31, 67, 68, 75, 76, 81, 83–5, 90, 94n11
Chappelle, Dave, 95
Charlie Hebdo, 9–10, 20, 23
Chasar, Mike, 96, 100
Cho, Margaret, 135, 148
civility, 59
Cixous, Hélène, 131
  account of laughter, 22, 32, 124–36, 138, 155, 156n3, 156n4, 169
  écriture féminine, 127–9, 157n5, 157n6
  'The Laugh of the Medusa', 124–30, 155
C. K., Louis, 150, 153
classical music, 112–15, 116

clowning (Adorno), 83–5
The Colbert Report see Colbert, Stephen
Colbert, Stephen, 1, 8–9, 13, 19, 29, 42, 58–60, 76, 87, 167
  see also Rally to Restore Sanity and/or Fear
colonialism, 102, 118
comedy, 13, 28–9, 59–60, 66, 83, 98, 102, 107
  authoritarianism and, 2, 75–6, 94n11
  of Black women, 38n30
  critique and, 165, 168
  fascism and, 75–6, 161, 162–3, 166–7
  female comedians, 147–9, 152, 154
  feminist politics and, 135, 147–54
  form of, 151–4, 159n15
  Gadsby's critique of, 150–5, 159n15
  gender and, 148–50
  Get Out as, 86–7
  in hetero-patriarchal social order, 147–54
  identity politics and, 150–4
  liberal discourse of gelopolitics and, 19–20
  marginalised comics and, 150–5
  masculine nature of, 147–9, 152–3, 169
  Mizejewski's account of, 147–9
  moral and political costs of, 164–5
  Nietzschean discourse of gelopolitics and, 24
  patriarchy and, 32, 135, 147–54, 169
  political theory and, 7, 28–9
  pretty vs funny logic in, 147–50, 152
  sex and gender politics of, 146–55
  sexuality and, 147–54
  storytelling and, 152, 154
  as subversive, 152, 153
  trauma and, 151–4
  Trump and, 1–2, 9, 13, 14–16, 19–20, 33, 66, 74, 76, 161–4, 166, 171n1
  Tyler Perry and, 102, 120n9
  see also jokes
comedy studies, 28
comic fascism, 166–7
Connolly, William, 24, 56
  Hobbesian sovereignty, 54
  neofascism, 2, 166
Cosby, Bill, 153
Coulson, Shea, 85, 90
counter-sovereignty, 31, 41, 53, 56–61, 168–9
  sovereignty and, 56–7, 64n12
  see also Hobbes's theory of laughter
counter/sovereignty, 31, 41–2, 56–61, 64n10, 64n12, 168–9; *see also* Hobbes's theory of laughter; laughing body politic; political logic of laughter
critical laughter, theory of, 85–6, 90–2, 165, 169; *see also* critical theory of laughter (Adorno)
critical theory, 91, 161, 165, 171
critical theory of laughter, 25–30, 39, 65, 161, 169–71, 172n1
  gelopolitics and, 17, 27–8, 34, 92, 102–3, 118, 125–6, 149, 155, 169–71
  inside/outside dialectic in, 26–8, 30
  race and, 31, 92, 96, 102–3, 118, 155, 169
  sex and gender politics and, 125–6, 132, 136–8, 146, 149, 155, 169
  style of presentation, 29
  tools of, 30–1, 61, 92, 96
critical theory of laughter (Adorno), 31, 61, 65–8, 70–92, 169
  as practice, 67, 86
  see also critical laughter, theory of
critical theory of society (Adorno), 25–8, 36n17, 66–70, 91, 96
Critique of Judgment, 160
cruel laughter, 72–3, 76, 88, 109–10, 145
  reconciliation and, 84–5
culture industry, 31, 81
  Benjamin's account of, 71–3, 78–9, 94n10
  cruel laughter in, 72–3, 76, 84–5
  laughter manufactured by, 65–8, 70–3, 75, 76, 77, 88, 90, 94n10

Daly, Mary, 123
The Daily Show, 78, 164, 166
   see also Stewart, Jon
Danish cartoon controversy, 10
Davidson, Arnold, 143
Davis, Angela, 32
Davis, D. Diane, 24, 126, 132–8, 157n7, 159n14
De Cive, 40, 42, 62n5
   laughter and the law of nature in, 47–53, 62n6
De Corpore, 62n5
De Homine, 42, 44–6, 62n5
deconstruction, 22–4, 26, 39, 66, 104–5, 118, 122n18, 125, 132–3, 156n3, 158n7, 159n15
DeGeneres, Ellen, 148
Deleuze, Gilles, 22, 36n18, 161
deliberation, 152
Deloria, Vine, Jr, 38n30
democracy, 11–12, 23, 24, 27, 33, 34, 152, 162, 171
   as antagonistic cooperation, 32, 98, 111–12, 114, 115–19, 122n18, 169
   Black laughter and, 31–2, 96–8, 105–12, 115–16, 118–19, 120n10, 122n18, 169
   as dialectical, 116–18
   Ellison's account of, 32, 96–8, 105–19, 120n10, 122n18, 169
   as form of political life, 111–12, 117–18
   individualism and, 98, 111–12, 117–18
   as mode of political life, 98, 112, 116–18
   Rancière and, 120n10
   white supremacy and, 97–8, 105–7, 110–11, 115–19, 120n10, 122n18, 169
depoliticisation of laughter, 33, 136–8, 154, 170
   in Hobbes, 41, 44–5, 52, 64n10
   see also repoliticisation of laughter; under-politicisation of laughter
Derrida, Jacques, 6, 22, 62n1, 132, 157n5

Descartes, René, 6
Dialectic of Enlightenment, 65, 68–70, 71, 78, 94n9, 119n3
dialectic of feminist/queer laughter, 126, 147, 149, 154
dialectical quality of laughter, 25–8, 67, 82, 86, 89, 91–2
   Black laughter, 32, 96–8, 103–7, 169
   feminist and queer politics, 126, 147, 149, 154
dialectics
   Adorno and, 37n19, 65, 91, 120n11
   antagonistic cooperation and, 113–18, 122n17
   democracy and, 116–18
dialectics of gelopolitics, 27–8, 30;
   see also experience/event dialectic; inside/outside dialectic; *logos/ phōnē* dialectic
differend (Lyotard), 3
Dionysus, 4, 168, 170
disciplinary power, 146
Disney, 71–3, 78, 94n10
dissensus, 32, 98, 105
Dolar, Mladen, 25
domination *see* social power
Douglas, Emily, 146
Du Bois, W. E. B., 95, 119n5
Dundes, Alan, 107
Durkheim, Émile, 71

Eagleton, Terry, 29
écriture féminine, 127–9, 157n5, 157n6
education, 8–9, 16
Egan, Timothy, 1–2, 4–5, 19
The Elements of Law, 39, 42–6, 48, 63n8
Ellison, Ralph, 5, 17, 28, 29
   Adorno and, 121n16
   'An Extravagance of Laughter', 31–2, 96, 98–101, 103–11, 115, 116, 118
   antagonistic cooperation, 32, 98, 111–19, 122n17, 122n18, 169
   Black nationalism, 117
   capitalism, 119n3
   classical music, 112–15, 116
   democracy, 32, 96–8, 105–19, 120n10, 122n18, 169

equality and, 97, 101, 105, 107, 111, 113, 116, 117, 119, 120n10
extravagance of laughter, 99, 105–7, 110
freedom, 108–9, 117–18, 121n13
individualism, 117–18
Invisible Man, 96, 111, 119n4
jazz, 112–16, 121n16
laughing barrels, 32, 96, 98–111, 115–16, 118–19, 120n9, 120n10, 121n12, 169
laughter, 31–2, 96–107, 108–12, 115–16, 118–19, 169
laughter of, 98–100, 105–7, 109–11, 119n4
liberalism, 111, 117
Rancière and, 120n10
rights, 97, 108–10, 119
white laughter, 98, 99–100, 102–7, 118, 122n18
emancipation
Black laughter and, 32, 98, 103, 105, 169
feminine/queer laughter and, 32–3, 125–6, 129–30, 132–8, 146–7, 149, 153–4, 155, 169
laughter and, 27, 31, 65, 75, 78–9, 86, 89, 91, 146–7, 149, 161, 166–7, 168, 169–71
as nature of laughter, 24, 26, 29, 66–7, 73, 93n2, 98, 105, 125, 129–30, 132–8, 144, 153–4, 155, 162–3, 169–70
empiricism, 66–7
end of laughter, 161, 163, 165, 168, 171
liberalism and, 163
see also new agelasty
Endgame, 74–5, 82–3, 88
enlightenment (Adorno), 68–70, 77, 83, 84
authoritarianism and, 69, 93n3
reconciliation and, 77
see also capitalism; logic of identity (Adorno)
equality, 97
antagonistic cooperation and, 117, 119

Black laughter and, 101, 105, 107, 111, 116, 120n10
feminist comedy and, 135, 136
jazz and, 113
see also democracy
event
aesthetic experience as, 81
laughter as, 36n18
see also experience/event dialectic
Ewin, R. E., 46–7, 52
experience/event dialectic, 27, 30–1, 67, 73, 81, 110, 168
extravagance of laughter, 99, 105–7
as experience/event, 110

fascism, 16, 69
a/gelasty dispute and, 2, 5, 33, 161–4, 166–7, 168, 170–1
capitalism and, 71–3, 76
comedy and, 75–6, 161, 162–3, 166–7
laughter and, 2, 4–5, 33, 34, 65, 71–3, 75–6, 86, 133, 161–4, 166–7, 168, 169–71, 171n1
liberal discourse of gelopolitics and, 162–3, 167, 171n1
logic of identity, 68–70, 76
logos/phōnē dialectic and, 161, 162–3, 170
parody and, 75, 161
white supremacy and, 32
Fassin, Didier, 10
feminine laughter, 32–33, 124–6, 129–37, 146–7, 149–50, 153–5, 156n3, 169
dialectic of, 147, 149, 154
feminine writing see *écriture féminine*
feminist and queer discourse of laughter, 22, 31, 32–3, 124–38, 146, 155, 156n3, 157n4, 169
comedy and, 135, 147–54
genealogy of, 126–38
as under-politicised, 125, 136–8
feminist politics
comedy and, 135, 147–54
laughter and, 5, 17, 22, 32–3, 125–38, 146, 155, 156n4, 169

feminist theory
   a/gelasty dispute and, 32–3
   laughter and, 28, 29, 124–38, 146, 156n3, 156n4, 169
   phallogocentrism and, 128–30, 132–4, 157n6, 157n7
Fey, Tina, 9, 148
film *see* culture industry
Ford, Christine Blasey, 123–5, 136, 141, 155
form of political life, 111–12, 117–18; *see also* mode of political life
Foucault, Michel, 4, 6, 64n12, 102, 132
   account of laughter, 22
   genealogy, 137
   power, 144
   repressive hypothesis, 143
Fox News, 59–60
Francis, Fred, 165
Frank, Jason, 42, 60
Frankfurt School, 25, 36n17, 93n2; *see also* Adorno, Theodor; critical theory
Fraser, Mariam, 36n18
Freedland, Jonathan, 1–2, 4, 5
freedom
   Ellison's account of, 108–9, 117–18, 121n13
   enlightenment and, 69, 93n3
   laughter and, 17–21, 36n15, 135–6, 150, 152, 162–3
   white supremacy and, 108–9, 117–18, 121n13
Freud, Sigmund
   account of laughter, 5, 17, 33, 126, 138–46, 155, 158n9, 169
   bawdry, 139–41, 143–6, 158n11, 159n12
   The Joke and Its Relation to the Unconscious, 33, 126, 138, 142, 143, 145, 155, 158n9
   jokes, 138–46, 158n9, 158n10, 159n12
   libido, 141–6, 159n13
   masculine laughter, 139–41, 145
   Medusa, 129
   repression, 140, 143–44
   sexual character, 141–5, 159n13
   sexual development, theory of, 141–6
   Three Essays on the Theory of Sexuality, 142

Gadsby, Hannah, 123, 169
   Douglas, 159n15
   Nanette, 33, 126, 147, 150–5, 159n15, 161
gaga feminism (Halberstam), 124
gelopolitics, 29, 160–1, 171
   vs a/gelasty dispute, 6–7, 16–17, 24–5, 27–8, 34, 91, 167, 168–71
   Adorno and, 65–8, 91
   of affective circulation, 14–16
   critical theory of laughter and, 17, 27–8, 34, 92, 102–3, 118, 125–6, 146, 149, 155, 169–71
   dialectical quality of, 79, 92, 105, 169
   dialectics of, 27–8, 30
   of education, 8–9, 16
   of escape, 12–14, 16, 78, 81
   feminist and queer account of, 125–6, 149, 155, 169
   feminist and queer discourse of, 124–38, 146, 156n3, 156n4, 169
   Freud and, 138–46
   Hobbesian, 42–5
   liberal discourse of, 17–21, 24, 27, 29, 33, 34, 35n14, 36n15, 65–6, 67, 73, 93n2, 102, 171n1
   Nietzschean discourse of, 17, 21–27, 29, 33, 34, 36n18, 39, 66, 67, 73, 82, 93n2, 129, 132, 160–1, 171n1
   politics as, 163, 168, 170
   race and, 31, 87–91, 95–112, 115–19, 126, 155, 169
   of rupture and transformation, 10–12, 16
   sex and gender, 136–7, 149, 155, 169
   social logic of, 31, 61, 65–7, 89, 92, 169
   social order and, 26–8, 30–4, 61, 66–7, 86, 102, 125, 169

sovereignty and, 64n12
  of struggle and contestation,
    9–10, 16
gelōs, 3
  polis and, 7, 33, 165, 167, 168
  see also gelopolitics; laughter
gender identity, 158n7
  comedy and, 148–50
  laughter and, 24, 31–3, 92, 96,
    124–6, 131–2, 134, 136, 138,
    146, 154, 155, 156n3, 169
  as performance, 130–1
gender politics *see* sex and gender
    politics
Gender Trouble, 33, 130–2, 158n7
genealogy
  of feminist and queer discourse of
    laughter, 126–38
  Foucault and, 137
  of power, 131, 158n7
Get Out, 29
  Adorno and, 90–1
  genre of, 86–7
  laughter at, 31, 68, 87–91
Giappone, Krista, 165
glory (Hobbes), 42–8, 55–6, 62n4;
  see also power (Hobbes)
Gorris, Marleen, 134, 135–6, 138, 169
  A Question of Silence, 134
Gray, Frances, 135
Griffin, Kathy, 148
Guattari, Félix, 22

Habermas, Jürgen, 4, 6
Hacking, Ian, 143
Halberstam, Jack, 32, 124
Halliwell, Stephen, 6
Hansen, Miriam, 71–2
Harding, James, 121n16
Hegel, Georg Wilhelm Friedrich, 4,
  22, 37n19, 70, 120n11, 157n5
  reconciliation, 77
hetero-patriarchy, 146–55, 169
  comedy and, 147–54
  see also heteronormativity; patriarchy
heteronormativity, 32–3, 124–6,
  131–2, 135–8, 146–55, 169
  see also hetero-patriarchy

Hickey-Moody, Anna, 146
Hietalahti, Jarno, 84
Hitchens, Christopher, 147–8
Hobbes, Thomas, 5, 6, 17, 28, 29
  a/gelasty dispute, 4, 31, 61, 169
  appetites and aversions, 49–50
  Aristotle and, 39–40, 47
  as author, 41, 52
  body politic, 31, 53–7
  De Cive, 40, 42, 47–53, 62n5, 62n6
  De Corpore, 62n5
  De Homine, 42, 44–6, 62n5
  The Elements of Law, 39, 42–6, 48,
    63n8
  gelopolitics, 42–5
  glory, 42–8, 55–6, 62n4
  God, 63n8
  humour in, 64n11
  joy, 44
  laughing body politic, 30, 41–2,
    55–61
  laughter *see* Hobbes's theory of
    laughter
  law of nature, 41, 47–53, 54, 63n7,
    63n8, 63n9
  Leviathan, 42–4, 46, 48, 51, 52,
    53–4, 55, 62n5
  logos/phōnē dialectic, 30, 39–41,
    45, 61, 92, 169
  moral philosophy, 48–53, 62n5,
    63n9
  natural philosophy, 62n5
  passions, 42–6, 48, 55, 62n5
  peace, 48–53, 56, 64n11, 168
  philosophical system, 62n5
  political philosophy, 39–40, 45,
    53–7, 60, 61, 62n2, 62n5, 63n9
  power, 30, 41, 42–5, 53, 56
  reason, 39–40, 48–52, 54, 62n2,
    63n8
  social contract, 41–2, 53–6; *see also*
    body politic (Hobbes)
  sovereignty, 30, 40–1, 45, 51–7, 61,
    64n9, 64n11, 168–9
  state of nature, 47–50, 52, 55–6
  as textual sovereign, 52, 64n9
  vainglory, 30, 39, 41, 45–50, 56,
    58, 61, 62n3, 62n6

Hobbes's theory of laughter, 31,
  39–57, 61, 62n3, 66, 92, 96, 118,
  168–9
  depoliticisation of laughter in, 41,
    44–5, 52, 64n10
  gelopolitical reading of, 40–1,
    57, 61
  Hobbes's political philosophy and,
    53, 55–7
  moral vs political critique of
    laughter, 46–7, 52–3
  shifting conceptions of gelopolitics
    within, 44–5
Holm, Nicholas, 59, 93n2, 165–6
homosocial ritual, 141, 145
Horkheimer, Max, 25, 65, 68–73,
  77–8, 82, 93n3, 93n5, 94n9
horror, 70, 81, 83, 88, 94n10
  Get Out and, 86–8, 90
  white supremacy as, 88
Hughes, Langston, 32, 95, 98–9
Hulatt, Owen, 79
human/non-human distinction, 5–7,
  62n2, 100, 166, 168;
  see also laughing animal
humour, 24, 28, 164–5
  in Adorno, 75, 82, 84
  critique and, 165, 168
  fascist, 161, 162–3, 165, 166,
    171n1
  feminist, 135, 137
  folk, 23
  in Hobbes, 64n11
  Native American, 38n30
  political theory and, 7, 28–9
  racist, 99
  self-deprecating, 150–2
  violence of, 84, 162
humour studies, 28

idealism, 66–7, 68–70, 77, 83
  falsity of, 79
identity politics, 150–4
ideology, 25, 29, 74–5, 89, 153, 171
  liberalism and, 59–60
  of white supremacy, 97
imperialism, 102, 118
'In Malibu', 83–4

inside/outside dialectic, 26–8, 30
interracial laughter, 103–7
Invisible Man, 96, 111, 119n4
Irigaray, Luce, 22, 32, 124, 126, 130–
  1, 133, 134, 135–6, 138, 156n3,
  157n6, 157n7, 169
  This Sex Which Is Not One, 130
irony, 24, 28, 164–5
  Adorno and, 74
  political theory and, 7, 28–9
  Socratic, 3
'Is Art Lighthearted?', 75–6, 81–2
Isaak, Jo Anna, 136–7

jazz
  Adorno and, 121n16
  antagonistic cooperation and,
    112–16
  classical music and, 112–15, 116
Jennings, Ken, 33, 161, 163–5, 167–8
Johnson, Boris, 10, 12, 35n12, 164
*The Joke and Its Relation to the
  Unconscious*, 33, 126, 138, 142,
  143, 145, 155, 158n9
jokes
  class and, 140, 159n12
  fascism and, 162–3
  female comedy and, 147–8, 154
  form of, 151–4, 159n15, 162
  Freud and, 138–46, 158n9, 158n10,
    159n12
  Gadsby and, 150–4, 159n15
  hostile, 139–40
  libido and, 142–3, 145–6
  new agelasty and, 164–5
  obscene, 139–41, 143–6
  rape, 146
  sexist, 127, 135, 139
  storytelling and, 152, 154
  trauma and, 151–4
  see also comedy
joy (Hobbes), 44
Judge, Mark, 123–4
justice, 2–3
Juvenal, 73–4

Kant, Immanuel, 160–1
  Critique of Judgment, 160

Kavanaugh, Brett, 123–4
knowledge
  laughter and, 22
  power and, 102
Kristeva, Julia, 22, 156n3
Kundera, Milan, 22

Lacan, Jacques, 36n18
Last Week Tonight see Oliver, John
Latour, Bruno, 161
'The Laugh of the Medusa', 124–30, 155
laughing animal, 6–7
laughing barrels, 32, 96, 98–111, 115–16, 118–19, 169
  in African American folklore, 96, 101, 107–8, 119n6
  antagonistic cooperation and, 115–16
  comedy and, 102, 120n9
  crisis generated by, 103–7, 118
  as empowering, 107–8
  equality and, 101, 105, 107, 116
  Rancière and, 120n10
  regulation of Black laughter, 100–7, 110, 116, 118–19, 119n6, 120n9, 121n12, 169
  see also white supremacist regime of laughter
laughing body politic, 30, 41–2, 55–61
laughter
  Adorno's critique of, 70–6, 78–9, 82, 162, 169
  affective economy of, 14–16, 20
  Benjamin's account of, 71–3, 78–9, 94n10
  Black laughter, 31–2, 87–91, 95–112, 115–16, 118–19, 122n18, 169
  body and, 6, 19, 45, 160, 166
  Butler's account of *see* Butler, Judith
  at capitalism, 73, 75
  capitalism and, 29, 31, 79, 86, 92, 97
  Cixous's account of *see* Cixous, Hélène
  class and, 140, 159n12
  clowning and, 83–5
  constituting *polis*, 7, 33, 161, 168, 169–71
  as counter-sovereign, 31, 41, 53, 56–61, 64n12, 168–9
  as counter/sovereign enactment, 31, 41–2, 57–61, 64n10, 64n12, 168–9
  critical, 85–6, 90–2, 165, 169
  critical theory of *see* critical theory of laughter
  critique and, 165, 168
  cruel, 72–3, 76, 84–5, 88, 109–10, 145
  culture industry and, 65–8, 70–3, 75, 76, 77, 88, 90, 94n10
  deconstruction and, 22–4, 26, 39, 66, 104–5, 118, 122n18, 125, 132–3, 156n3, 159n15
  democracy and, 11–12, 23, 24, 27, 33, 34, 96–8, 105–12, 115–16, 118–19, 120n10, 122n18, 152, 162, 169, 171
  depoliticisation of, 33, 41, 44–5, 52, 64n10, 136–8, 154, 170
  dialectical quality of, 25–8, 32, 67, 82, 86, 89, 91–2, 96–8, 103–7, 126, 147, 149, 154, 169
  disciplinary power and, 146
  as dissensus, 32, 98, 105
  écriture féminine and, 129
  education and, 8–9, 16
  effects on political discourse, 10–12, 13, 16, 23–4, 36n18, 168, 171n1
  of Ellison, 98–100, 105–7, 109–11, 119n4
  Ellison's account of, 31–2, 96–107, 108–12, 115–16, 118–19, 169
  emancipation and *see* emancipation
  end of, 161, 163, 165, 168, 171
  equality and, 101, 105, 107, 111, 116, 120n10, 135, 136
  as escape from politics, 12–14, 16, 78, 81
  as exogenous to *polis*, 7, 163, 164–5, 166, 168, 170–1
  as experience, 27, 67, 73, 110
  as experience/event, 27, 30–1, 67, 73, 81, 110, 168, 170–1

laughter (*cont.*)
  fascism and, 2, 4–5, 33, 34, 65, 71–3, 75–6, 86, 133, 161–4, 166–7, 168, 169–71, 171n1
  feminine, 32–3, 124–6, 129–37, 146–7, 149–50, 153–5, 156n3, 169
  feminist and queer discourse of, 22, 31, 32–3, 124–38, 146, 155, 156n3, 157n4, 169
  feminist politics and, 5, 17, 22, 32–3, 125–38, 146, 155, 156n4, 169
  feminist theory and, 28, 29, 124–38, 146, 156n3, 156n4, 169
  Foucault's account of, 22
  freedom and, 17–21, 36n15, 135–6, 150, 152, 162–3
  Freud's account of, 5, 17, 33, 126, 138–46, 155, 158n9, 169
  Gadsby's account of, 33, 123, 126, 147, 150–5, 159n15, 161, 169
  gender and, 24, 31–3, 92, 96, 124–6, 131–2, 134, 136, 138, 146, 149, 150, 154, 155, 156n3, 169
  at *Get Out*, 87–91
  as glory, 42–8, 55–6
  in hetero-patriarchal social order, 146–55, 169
  heteronormativity and, 32–3, 124–6, 131–2, 135–8, 146–55, 169
  history and, 10, 23
  Hobbes's account of *see* Hobbes's theory of laughter
  as homosocial ritual, 141, 145
  human/non-human distinction and, 5–7, 100, 166, 168
  identity politics and, 150–4
  ideology and, 25, 29, 74–5, 89, 153, 171
  inside/outside dialectic and, 26–8, 30
  interracial, 103–7
  Irigaray's account of *see* Irigaray, Luce
  irrational, 98, 100–5, 118, 122n18, 127, 169
  justice and, 2–3
  Kant's account of, 160–1
  knowledge and, 22
  law and, 132, 134, 137, 159n14
  law of nature and, 41, 47–53, 62n6
  liberalism and, 163, 167
  libido and, 142–3, 145–6
  limits on, 161–2, 161–5, 167, 171, 171n1
  logos/phōnē dialectic and, 5–7, 17, 19–24, 26–7, 30, 39–41, 45, 61, 92, 118, 120n10, 127–30, 133, 155, 159n12, 160–1, 162–3, 168–70
  male power and, 124, 136, 146, 149, 169
  masculine, 139–41, 145, 146, 149, 152–3
  at men, 136, 146
  as metaphor, 136–7
  mimesis and, 83–4, 166–8, 170
  Mizejewski's account of *see* Mizejewski, Linda
  nature and, 146, 170
  new agelasty and, 33, 161–8, 170–1, 171n1
  non-identity and, 26, 31, 78, 83, 88–9, 91–2, 169, 170
  as a passion, 42–6, 48, 55
  pathological forms of, 18–20, 166–7, 170
  patriarchy and, 32–3, 66, 124–6, 127, 129–36, 133–4, 135–8, 147–55, 169; *see also* hetero-patriarchy
  peace and, 52–3, 168
  phallogocentrism and, 132–4
  place in the *polis*, 2–5, 7, 17, 18, 24–5, 27–8, 34, 61, 161–8, 170–1
  Plato's account of, 2–5, 24, 35n14
  as pluralising, 133
  polemical, 68, 70–1, 73–6, 81, 82, 84, 88
  political logic of, 28, 30–1, 39–42, 56–61, 92, 168; *see also* counter/sovereignty
  political polyvalence of, 26–8, 67, 78–9, 89–92, 105, 107, 116, 125–6, 136–7, 155
  political productivity of, 125–6, 138, 144–6, 155, 169

popular laughter, 23, 36n16, 58
power and, 4, 10, 24, 26–7, 30–1, 39, 41, 42–5, 53, 57–61, 64n12, 67, 102, 146, 169; *see also* male power; social power
psychoanalysis and, 127, 138–46
public opinion and, 9
queer/ing, 131–2, 134, 136, 149–50, 153, 154, 156n3
queer politics and *see* queer politics
queer theory and *see* queer theory
race and, 31, 86–92, 95–112, 115–19, 126, 155, 169
rational, 101, 102, 104–5, 118, 122n18, 127
reason and, 6, 19, 20, 23, 26–7, 32, 35n14, 36n15, 39, 84, 160–1
reconciled laughter *see* reconciled laughter (Adorno)
regime of, 102, 120n8; *see also* white supremacist regime of laughter
regulation of *see* regulation of laughter
religion and, 9–10, 20
repoliticisation of, 32–3, 125–6, 138, 146, 154, 170
rupture and, 10–12, 16, 26–7
salvational power of, 84–5, 89
self-reflexive, 82–5
self-regulation of, 106, 167
sex and gender politics of *see* sex and gender politics
sexual violence and *see* sexual violence
sexuality and, 24, 32–3, 92, 96, 124–6, 130–1, 132, 134, 136, 138, 139–46, 147–55, 156n3, 169
as site of politics, 4–5, 7, 17, 26–8, 29, 33, 34, 39, 61, 65–7, 86, 92, 97, 100, 105, 118, 125, 137, 155, 162, 168–71, 172n1
social contract and, 55–6
social order and, 25–8, 33, 34, 36n18, 39, 61, 65–7, 70–92, 96–8, 100, 102, 118, 125–6, 146–7, 151, 155, 169–71
sovereignty and, 30, 40–1, 45, 53, 55–61, 62n1, 64n11, 64n12, 168–9

spontaneous, 66, 73
Stoic, 19
storytelling and, 152, 154
subject-centric accounts of *see* subject-centrism
subversive, 67, 71–3, 89, 105, 110–11, 125–6, 129, 132, 135, 137, 146, 149, 150, 153
temporality of, 55
trauma and, 151–4
truth and, 18–21, 23–4, 26–7, 35n14, 66, 73, 102, 161, 162–3, 168, 171n1
under-politicisation of, 125, 136–8
as vainglory, 30, 39, 41, 45–50, 56, 58, 61, 62n3, 62n6
violence and, 9–10, 16, 31, 72–3, 75, 78, 84–5, 88–91, 94n10, 101, 107, 109, 119n1, 123–5, 136, 141, 145, 146, 155, 155n1, 161, 169; *see also* sexual violence
white laughter, 31, 87–91, 98, 99–100, 102–7, 118, 122n18
white supremacist regime of, 32, 98, 102, 104–8, 110–11, 115, 118, 120n10, 121n12
white supremacy and, 32, 86–90, 96–112, 115–19, 169
at women, 123–4, 126–7, 139–41, 145–6, 147–9, 152
women's, 123, 125, 127, 129–30, 134, 136–8, 156n4, 163
wrong laughter *see* wrong laughter (Adorno)
yoga and, 93n6, 164
laughter studies, 29
laughter yoga, 93n6, 164
Laurie, Timothy, 146
law, 132, 134, 137, 159n14
law of nature (Hobbes), 41, 47–53, 54, 62n6, 63n7, 63n9
Lawtoo, Nidesh, 33, 161, 166–8, 170–1, 171n1
Leahy, Patrick, 123–4
Leclerc, Annie, 156n4
Lenin Shipyard Strike, 31, 42, 57–60
Leviathan, 42–4, 46, 48, 51, 52, 53–4, 55, 62n5

liberal discourse of gelopolitics, 17–21, 24, 27, 29, 34, 35n14, 36n15, 65–6, 67, 73, 93n2, 102, 171n1
   a/gelasty dispute and, 19–20, 24–5, 33, 161, 162–3, 167
   comedy and, 19–20
   crisis in, 162–3, 165
   dialectic of, 20, 24, 25
   fascism and, 162–3, 167, 171n1
   limits of, 20, 24, 26–7
   logos/phōnē dialectic in, 19–20, 21, 24, 162–3
   race and, 102
   social order and, 93n2
   as subject-centric, 65–7, 73, 93n2
   Trump and, 60, 162–3, 171n1
liberalism, 80–1
   Ellison and, 111, 117
   end of laughter and, 163
   ideology and, 59–60
   laughter and, 163, 167
   logos/phōnē dialectic and, 163
   race and, 86–8, 94n12, 102, 117
libido (Freud), 141–6, 159n13
light-hearted art (Adorno), 31, 67, 68, 76, 81–2
Lockyer, Sharon, 146
logic of identity (Adorno), 68–70, 73, 75–6, 77, 83; *see also* capitalism; enlightenment (Adorno)
logos, 161
   Adorno and, 68
   Aristotle and, 5–7, 39–40
   class and, 159n12
   Hobbes and, 30, 39–41, 45, 92, 169
   in liberal discourse of gelopolitics, 20–1, 24, 162–3
   patriarchy and, 22, 127–30, 133, 155, 159n12; *see also* phallogocentrism
   polis and, 7, 17, 26–7, 37n22, 61, 92, 163, 168, 169–70
   race and, 118, 120n10
   social order and, 26–7, 37n22, 39, 92, 102, 118, 120n10, 127–9, 155, 159n12
   sovereignty and, 31, 40–1, 45, 61, 169
   see also logos/phōnē dialectic; reason

logos/phōnē dialectic, 27
   Aristotle and, 5–7, 39–40
   Bakhtin and, 23
   class and, 159n12
   écriture féminine and, 129
   fascism and, 161, 162–3, 170
   Hobbes and, 30, 39–41, 45, 61, 92, 169
   liberal discourse of gelopolitics and, 19–20, 21, 24, 162–3
   Nietzschean discourse of gelopolitics and, 21–24, 26, 39, 66, 160–1
   patriarchy and, 22, 127–30, 133, 155, 159n12
   polis and, 7, 17, 26–7, 37n22, 61, 92, 163, 168, 169–70
   race and, 118, 120n10
   in Rancière, 120n10
   social order and, 26–7, 37n22, 39, 92, 102, 118, 120n10, 127–9, 159n12
Lyotard, Jean-François, 3–5, 22, 24, 157n5

MacKenzie, Iain, 165
male power, 124, 136, 146, 149
Martel, James, 41, 52, 54, 56
Marx, Karl, 65, 66, 93n2, 122n17
masculine laughter, 139–41, 145, 146, 149, 152–3
Mbembe, Achille, 120n11
Medusa, 129; *see also* Cixous, Hélène
Meyers, Seth, 14
middle voice, 110
Mill, John Stuart, 17, 36n15
mimesis
   Adorno and, 83–4
   Lawtoo and, 166–8, 170
Minima Moralia, 70, 72, 73–4, 78, 91
minstrelsy, 102, 104
Mizejewski, Linda, 126, 147–9, 152, 154, 155, 159n14, 169
mode of political life, 98, 112, 116–18; *see also* form of political life
Morel, Lucas, 109, 111–12, 117
Morreall, John, 46, 52

Nancy, Jean-Luc, 22
Nanette, 33, 126, 147, 150–5, 159n15, 161
Napa Valley Wine Train, 95, 101, 102, 119
nature, 146, 170
negative dialectics, 25, 37n19, 91, 120n11; *see also* critical theory
Negative Dialectics, 69, 77, 91
neoliberalism, 13, 26, 28, 165, 171
new agelasty, 33, 161–8, 170–1, 171n1; *see also* end of laughter
Ngai, Sianne, 10
Ngangura, Tari, 87–8
Nietzsche, Friedrich
 autonomy and, 80–1
 Hobbes and, 31
 see also Nietzschean discourse of gelopolitics
Nietzschean discourse of gelopolitics, 17, 21–7, 29, 33, 34, 36n18, 129, 132, 171n1
 a/gelasty dispute and, 4, 24–5, 33, 161, 171n1
 comedy and, 24
 limits of, 24–5, 26–7
 logos/phōnē dialectic in, 21–24, 26, 39, 66, 160–1
 social order and, 93n2
 as subject-centric, 66–7, 73, 82, 93n2
Noerr, Gunzelin, 93n5
noise *see phōnē*
non-identical, the (Adorno), 25, 37n19, 57, 69, 120n11
 aesthetic experience and, 79–81
 laughter as, 26, 31, 78, 91, 169, 170
 reconciled laughter and, 81–5, 88–9, 91–2
 reconciliation and, 77–81, 91–2
Nussbaum, Emily, 33, 161, 162–3, 165, 167–8, 171n1
Nussbaum, Martha, 4, 19

Oakeshott, Michael, 48–9, 64n9
Obama, Barack, 9, 60
 as comedian, 14–15, 164

obscene joking, 139–41, 143–6
 as homosocial ritual, 141, 145
 see also bawdry (Freud)
Oliver, John, 8–9, 19
The Order of Things, 22
O'Reilly, Bill, 19–20

Parikh, Tej, 13
parody, 24, 83–5, 131–2, 133, 137, 148
 fascism and, 75, 161
 political theory and, 7, 28–9
Parvulescu, Anca, 21, 110, 121n12
passions (Hobbes), 42–6, 48, 55, 62n5
 vs signs of passions, 45, 48
patriarchy
 comedy and, 32, 135, 147–54, 169
 laughter and, 32–3, 66, 124–6, 127, 129–36, 133–4, 135–8, 147–55, 169
 logos and, 22, 127–30, 133, 155, 159n12
 see also phallogocentrism; hetero-patriarchy
Paxman, Jeremy, 10–12, 17
peace (Hobbes), 48–53
 sovereignty and, 51–3, 56, 64n11, 168
Peele, Jordan, 29, 68, 86–9; *see also* Get Out
Perry, Tyler, 102, 120n7, 120n9
phallogocentrism, 128–30, 157n6, 157n7
 laughter and, 132–4
phōnē
 Black laughter as, 100, 169
 women's laughter as, 127, 156n4
 see also logos/phōnē dialectic
Plato, 2–5, 24, 35n14
pluralism, 133
Poehler, Amy, 148
polemical laughter (Adorno), 68, 70–1, 73–6, 81, 82, 84, 88; *see also* wrong laughter (Adorno)
police *see* regulation of laughter
polis
 constituted by laughter, 7, 33, 161, 168, 169–71
 exogenous to laughter, 7, 163, 164–5, 166, 168, 170–1

polis (cont.)
   laughter's place in, 2–5, 7, 17, 18, 24–5, 27–8, 34, 61, 161–8, 170–1
   logos and, 7, 17, 26–7, 37n22, 61, 92, 163, 168, 169–70
   social order and, 37n22, 105
political correctness, 162
political logic of laughter, 28, 30–1, 39–42, 56–61, 92, 168; *see also* counter/sovereignty
political theory
   a/gelasty dispute and, 4, 7, 17, 29, 161, 167, 168, 170–1
   genres of laughter and, 7, 28–9
   gelopolitics and, 17
popular sovereignty, 42, 60
power, 4, 10, 24, 26–7, 31, 39, 64n12, 67, 93n4, 102, 169
   disciplinary, 146
   enlightenment and, 68–9
   genealogy of, 131, 158n7
   knowledge and, 102
   laughing body politic and, 57–61
   logic of identity and, 68–70, 73, 75
   male, 124, 136, 146, 149
   sexuality and, 144, 146
   white supremacy and, 96–7
   see also power (Hobbes); social power
power (Hobbes), 30, 41, 42–5, 53, 56; *see also* glory (Hobbes)
pretty vs funny (Mizejewski), 147–50, 152
psychoanalysis, 127, 138–46

queer/ing laughter, 131–2, 134, 136, 149–50, 153, 154, 156n3
   dialectic of, 126, 147, 149, 154
queer politics, 22, 32–3, 125–6, 132, 134, 138, 146, 155, 169
queer theory
   a/gelasty dispute and, 32–3
   laughter and, 28, 29, 124, 130–8, 146, 156n3, 156n4, 169

Rabelais, François, 1, 3, 4, 23
race
   Adorno and, 119n3
   critical theory of laughter and, 31, 92, 96, 102–3, 118, 155, 169
   freedom and, 108–9, 117–18, 121n13
   innocence and, 87–90
   laughter and, 31, 86–92, 95–112, 115–19, 126, 155, 169
   liberalism and, 86–8, 94n12, 102, 117
   logos and, 118, 120n10
   racial order, 86–92, 96–100, 102, 104–8, 110, 111–12, 116–19, 122n18, 169
   see also white supremacy
raillery *see* ridicule
Rally to Restore Sanity and/or Fear, 29, 31, 42, 58–60
Rancière, Jacques, 105, 120n10
reason, 59
   in Adorno, 68–70, 77, 83–4
   enlightenment and, 68–70, 84, 93n3
   hetero-patriarchy and, 147
   in Hobbes, 39–40, 48–52, 54, 62n2, 63n8
   laughter and, 6, 19, 20, 23, 26–7, 32, 35n14, 36n15, 39, 84, 160–1
   mimetic, 83–4
   sovereignty and, 51, 54
   violence of, 84, 93n3
   see also logos
reasoned speech *see logos*
reconciled laughter (Adorno), 68, 76–9, 81–6, 88–92
   as aesthetic experience, 81–5
   as dialectical concept, 86, 91–2
   see also wrong laughter (Adorno)
reconciliation (Adorno), 77–8, 83, 85, 91–2, 94n8
   art and, 80–1
regime of laughter, 102, 120n8; *see also* white supremacist regime of laughter
regime of truth (Foucault), 102
regulation of laughter, 2–5, 7, 16–7, 24, 27
   gender and, 136, 146, 169
   new agelasty and, 161–5, 167, 168
   white supremacy and, 95–6, 98, 100–8, 110, 116, 118–19, 119n1, 119n6, 120n9, 121n12, 169
   see also white supremacist regime of laughter

religion, 9–10, 20
repoliticisation of laughter, 32–3,
    125–6, 138, 146, 154, 170; *see
    also* depoliticisation of laughter;
    under-politicisation of laughter
repression, sexual, 140, 143–4
repressive hypothesis (Foucault), 143
Republican Party, 60
ridicule, 18–19, 23, 166
rights, 97, 108–10, 119
Rogers, Will, 8
Rowson, Martin, 9
Rudolph, Maya, 148
Russell, Danielle, 147
Russell, Harold, 84

Sanders, Lynn, 152
satire, 24, 149
    Adorno and, 74–5
    authoritarianism and, 2
    liberalism and, 9–10, 59
    new agelasty and, 165–6, 171n1,
      172n2
    political theory and, 28–9
    race and, 9–10
Saturday Night Live, 1, 9, 13, 20, 164
Savigny, Heather, 146
Schiller, Friedrich, 81
Schoolman, Morton, 77–8
The Second Sex, 156n4
segregated laughter *see* regulation of
    laughter
segregation, 97, 101
self-reflexive laughter (Adorno), 82–5
'Sensus Communis', 18–20; *see also*
    Shaftesbury, Third Earl of
Servant of the People see Zelensky,
    Volodymyr
sex and gender politics, 24, 31–3, 92,
    96, 125–6, 136–7
    comedy and, 146–55
    critical theory of laughter and,
      125–6, 132, 136–8, 146, 149,
      155, 169
sexual character (Freud), 141–5,
    159n13
sexual politics *see* sex and gender politics
sexual violence, 123–5, 136, 141, 145,
    146, 151, 155, 155n1

sexuality, 158n7
    comedy and, 147–54
    Freud's account of, 141–6
    laughter and, 24, 32–3, 92, 96,
      124–6, 130–1, 132, 134, 136,
      138, 139–46, 147–55, 156n3,
      169
    power and, 144, 146
    social regulation of, 143–4
Shaftesbury, Third Earl of, 18–20,
    23, 36n15, 75, 162; *see also*
    liberal discourse of gelopolitics
Sherman, Yael, 134–5
Silverman, Sarah, 148
Skinner, Quentin, 41, 46–7, 50–1, 52
slavery, 97, 101, 102, 107, 118,
    121n13; *see also* white supremacy
social contract (Hobbes), 41–2, 53–6
    laughter and, 55–6
    see also body politic (Hobbes)
social logic of gelopolitics, 31, 61,
    65–7, 89, 92, 169
social order
    Adorno's account of, 25–7, 36n17,
      61, 66–70, 73, 92n1, 93n2, 169
    aesthetic organisation of, 105
    antagonistic cooperation and,
      115–19, 122n17, 169
    art and, 79–82
    autonomy in, 79–82
    culture industry and, 71–3
    enlightenment and, 70
    fascism and, 72–3, 75–6
    as 'fractured totality', 67, 89
    gelopolitics and, 26–8, 30–4, 61,
      66–7, 86, 102, 125, 169
    gender identity and, 31–3, 92, 96,
      126, 130–1, 146, 148, 150, 154,
      155, 169
    hetero-patriarchal, 146–55
    heteronormative, 32–3, 124–6,
      146–55
    horror and, 70, 81, 83, 88
    ideology and, 29, 74–5, 89, 153
    laughter as site of politics in,
      26–8, 33, 34, 36n18, 39, 61,
      65–7, 86, 92, 97, 100, 105,
      118, 125, 137, 155, 162,
      168–71, 172n1

214 Index

social order *(cont.)*
  laughter in, 70–92, 96–8
  liberal discourse of gelopolitics and, 93n2
  logic of identity and *see* logic of identity (Adorno)
  logos and, 26–7, 37n22, 39, 92, 102, 118, 120n10, 127–9, 155, 159n12
  Nietzschean discourse of gelopolitics and, 93n2
  patriarchal, 32–3, 124–6, 127–30, 146–55
  polis and, 37n22, 105
  racialised, 86–92, 96–100, 102, 104–8, 110, 111–12, 116–19, 122n18, 169
  repression and, 140, 143–4
  sexuality and, 31–3, 92, 96, 126, 130–1, 143–4, 146, 150, 154, 155, 169
  structures of power in, 4, 24, 26–7, 31, 39, 67, 76, 92, 93n4, 96, 102, 125–6, 131, 135, 146, 150, 154, 159n12, 169; *see also* hetero-patriarchy; heteronormativity; patriarchy; power; social power; white supremacy
  trauma and, 151–4
  violence of, 31, 71–3, 75–6, 84–5, 88–9, 151, 169
  white supremacist, 96–7, 99–111, 108, 115–19
social power, 67–8, 70–1, 73, 75–6, 77–8, 87–90, 93n4, 154, 169
socialism, 93n3
society *see* social order
sovereignty
  aesthetic dimensions of, 60–1
  counter-sovereignty and, 56–61, 64n12
  gelopolitics and, 64n12
  Hobbes and, 30, 40–1, 45, 51–7, 61, 64n9, 64n11, 168–9
  human subject and, 68–70
  laughter and, 30, 40–1, 45, 53, 55–61, 62n1, 64n11, 64n12, 168–9

  logos and, 31, 40–1, 45, 61, 169
  peace and, 51–3, 56, 64n11, 168
  as performance, 52
  popular, 42, 60
  reason and, 51, 54
  social contract and, 53–5
  Trump and, 16
  see also counter-sovereignty; counter/sovereignty
stand-up comedy *see* comedy
Stanley, Alessandra, 148
state of nature (Hobbes), 47–50, 52, 55–6
Stewart, Jon, 4, 8–9, 13, 29, 42, 58–60; *see also* Rally to Restore Sanity and/or Fear
Stoic laughter, 19; *see also* liberal discourse of gelopolitics
storytelling, 152, 154
subject-centrism, 31, 61, 65–7, 73, 75–6, 82, 88–90, 92, 93n2
sudden glory *see* glory (Hobbes)
sudden vainglory *see* vainglory (Hobbes)
Sykes, Wanda, 135

Tea Party, 59–60
This Sex Which Is Not One, 130
Three Essays on the Theory of Sexuality, 142
Tobacco Road, 98–9, 105
tolerance, 59
Tønder, Lars, 24
The Tonight Show, 9
trauma, 151–4
trolling, 161, 163
Trump, Donald, 12, 23, 35n11, 35n13
  a/gelasty dispute and, 1–2, 33, 161–5, 171n1
  comedy and, 1–2, 9, 19–20, 74, 76, 166
  as insult comic, 13, 15–16, 33, 66, 161–3, 164, 166, 171n1
  laughing at, 1–2, 14–16, 74, 76, 162, 166
  liberal discourse of gelopolitics and, 60, 162–3, 171n1

truth
  laughter and, 18–21, 23–24, 26–7, 35n14, 66, 73, 102, 161, 162–3, 168, 171n1
  regime of, 102; *see also* liberal discourse of gelopolitics; Nietzschean discourse of gelopolitics
'Trying to Understand *Endgame*', 74–5, 82–3
Turner, Jack, 111, 117
Tuskegee Institute, 98, 109–10
Twain, Mark, 17

Ukraine, 12–14
under-politicisation of laughter, 125, 136–8; *see also* depoliticisation of laughter; repoliticisation of laughter

vainglory (Hobbes), 30, 39, 41, 45–50, 56, 58, 61, 62n3, 62n6
violence
  enlightenment and, 69–70, 77, 84, 93n3
  humour and, 84, 162
  laughter and, 9–10, 16, 31, 72–3, 75, 78, 84–5, 88–91, 94n10, 101, 107, 109, 119n1, 123–5, 136, 141, 145, 146, 155, 155n1, 161, 169
  logic of identity and, 68–70, 73, 75, 77
  sexual *see* sexual violence
  of social order, 31, 71–3, 75–6, 84–5, 88–9, 151, 169
  white supremacy and, 86–91, 97, 101, 119n1
voice *see phōnē*

Webber, Julie, 165
Weber, Samuel, 158n9
White House Correspondents' Dinner, 1, 14–16
white laughter
  vs Black laughter, 98, 99–100, 102–7, 118, 122n18
  at *Get Out*, 31, 68, 87–91
  white supremacist regime of laughter, 32, 98, 102, 104–8, 110–11, 115, 118, 120n10, 121n12; *see also* laughing barrels
white supremacy
  democracy and, 97–8, 105–7, 110–11, 115–19, 120n10, 122n18, 169
  fascism and, 32
  freedom amid, 108–9, 117–18, 121n13
  laughter and, 32, 86–90, 96–112, 115–19, 169
  laughter at, 98, 109–10
  rights and, 97, 108–10, 119
  violence and, 86–91, 97, 101, 119n1
  see also race; white supremacist regime of laughter
whiteness, 97
  contingency of, 99–100
  see also white supremacy
Whitford, Bradley, 94n12
Willett, Cynthia, 32, 124–6, 134–8, 154, 169
Willett, Julie, 134–5
wokeness, 90
Wolin, Sheldon, 4, 54, 56
women's laughter, 123, 129–30, 163
  emancipation and, 32–3, 125–6, 129–30, 134, 136–8, 169
  'irrationality' of, 127, 156n4
wrong laughter (Adorno), 77–8, 85–6, 87–91
  as dialectical concept, 86, 91
  see also culture industry; polemical laughter (Adorno)

Yurchak, Alexei, 172n2

Zelensky, Volodymyr, 12–14, 17, 23, 35n11
Zupančič, Alenka, 24, 93n2

EU representative:
Easy Access System Europe
Mustamäe tee 50, 10621 Tallinn, Estonia
Gpsr.requests@easproject.com

www.ingramcontent.com/pod-product-compliance
Lightning Source LLC
Chambersburg PA
CBHW070353240426
43671CB00013BA/2488